MARIAN ENGEL: LIFE IN LETTERS

Marian Engel
Life in Letters

EDITED BY

Christl Verduyn and Kathleen Garay

UNIVERSITY OF TORONTO PRESS
Toronto Buffalo London

University of Toronto Press
Toronto Buffalo London
Printed in Canada

ISBN 0-8020-3687-2

Printed on acid-free paper

National Library of Canada Cataloguing in Publication

Engel, Marian, 1933–1985
 Marian Engel : life in letters / edited by Christl Verduyn and
Kathleen Garay.

 Includes bibliographical references and index.
 ISBN 0-8020-3687-2

 1. Engel, Marian, 1933–1985 – Correspondence. 2. Novelists,
Canadian (English) – 20th century – Correspondence. I. Verduyn,
Christl, 1953– II. Garay, Kathleen E., 1945– III. Title.

PS8559.N5Z48 2004 C813'.54 C2004-900470-0

University of Toronto Press acknowledges the financial assistance to
its publishing program of the Canada Council for the Arts and the
Ontario Arts Council.

This book has been published with the help of a grant from the
Canadian Federation for the Humanities and Social Sciences
through the Aid to Scholarly Pulications Programme, using funds
provided by the Social Sciences and Humanities Research Council
of Canada.

University of Toronto Press acknowledges the financial support for
its publishing activities of the Government of Canada through the
Book Publishing Industry Development Program (BPIDP).

Contents

Illustrations follow page xxxii

Preface

This collection of letters to and from Canadian novelist Marian Engel (1933–85) presents a unique perspective on Canada's literary scene during the period 1960–85. Engel belonged to the generation of Canadian writers who came to prominence during the 1970s. Her contemporaries included many well-known figures, such as Margaret Laurence, Margaret Atwood, Timothy Findley, and Austin Clarke. Engel's correspondence with these and other writers forms part of the wealth of letters exchanged by friends, family, and acquaintances deposited in the Marian Engel Archive at McMaster University as well as in other archival collections in Canada and the United States.

Both editors of this collection have long been aware of the importance of the correspondence in the Marian Engel Archive. Archivist Kathy Garay arranged and described Engel's papers and knows their contents intimately. Christl Verduyn has worked extensively with the archive in completing a number of projects on Engel's writing, including a study of the author's fiction, *Lifelines: Marian Engel's Writing* (1995), an edition of her writing *cahiers*, *Marian Engel's Notebooks* (1999), and an earlier selection of letters, *Dear Marian, Dear Hugh: The MacLennan-Engel Correspondence* (1995). These projects and a mutual interest in the Marian Engel Archive generated many hours of conversation, and in time the idea emerged to do a collaborative research project. When, in spring 2001, McMaster received an exciting new instalment of Engel correspondence, we knew what the project would be. This book is the result of our collaboration.

A number of individuals and organizations assisted in the production of this volume, and we would like to acknowledge and thank them for their help. First and foremost, we wish to thank Charlotte Engel and her brother, William Engel, for permission to publish materials from the Marian Engel Archive at McMaster University. Without their cooperation, this book would not have been possible, and we are most grateful to them. We are also very grateful for permissions received from the large number of contributors to the collection. Many expressed enthusiasm for our undertaking and shared their memories of Marian Engel. Clearly she figured prominently in the minds and hearts of many. For their timely assistance, we would like to thank the archivists at the University of British Columbia, the National Archives of Canada, the University of Toronto, York University, Concordia University, Amherst College, the University of Michigan, and the University of Queensland, Australia as well as those at McMaster University. We wish to thank the editors and staff at University of Toronto Press, and in particular Siobhan McMenemy for her early interest in the project. Thanks also to Liz Blackwell for transcription help in the early stages, and to the Social Sciences and Humanities Research Council for a grant to Christl Verduyn which helped fund that assistance. We are also grateful to Kerry Cannon and Sally Heath for late-stage research and technical assistance. Various colleagues and individuals generously provided leads for some of the more difficult to locate permissions. Finally, we would like to express heartfelt thanks to our spouses, Robert Campbell and Nick Garay, and to our families for their ongoing support and understanding. Nothing corresponds to that!

Introduction

The correspondence collected in this volume offers a view of the literary landscape in Canada from 1960 to 1985 as seen in letters to and from a key contributor to the writing community of the time – novelist Marian Engel (1933–85). Author of seven novels, including the Governor General's Award–winning *Bear* (1976), two collections of short stories, two books for children, a non-fiction book on islands, and many essays and articles, Engel was also a lively and prolific letter writer. Active and visible on the Canadian literary scene throughout her career, a key proponent of Public Lending Right for writers, Engel became the first Chair of the Writers' Union of Canada. Her correspondence, most of which is located in the Marian Engel Archive at McMaster University, includes a treasure trove of letters to and from prominent personalities of the Canadian writing community, as well as exchanges with family members and other friends, acquaintances, and professional contacts. This volume presents selections from that correspondence.

Life and Letters

Marian Engel was born in Toronto on 24 May 1933. She was the second of twin girls, whose mother, eighteen and unmarried, confronted the almost impossible task of raising her daughters in the face of the disapproving social mores and difficult economic circumstances of the time. 'First World War and Depression women,' Engel later observed, 'knew what happened to women without men':[1] 'Respectable was ... the key word.'[2] Society frowned on unwed mothers. Given this context, it is hardly surprising that the twins, Eleanor and Ruth, spent the first three years of their lives in foster care until they were adopted separately.

Ruth became a member of the Passmore family. Frederick Passmore, an auto-mechanics teacher, and his wife, Mary, a homemaker and former secretary, already had one daughter, Helen, and named their new daughter Marian. The Passmores lived in various southwestern Ontario towns as Frederick took up a series of teaching positions in centres such as Brantford, Galt (now Cambridge), and Sarnia.

Marian Engel was a determined ten-year-old when she made up her mind to become a writer. In later years, the author recalled purchasing a small notebook and informing her mother that she was going to be a writer. 'She said, "That's very hard." I said, "I don't care."'[3] Engel's apprenticeship and self-discovery as a novelist were recorded in her notebooks, or *cahiers* as she called them, and played out in her letters, as illustrated in the chapters that follow.[4] The author's letters explain, promote, question, and reflect on her lifelong practice of the craft of writing

Engel's first published work appeared in the 'Girls' Own' pages of the United Church Sunday school paper, *Canadian Girl.* She continued to submit poetry, stories, and articles to magazines and papers throughout her teenage years. Her submissions won awards, citations, and prizes. She received honourable mention for a story she sent to the popular teen magazine *Seventeen* in July 1952, for example, and third prize for a story published in the same magazine in July 1953.

Upon graduating from Sarnia Collegiate Institute and Technical School in 1952, Engel entered McMaster University in

Hamilton. While pursuing a B.A. in French and German, she worked on and published in the university student publications, the *Silhouette* and the *Muse*. University life offered Engel the intellectual environment and artistic nourishment she craved. From McMaster, she proceeded to McGill University in Montreal, where she completed a master's degree in 1957 with a thesis on the Canadian novel under the supervision of Hugh MacLennan.[5] MacLennan became a mentor and, in due course, a friend and colleague. He encouraged Engel's writing. To support herself in her chosen profession, Engel accepted a one-year teaching appointment at the University of Montana in 1957. There she completed her first novel with the help of another newly appointed instructor, Leslie Armour. Armour provided the plot, and Engel produced the prose. The result, 'The Pink Sphinx' (1958), would never be published, but it afforded Engel the valuable experience of writing a full-length manuscript. At the end of her year in Montana, Engel returned to Montreal, where she landed a teaching position at The Study, a private school for girls. For the next two years, she honed her writing skills, adding plays to her literary repertoire. In 1960, on MacLennan's recommendation, she applied for and was awarded a Rotary Foundation Fellowship to study for a year at the Université d'Aix-Marseilles in Aix-en-Provence.[6] Her travels in France and other parts of Europe generated the letters with which this volume begins.

The selection of letters in chapter 1, for the period 1960–5, is particularly rich in family material. Writing to her mother, her aunt, her sister, and family friend Mrs A.W. Mills,[7] first from France and then from England, Engel reflected upon her journeys, developing her writer's voice in lively descriptions of her travels. After initial contact through Hugh MacLennan, and in an era before there were any significant Canadian counterparts, she persuaded the distinguished New York literary agents Russell and Volkening to represent her work. Engel entered into a fruitful dialogue with their discerning editors, Diarmuid Russell,[8] and later Timothy Seldes, with the object of producing a publishable, saleable novel.

When her fellowship at the Université d'Aix-Marseilles ended, Engel did not return to Canada. Instead, she found a job in a tax credit firm in London to support herself while she continued to write. Her second attempt at a novel, 'Women Travelling Alone' (1962), like her first, remained unpublished. Both initial literary efforts, however, begin to trace Engel's literary journey. While Russell and Volkening declined her first two manuscripts, Engel was sustained by the highly encouraging words that accompanied the rejections.

On 27 January 1962, the author married Howard Engel in London. The couple relocated to Cyprus, where for the next two years Howard freelanced for the CBC and Marian taught while continuing to write and to correspond about her work. In the fall of 1964, the Engels returned to Canada and settled in Toronto. Twins Charlotte and William were born 30 April 1965. The early 1960s marked the beginning of Engel's two-decade-long correspondence with the 'godfather'of Canadian literature, Robert Weaver.[9] Meanwhile, her experiences abroad and her return home became the basis for letters and for the novels which soon began to appear.

Chapter 2 covers the period of Engel's breakthrough onto the Canadian literary scene – 1965 to 1970. Her first novel, *Sarah Bastard's Notebook*, was published to critical acclaim in 1968, and her second novel, *The Honeyman Festival*, followed in 1970. Engel's professional letters to her agents, to her publishers, and to the Canada Council dominate these busy, creative years.[10]

With the successful publication of *The Honeyman Festival*, Engel had avoided the dreaded 'second novel syndrome.' But she was concerned that there might be 'too much of herself' in her novels. *Monodromos*, published in 1973, marked the author's attempt to get out of the 'skin' of subjectivity and into the realm of ideas, and to dismember and reconstruct the traditional novel form. Her letters in chapter 3, covering the period 1971 to 1975, especially those to Diarmuid Russell and Dennis Lee,[11] map her struggle with *Monodromos*, which appears to have been the most challenging of her books to write. She was also grappling with a dead marriage.

The publication in 1976 of her fourth novel, *Bear,* transformed Engel's career. During the years 1976 to 1980, the focus of chapter 4, the author became much more widely known – if not more widely read. *Bear*'s story of a librarian's love affair with a bear was succeeded, in 1978, by the story of a Protestant nun. Less sensational and less commercially successful, *The Glassy Sea* remains one of Engel's most spiritual explorations.

The 1970s also coincided with the development of Engel's literary activism. She became the first Chair of the Writers' Union of Canada in 1973 and served on the Board of the Toronto Public Library from 1975 to 1978. In both contexts, Engel helped define and defend the important question of royalties for authors, the issue which later became established as Public Lending Right. Now a single mother, following her divorce from Howard Engel in 1977, Engel donated what time she could rescue from her writing and raising the twins to causes for which she felt her voice might make a difference and help achieve change.

Engel's last published novel, *Lunatic Villas,* appeared in 1981. As is evident from the letters in chapter 5, however, she continued to write throughout the final phase of her life, 1981 to 1985. In addition to multiple drafts of a new novel, tentatively entitled 'Elizabeth and the Golden City,' Engel completed a non-fiction book about islands, short stories, a year's worth of weekly newspaper columns for the *Toronto Star,* book reviews, and, always and especially, letters. As it became clear that she would not survive the cancer with which she had been diagnosed in 1979, her friends – many of them companions in the struggle to 'hack away at the shape of paragraphs'[12] – sent their words to help sustain her.

A primary focus of this collection of letters is Marian Engel's emergence, development, and contribution as a writer. In addition, however, through her words and those of her correspondents, new perspectives are revealed on the practice of writing in Canada during the quarter century between 1960 and 1985. This was a fertile and formative time which, some have suggested, marked the birth of the elusive 'Canadian identity' in the arts, and particularly in literature. The wider national cultural picture is illuminated by the letters in the collection, including the germination, in Engel's home, of the Writers' Union of Canada. Novelist Matt Cohen recalled early meetings of the Writers' Union in his memoir *Typing: A Life in Twenty-Six Keys:*

> I felt both privileged and lucky to be included when the early meetings took place; they were held on Brunswick Avenue, either at Marian Engel's house or just up the street at Austin Clarke's.[13] Despite the fact they were only separated by a few dozen paces, the two meeting places were totally unlike. Marian Engel's large and pleasant living room fell into the harried housewife category. It was so emphatically disorganized that it in fact overflowed the category to become its own archetype. Its furnishings were the inevitable result – though unfortunately at the time I couldn't know it – of co-existence with vigorous young children. Her ground floor workroom was behind glass doors in what had been the dining room. It looked to me like the site of a hurricane disaster, but somehow it yielded the unending stream of amazingly elegant reviews and fictions that I had thought, before meeting her, must issue from some museum of perfect orderliness.[14]

Cohen contrasts Engel's workplace with that of her colleague, friend, and neighbour, Austin Clarke, whose study was 'the ultimate male bastion and fantasy': 'It was large enough to seat a dozen people (some on the floor), and lined with beautiful shelves containing a whole library's worth of books, including various editions of his own already considerable publications ... Austin would sit in solitary and contented splendour behind a huge desk, his study in every way a suitable haven for "the writer."'[15] Cohen's comments echo an earlier observation by Hugh MacLennan of the differing circumstances for men and women writers of Engel's generation in Canada. 'When I knew you in the old days,' MacLennan wrote 16 May 1981, 'I was a good judge of ability. I knew Mordecai [Richler] had it, and I got him a Canada Council Grant that enabled him to write *Duddy Kravitz*. I knew you had it, and did nothing for you except give you encouragement and an electric blanket.'[16] Marian Engel and other literary women of her generation – Margaret Laurence, Phyllis Webb, Margaret Atwood, Carol Shields, among many others – were keenly conscious of the imbalance in the writing lives of women as compared to men and have written of the special challenges faced by women writers.[17] In *Negotiating with the Dead: A Writer on Writing* (2002), Margaret Atwood points out that 'a man playing the role of Great Artist was expected to Live Life – this chore was part of his consecration to his art – and Living Life meant, among other things, wine, women, and song. But if a female writer tried the wine and the men, she was likely to be considered a slut and a drunk, so she was stuck with the song; and better still if it was a swan song.'[18] Ordinary women were supposed to get married, Atwood recalls, but not women artists: 'When I was an aspiring female poet, in the late 1950s ... you couldn't be a wife and mother and also an artist, because each one of these things required total dedication ... Love and marriage pulled one way, Art another ... it would destroy you as an ordinary woman.'[19]

The struggle of ordinary women to live creatively on their own terms, as artists or writers as well as mothers and lovers, is a central theme of Engel's work and her letters.[20] The author formulated the project for an artistic life early on. 'Live so that the pattern you make of your life is a work of art in itself,' she noted in a *cahier* at age sixteen.[21] Engel's novels, short stories, and articles represent the effort and desire for a creative life, as well as the everyday realities of women's experience and the constraints on female creativity. The representation of women's reality and day-to-day lives is an integral aspect of Engel's writing. 'I think there is a point in recording female experience, which is different from male experience,' she asserted.[22] 'Half a century ago, women had to disguise everything about their heroines. Nobody menstruated, no one came closer than embrace or disgrace, childbirth was veiled. Women's lives were half blocked-off.'[23] Social conventions, family expectations, and economic and emotional insecurity can conspire to constrain women's lives and to funnel female desire toward either-or rather than both-and options. Engel's literary vision resisted duality and dichotomized experience in favour of a synthesis of the mundane and the magical, the ordinary and the extraordinary, life and art. Her protagonists strive to fuse oppositional forces in their lives. In *Sarah Bastard's Notebook,* Sarah rejects the view that 'life is a simple dichotomy'; she 'want[s] it all both ways.'[24] Likewise in *The Glassy Sea,* Rita 'always wanted to have things both ways.'[25] Engel's female characters are simultaneously drawn to the interest of everyday reality for women and to the attraction of intellectual and artistic pursuits. A 'both-and' approach to life is what fiction allowed Engel to create. In life, as in fiction, writing was a way of living and working on one's own terms, creatively as an artist and a woman. The theme of female creativity presides over all Engel's work, from her notebooks to her novels, from her short stories to her letters.

Engel's achievements were recognized by numerous awards and honours during her lifetime. In addition to the Governor General's Award for fiction in 1976, for *Bear,* she won the 1978 Canadian Authors Association Silver Medal for fiction for *The Glassy Sea;* the 1979 McClelland and Stewart Award for fiction writing in a Canadian magazine for her short story 'Father Instinct';[26] and the 1981 City of Toronto Book Award for *Lunatic*

Villas. In 1982, Engel was appointed Officer of the Order of Canada, and in 1984 she was honoured as the Metro Toronto YWCA Woman of Distinction in Arts and Letters. Throughout the early 1980s, even as she struggled with the cancer that would take her life prematurely, Engel continued to write and travel. Her non-fiction book *The Islands of Canada* appeared in 1981, and for a year beginning in November 1981, she wrote a weekly column called 'Being Here' for the *Toronto Star.* She was a Canadian representative at the biennial Adelaide Festival in Australia in March 1980, and in October 1981 she represented the Writers' Union of Canada at a conference in Germany. Her writing projects during this period included a new novel, 'Elizabeth and the Golden City,' and a collection of short stories, *The Tattooed Woman,* published posthumously. In December 1984, Engel travelled to Paris with her children. Her final journey followed soon after. Marian Engel died 16 February 1985.

Archival and Editorial Note

The main repository of letters to and from Marian Engel can be found in the Marian Engel Archive in the William Ready Division of Archives and Research Collections at McMaster University, Hamilton, Ontario. The McMaster collection, as well as manuscripts, journals, notebooks, and published materials, contains almost 3,000 letters written to and by the author. Although it appears that Engel did not systematically keep copies of her correspondence, some have survived in her archive and appear in this selection. The greater part of the collection was acquired by McMaster in two lots, one in 1982 from Engel herself and another from her estate in 1992. Individual letters came from several donors between 1995 and 2000, and a third major accrual of some 360 letters was added to the collection in April 2001. This last addition had a highly unusual pedigree. Sara Sutcliffe, who purchased Engel's house on Marchmount Road after her death, found the letters in a garbage bag and eventually decided to donate them to McMaster, just at the time we were planning this edition.

We have also been fortunate in locating Engel letters in other repositories, a process greatly facilitated by the availability of archival web pages and entire finding aids on the Internet. As well as the Engel letters in the Margaret Laurence Archive at York University, we located Engel's letters to Jane Rule at the University of British Columbia, her letters to Judith Rodriguez at the University of Queensland, Australia, and her correspondence with Timothy Findley, Lovat Dickson, and Robert Weaver at the National Archives of Canada. In all cases, we have had the benefit of prompt and professional help from archivists, and in some cases, when contacted for permission to publish, correspondents have even supplied us with additional letters.[27]

Making a final selection from among such a wealth of material has been difficult, but we have been guided in our choice by three criteria: we have sought letters that map the various stages in Engel's life; those which cast light on the literary circle of which she was an increasingly vital member; and those which are simply a joy to read. Editorially we have interfered as little as possible with the correspondence presented here. Most of the letters are presented in their entirety (all ellipsis or suspension points are in the originals); the only deletions have been made at the request of the authors or their estates. Such requests have been few, and the brief excisions have been done silently, without ellipsis points. In occasional cases, when more extensive deletions have been requested, we have chosen instead not to use the letters. Except where noted, we have silently corrected obvious spelling and punctuation errors, and have regularized all dates and other common elements such as the italicization of book titles and the positioning of signatures on the page. Correspondents' mailing addresses have been abbreviated, but Engel's have been left in full to enable the reader to follow her movements through the years. We have removed page divisions and page numbering from the original letters and have indicated any additions, omissions, or uncertain readings by the use of square brackets, thus: [uncertain reading].

Anticipating that this collection will find its readership well beyond the realm of literary scholars, we have not wished to encumber it with too large a number of notes or to stuff them with an excess of detail. We have adhered to the principle of adding a note only where the information it conveys may assist the reader's understanding. Accordingly, while we have attempted to identify proper names of all correspondents, where names mentioned in the letters are clearly those of family members or neighbours, we have not provided notes. Professional writers are identified by nationality in order to point readers to the many available literary reference works which provide detailed information concerning a writer's publications, primary themes, and major awards.[28]

Copyright ownership of the letters included in this collection remains with the correspondents or with their estates.

Notes

1 Marian Engel Archive, William Ready Division of Archives and Research Collections, McMaster University, Hamilton, Canada, box 23, file 34, 'Oh Romance.'

2 Marian Engel Archive, box 26, file 12, 'The Greening of Toronto: A Footnote to Mordecai Richler.'

3 Marian Engel, 'Beginnings,' *Today Magazine*, 2 May 1981, p. 3.

4 Engel's *cahiers* may be read in *Marian Engel's Notebooks: 'Ah, mon cahier, écoute ...,'* ed. Christl Verduyn (Waterloo, ON: Wilfrid Laurier University Press, 1999).

5 Hugh MacLennan (1907–90), Canadian novelist. His *Two Solitudes* (1945), an exploration of French and English tensions in Montreal, is considered a classic of Canadian literature. MacLennan obtained

a part-time teaching position at McGill University in 1951 and became a full professor of English in 1968.

6 The Rotary Foundation is the largest private source of scholarships in the world. It seeks to promote international understanding through student exchanges and provides funds for travel and study in foreign countries.

7 Mrs A.W. Mills, mother of former Lieutenant-Governor Pauline McGibbon.

8 Diarmuid Russell (d. 1973) was the son of the George William Russell ('A.E.'), Irish writer, artist, and patriot. He was a founding partner of the distinguished New York literary agency Russell and Volkening, established in 1940.

9 Robert Weaver (1921–), Canadian radio producer and literary editor. Though Weaver officially retired in 1985 after a lengthy career at the CBC, he continues to oversee its annual literary competition.

10 *Sarah Bastard's Notebook* is also known by its original Canadian-release title, *No Clouds of Glory*.

11 Dennis Lee (1939–), Canadian editor, poet, and critic, co-founder in 1967 of House of Anansi Press. Lee is also an acclaimed author of children's verse, including the popular *Alligator Pie* (1974) and *Garbage Delight* (1977).

12 Marian Engel Archive, box 34, file 41.

13 Austin Clarke (1934–), Canadian novelist. Clarke won the 2002 Giller Prize for his most recent novel, *The Polished Hoe* (Toronto: Thomas Allen, 2002).

14 Matt Cohen, *Typing: A Life in Twenty-Six Keys* (Toronto: Vintage Canada, 2000), 182–3.

15 Ibid., 183.

16 *Dear Marian, Dear Hugh: The MacLennan-Engel Correspondence*, ed. Christl Verduyn (Ottawa: University of Ottawa Press, 1995), 20.

17 See Sandra Gilbert and Susan Gubar, *The Madwoman in the Attic: The Woman Writer and the Nineteenth-Century Literary Imagination* (New Haven: Yale University Press, 1979); Carol Shields, *Jane Austen* (New

York: Viking, 2001); and letters by Margaret Laurence in this
volume.

18 Margaret Atwood, *Negotiating with the Dead: A Writer on Writing* (Cambridge: Cambridge University Press, 2002), 83–4. Award-winning
poet, novelist, short story writer, and critic Margaret 'Peggy' Atwood
(1939–) is internationally renowned for such influential works as
Survival: A Thematic Guide to Canadian Literature (1972), *Surfacing*
(1972), *The Handmaid's Tale* (1985), *Cat's Eye* (1988), *Alias Grace*
(1996), and *Oryx and Crake* (2003), to name only these. During the
1970s, Atwood was involved with both House of Anansi Press and
This Magazine, as well as the development of the Writers' Union, of
which she became vice-chair in 1980. Atwood is recognized for her
writerly craft, her keen observation of contemporary issues, and her
cutting wit. She continues to produce and to garner awards for her
literary oeuvre.

19 Ibid., 85.

20 For more analysis of Engel's fiction, see Christl Verduyn, *Lifelines:
Marian Engel's Writings* (Montreal and Kingston: McGill-Queen's
University Press, 1995).

21 Verduyn, ed., *Marian Engel's Notebooks*, 26.

22 Cathy Matyas and Jennifer Joiner, 'Interpretation, Inspiration and
the Irrelevant Questions: Interview with Marian Engel,' *University of
Toronto Review 5* (Spring 1981): 4–8.

23 Marian Engel, 'The Woman As Storyteller,' *Communiqué 8* (May
1975): 6–7, 44–5.

24 *Sarah Bastard's Notebook* (New York: Harcourt Brace & World, 1968),
12, 99.

25 *The Glassy Sea* (Toronto: McClelland and Stewart, 1978), 58.

26 'Father Instinct,' *Chatelaine*, August 1979, pp. 32, 48, 50, 52.

27 Sharon Riis and Judith Rodriguez generously gave us letters from
their personal archives.

28 A fine example is William H. New, ed., *Encyclopedia of Literature in
Canada* (Toronto: University of Toronto Press, 2002).

Chronology

1933
Born 24 May, second of twin girls, Eleanor and Ruth, in Toronto, Canada.

1936
Adopted by the Passmore family, as Marian.

1936–46
Lives with her adoptive family in various Ontario towns, including Port Arthur, Brantford, Galt (now Cambridge), Hamilton, and Sarnia.

1946–52
Sarnia Collegiate Institute and Technical School.

1952–5
McMaster University: B.A. (French and German).

1955–7
McGill University: writes M.A. thesis, 'A Study of the English-Canadian Novel since 1939,' under the supervision of Hugh MacLennan.

1957–8
Teaches at the University of Montana; writes 'The Pink Sphinx' (unpublished novel).

1958–60
Teaches at The Study, Montreal; writing includes plays (unpublished).

1960–1
Rotary Foundation Fellowship at the Université d'Aix-Marseilles, France.

1961–2
Supports herself in London, England, with office job and writes 'Women Travelling Alone' (unpublished novel).

27 Jan. 1962
Marries Howard Engel.

1962–4
Lives in Cyprus and teaches at St John's School, Nicosia; writes 'Death Comes for the Yaya' (unpublished novel).

1964
Returns to Toronto, Canada; writes 'Lost Heir and Happy Families' (unpublished novel).

30 April 1965
Gives birth to twins, William and Charlotte.

1968
Sarah Bastard's Notebook (novel).

1970
The Honeyman Festival (novel).

March 1971
Makes return visit to Cyprus.

1973
Monodromos (novel); elected Chair, Writers' Union of Canada.

1974
Adventure at Moon Bay Towers (book for children); conducts research on Major William Kingdom Rains.

·1975
Inside the Easter Egg (short stories); *Joanne: The Last Days of a Modern Marriage* (radio drama / novel); becomes Toronto Public Library Board trustee (until 1978).

1976
Bear (novel); receives Governor General's Award for fiction.

1977
My Name Is Not Odessa Yarker (book for children); divorces Howard Engel.

1978
The Glassy Sea (novel); receives Canadian Authors Association Silver Medal for fiction.

1978–9
Writer-in-residence, University of Alberta, Edmonton.

1979
Diagnosed with cancer.

1979–80
Lives in Edmonton, Alberta, where she teaches creative writing;
receives McClelland and Stewart Award for fiction writing in a
Canadian magazine.

March 1980
Travels to Australia as Canadian representative at the Adelaide
Festival.

Summer 1980
Travels to conduct 'Islands of Canada' research.

1980–1
Writer-in-residence, University of Toronto.

1981
The Islands of Canada (non-fiction); *Lunatic Villas* (novel); receives City of Toronto Book Award (presented 1982).

Oct. 1981
Travels to Germany as representative of the Writers' Union of
Canada; visits Sweden.

1981–2
Writes weekly column 'Being Here' for *Toronto Star.*

1982
Appointed Officer of the Order of Canada.

24 May 1982
Death of Mary Elizabeth Passmore.

June/July 1983
Vancouver 'Women and Words' conference.

1984
Named Metro Toronto YWCA Woman of Distinction in Arts and Letters; writes 'Elizabeth and the Golden City' and 'The Vanishing Lakes' (unpublished).

Dec. 1984
Makes return visit to Paris, France.

16 Feb. 1985
Dies of cancer.

Wedding day, 27 January 1962, London, England

Cyprus, April 1963

Expecting twins, Toronto, 1965

Return to Cyprus, 1971

Embraced by a 'bear' at a Writers' Union meeting, [1976?]

With her children, Charlotte and William, 1978

On Galiano Island, British Columbia, 1978

Marian Engel, 1981

MARIAN ENGEL: LIFE IN LETTERS

1

Woman Travelling, 1960–1965

Marian Engel's travels abroad in the early 1960s would have lasting impact on her life and writing. A prestigious Rotary Foundation Fellowship in 1960 allowed Engel to study for a year in Aix-en-Provence in the south of France. While abroad, she travelled and explored Europe from Sweden to Cyprus. A mature and not unsophisticated twenty-seven-year-old, Engel had already studied and worked outside her native Ontario.[1] This was her first experience, however, of life beyond North America, and letters from Sweden, England, France, and Italy express her delight with her widening world. She reported regularly on her travels, with details about foods, festivals, and cultural customs, as well as reflections on books and writing. Correspondence from this period also traces her developing relationship with Howard Engel. The former McMaster classmates crossed paths while abroad and travelled together to Cyprus, where they spent two years before returning to Canada in September 1964. The letters in this chapter, most of which were written to Engel's parents at home in Sarnia, begin with the young author's arrival in Europe and end with the couple's return to Canada.

Keen though she was to explore a wider world, she was not, Engel declared, a very good tourist. 'For one thing,' she wrote her parents shortly after her arrival in Europe, 'I like comfort too much, for another I'm a simply dreadful coward. I suppose it's being alone that makes me timorous' (16 October 1960). 'Women travelling alone' became the theme and title of a manuscript that Engel worked on during this period. Notwithstanding claims of cowardice, the author travelled through Europe without serious difficulty, relishing the rewards of timidity vanquished: 'clothes, cookery, books, politics' in France (5 March 1962); and, in Cyprus, 'a monastery, the ruins of an ancient city, and a hermit's cave! All this for a 45¢ bus ride!' (10 May 1963). Food is a recurring theme in the correspondence. Between mussels and snails, shish kebab and pâté de foie gras, croissants and chocolate, good coffee, and 'wine with all, naturally,' Engel became 'quite a food fancier' (24 October 1960). But travel was not all about physical comforts or discomforts. There were newspapers, books, films, and galleries to discover, as well as new perspectives on the world. Particularly striking is Engel's newfound view of the British Empire. 'I think [England] built that Empire on a myth,' she wrote to her parents 16 October 1960. 'What a laugh! I suppose I'm very angry because I was brought up thinking England was superior and singing "There'll always be an England" – but it's really no better than any place else – it just has that sublime confidence. What makes me mad is the talk about the colonies – you hear it everywhere' (16 October 1960).

Engel's critical views about colonialism placed her in a vanguard of Canadian artists and intellectuals who began to voice concerns about the country's cultural identity and future in the face of ongoing European influence and growing American presence during the post–Second World War period. Such prominent thinkers and theorists as George Grant, Marshall McLuhan, and Northrop Frye were joined by other writers and artists in observing the impact of the British, French, and American empires, past and present, on the political, cultural, and economic sovereignty of Canada and other former colonies.[2] In memoirs of the 1950s and 1960s, writers such as Margaret Atwood, William Weintraub,

Matt Cohen, and Douglas Fetherling identify the British and American dominance in cultural and curriculum developments of the time.[3] Atwood recalls poet Earle Birney's claim that most Canadians of those years had only three hardcover books in the house: 'the bible, the works of Shakespeare, and Fitzgerald's *The Rubaiyat of Omar Khayyam.*'[4] The concept of a distinctly Canadian literature did not yet exist. 'Jack Kerouac and the Beat Generation had hit the scene in the late 1950s,' Atwood recollects. 'You were supposed to be familiar with Faulkner and Scott Fitzgerald and Hemingway, and Tennessee Williams and Eugene O'Neill.'[5] Steinbeck, Whitman, Dickinson, Miller, Eliot, Pound, Joyce, Woolf, and Yeats, these were the authors to read. Peter Sellers, Elvis Presley, the Monty Python precursor *Beyond the Fringe,* these were the entertainers and entertainments. 'There were very few published Canadian novelists,' Atwood points out; 'few knew one another, and of these many were living in other countries, having gone there because they did not think they could function as artists in Canada.'[6] This was certainly the case with Mavis Gallant, Brian Moore, and Mordecai Richler, three of William Weintraub's correspondents in his reminiscence of the 1950s, *Getting Started.* Short story writer Mavis Gallant had given up her job as feature writer for the *Montreal Standard* to live in Paris and work as a full-time writer. Weintraub, her former newspaper colleague, visited her there, and she introduced him to Mordecai Richler, who also was living abroad at the time. 'Richler is the first Canadian who is also a novelist,' the English critic Walter Allen declared upon the publication of Richler's 1955 novel *Son of a Smaller Hero.*[7] The view that Canadian literature was barely entering its infancy was not limited to non-Canadians during the 1950s and 1960s. Canadians also tended to measure the quality of their country's literature and culture by European and American standards and by successes in Europe and the United States. Canadian publishers, still few in number, rarely risked a Canadian work that was not already under contract with an American or British house. 'Until the mid-sixties it was considered impossible for a novel published only in Canada to recoup its costs,' Matt Cohen observed, underlining the importance of Engel's later contact with the New York agents Russell and Volkening. Artists and writers like Gallant, Richler, or Quebec's Anne Hébert sought artistic confirmation and community abroad. 'In Canada at that time,' Cohen put it plainly, 'writing was not a career in any sense.'[8]

The challenges to Canadian cultural development would ease somewhat as various government and individual initiatives of the 1950s began to have effect. The 1951 Royal Commission on National Development in the Arts, Letters and Sciences, chaired by Vincent Massey and Henri Lévesque, provided a catalyst for change. The Massey Report, as the work of the commission came to be known, recommended federal government policies and support for the development and protection of the arts in Canada. The Report played a direct role in the creation of the National Library in 1953 and, in 1957, the Canada Council, which would provide assistance to individuals and groups for artistic and cultural production. The 1955 'Kingston Conference,' held at Queen's University, concluded with a resolution that 'urged all provinces to give a more prominent place to Canadian literature in school curricula, textbooks, colleges, and universities and to support Canadian libraries.'[9] Canadian literature began to be included slowly but surely as a separate course in school curricula rather than as a mere subset of 'North American' literature. At the ensuing Conference on B.C. Writing in January 1956, delegates discussed 'the situation of the Canadian writer, the difficulty of obtaining Canadian books, and a request that the CBC increase its coverage of Canadian writing.'[10] Discussions, resolutions, and commissions on Canadian culture during the 1950s made possible several striking developments on the cultural scene of the 1960s, such as the flowering of Canadian literary and arts magazines and the creation of the House of Anansi and Coach House publishing companies.[11] Cultural nationalism would peak with the Centennial celebrations of 1967. In the interim, however, the international scene remained the place to pursue arts and culture, and like her contemporaries, Engel travelled in search of them.

Travel brought additional intellectual developments. Engel read and wrote tirelessly throughout her time in Europe. Soon after arrival, she had already spent the last of her English money on books – 'serious things, gaps in my reading,' Engel assured her parents 16 October 1960. A week later, she writes happily that she has 'a typewriter in my paws again' (24 October 1960). Not just any typewriter, this one belonged to Howard Engel, whose reacquaintance brought an end to travelling alone. Engel expressed joy in the company. 'We both love adventure & islands,' she reported (20 August 1962). 'We are rotund, happy, and ON THE MOVE ... We are twins!' (18 November 1962). Typewriter at hand, Engel pursued her various writing projects, which included plays and novels. A letter of 9 December 1960 announces that she has 'mailed the play and started another one, and read a couple of books.' Her thesis supervisor and mentor, Hugh MacLennan, had encouraged Engel to try her hand at plays. She worked on two in particular: 'The Deception of the Thrush,' about a young woman's desire to be an artist, and 'Beat Up the Rain,' a variation on the same theme. 'Women Travelling Alone' was the title of the novel Engel worked on while in London. It told the story of a woman 'happily married to a painter who leaves, teaches, travels and tutors in order to find her feet,' as Engel described it to Diarmuid Russell (10 April 1962). The New York literary agency Russell and Volkening had agreed to consider her work. 'Women Travelling Alone' was destined to become Engel's second unpublished novel, after 'The Pink Sphinx,' written during her year teaching in Montana. While neither manuscript was retained for publication, both earned Engel praise for her writing, and she felt encouraged to undertake a new novel. 'Death Comes for the Yaya,' her third unpublished manuscript, was set on an island much like Cyprus, where Engel wrote it.

While her publishing breakthrough did not occur until she was back in Canada, Engel's writing apprenticeship abroad played an important role in her growth as a writer. Letters home map her professional development with references to manuscripts mailed off and progress on various literary projects. On 29 April 1962 she told her aunt and uncle that 'a publisher in New York wants to see part of my novel.' On 12 February 1963 she explained to her parents a lapse in the regularity of her letters home: 'chronicles' to Canada, she wrote, 'sop up my need to write.' On 10 May 1963 she expressed relief that her book had finally been received by her New York agents, and a copy was on its way to London.[12]

Writing to her parents, Engel was often surprisingly candid about her adventures. From Lund, she complained that lectures 'are not very absorbing – especially after a party every night' (1 September 1960). From Aix-en-Provence, she reported to her mother that her new French skirt was 'tighter in the waist than I used to be able to wangle from you' (9 December 1960), and from London came news of being evacuated in the middle of the night from a house fire so intense that the mirrors melted (20 August 1962). The author was more circumspect about her developing relationship with Howard Engel, particularly in the case of a trip they took at Christmas 1960 to Venice, where they became engaged.[13] Clearly content in one another's company, the couple enjoyed Paris as well as Venice and Ravenna together. When her scholarship year drew to an end, Marian and Howard travelled to London, rather than return to Canada.

In a letter copied to both the Passmore and the Engel parents on 18 November 1962, the newly married couple announced their plans to leave London for Cyprus. Howard expected to do freelance work for the CBC, and Marian anticipated finding a teaching job or office work. By the time of her letter to her parents on 10 May 1963, she was teaching on the RAF base in Nicosia. At the end of the summer of 1963, as they prepared to leave Cyprus and return to Canada, Engel wrote admiringly of her new husband to her parents: '... here I come with my miracle man ... He's really petrified of Passmores and we must bring him round gently because underneath the shell he's a fantastically good person, and he gives, gives and gives' (31 August 1963).

Travel abroad meant yet another form of personal development for Marian Engel. 'Going to France,' she observed to a new Rotary Scholarship recipient who had written to her from Sarnia, 'gave me more than anything else a new concept of myself. I realised for good and all that I was a girl! ... I learned a great deal, lived almost lyrically, and came to understand part at least of the French mentality. The year left me fantastically pro-French' (5 March 1962). Engel remained partial to France, and to its literature, language, and food, for the rest of her life. A return visit to Paris at Christmas 1984 was a wish fulfilled only weeks before her untimely death in February 1985.

The years abroad presented frequent financial concerns: money was needed for rent and dental bills, for brassieres and books. Engel's fulsome letter of 16 October 1960 closes with one of several requests home to arrange for funds to be sent. Letters from this period contain equally frequent thanks to family members and relatives for cash presented in lieu of Christmas or birthday gifts. Such assistance helped make life abroad possible.

Although clearly very happy in her newly married life, Engel was already feeling some of the strain of finding enough time to write. On 31 August 1963 she remarked that Howard had 'gone out so I can work on my new book' and observed that she had been 'terrible about housework and entertaining, but I am also trying to toughen myself up and not care what other people think.' Enclosing a short piece of writing for her New York agent, on 17 September 1964, Engel reported that she was 'working on two novels: one bosh about how deeply one can hate Toronto, another possibly quite good, remittance people on an island. This last will be quickly written, and sent to you before next year, I hope.' A week later, the couple left Cyprus for Toronto, where

Engel was to make her breakthrough into the world of published authors.

Notes

1 In Montreal, where she completed her M.A. at McGill, and in Montana, where she taught for a year at the University of Montana.

2 George Grant (1918–88), philosopher and professor, whose *Lament for a Nation* (1965) raised Canadian political consciousness in the 1960s; Marshall McLuhan (1911–80), celebrated media theorist and author of *The Medium Is the Message* (1967); Northrop Frye (1912–91), professor at University of Toronto, who influenced many future Canadian writers and intellectuals with works such as *The Anatomy of Criticism* (1955).

3 Atwood, *Negotiating with the Dead: A Writer on Writing*; William Weintraub, *Getting Started: A Memoir of the 1950s* (Toronto: McClelland and Stewart, 2001); Douglas Fetherling, *Travels by Night: A Memoir of the Sixties* (Toronto: McArthur & Co., 1994); Cohen, *Typing: A Life in Twenty-Six Keys*.

4 Atwood, *Negotiating with the Dead: A Writer on Writing*, 6.

5 Ibid., 19.

6 Ibid., 23.

7 See Weintraub, *Getting Started: A Memoir of the 1950s*, 125.

8 Cohen, *Typing: A Life in Twenty-Six Keys*, 82, 37.

9 Sandra Djwa, *Professing English: A Life of Roy Daniells* (Toronto: University of Toronto Press, 2002), 311.

10 Ibid., 312.

11 See below, p. 52.

12 For more information about Engel's early writings, see Verduyn, *Lifelines*, chapter 3.

13 For example, Engel fails to mention her engagement in the letter to Auntie Lola, 13 January 1961.

To Mr and Mrs F.S. Passmore
Sarnia, Ontario

Lund University
Lund, Sweden .

1 September (I think!) [1960][1]

Dear Mum and Dad –
I just received your letter of August 28th telling about the wedding. So sorry you hadn't had mine yet, but perhaps you have got the two by now. One from Paris, one from here – I think. Travelling so much, one gets confused. I also wrote a very long one to Helen[2] – kept adding to it. It was for all of you of course, but I sent it to her as it was her turn. Postcards are quite expensive so I hope the neighbours show you theirs!

They are keeping us very busy here. There was a big party at Malmö last night and today I slept in and missed a tour of a paper plant – needed the sleep more! I'm not much good at these long parties any more. Fortunately the students here don't drink as much as at home. They manage to be quite lively enough as it is. I kept having to escape from these characters who dance too close! (*NOT* Swedes.) It's most embarrassing.

The lectures haven't really got underway yet, but they are not very absorbing – especially after a party every night. The people who wish to preach are a bore, too. There is a *mad* Indian called Funchel who gives impassioned speeches in thick, staticky English no one can understand. The communists stick together, except for the Yugoslavs, who keep apart! As talking is more my forté than dancing I hope we have a good discussion this afternoon. I

---

1 'Sept. 3' is added at the end of the letter.
2 Helen Crawford (née Passmore), Engel's older sister.

haven't felt out of it at these parties, but I must admit they make me feel a little old. Usually I find some learned person and go off and talk!

The trip to Malmö also included a visit to the town planning office and to a ship-building enterprise. They are building *huge* apartment buildings there – with lots of park area – but it's all a little multiple for me. Housing is a problem here. There are also plans for a bridge across the sound from Copenhagen to Malmö. The shipyards gave us a grand view across to Copenhagen – on a beautiful blue, sunny day. They took us around their establishment – they build 10 ships a year, usually, and have 600 workers. They showed us a job they were doing for the Greek, Niarchos[3] – putting a new midships in an old American army tanker – amazing job. The generators and engines they build are of an amazing size!

I received the forwarded letters yesterday Mom – many thanks. They were from Maggie D., Michel, and Cynthia Wilson,[4] who apologized for not visiting us or saying she wasn't coming. She was an English girl I met at Geography summer school.

What else can I tell you about Sweden? Here in the south the land is flat and orderly. Rather like home but neater. A lot of red tile roofs, as is usual in northern Europe.
Friday.

Haven't had another chance to get at this letter, what with life bursting with lectures and parties. However, I have three whole hours to myself if I go without supper and since I'm eating too much might as well. On the way home this afternoon I bought a London *Times*, some nail polish remover, and a tube of pimple cream. Not enough greens and fruit, I guess – all we N. Americans are getting spotty. The food at the cafeteria is largely meat and

3 Stavros Niarchos (1908–96), billionaire Greek shipping magnate.
4 Engel friends. Michel Euvrard reappears in subsequent letters, along with spouse, Janine.

potatoes, which is why most of the girls do their own cooking. You can get delicious open-face sandwiches at the Student Union but I object to buying extra food!

Ye gods, it's raining again. About every two hours the sky simply opens! You can see why the Swedes are athletic – they run an awful lot.

I've been trying to find a present for Ruth and Ted, but glass is too expensive and I haven't yet seen any tablecloths I like. Some of us are going to Copenhagen on Sunday, though, and maybe I'll see something there. Swedish exports are probably cheaper at home. However, I did see a beautiful pewter bowl for about $10 and if I don't find something else that is suitable, I'll perhaps add a little souvenir of Sweden. I know you are not pewter-lovers, but this is *good* pewter and suitable for any decor. It would look marvellous with fruit. There are also very interesting lamps but they probably won't work on alternating current and the shop-keepers don't speak enough English to be sure. Pewter-working is a Lund industry.

I fell from grace and bought myself a present today – a dear little pottery hedgehog I've walked past every day in store windows! Such a sweetheart. I think Maggie D. has one also. Snub nosed and spiny! He may go for a present, perhaps.

Last night we were each invited to a student's 'digs' for a coffee party. There were six altogether at the party I attended and it was most interesting. The negro boys were persuaded to talk about their reception in the world. They were most bitter about having lost their countries' history – brought up as Englishmen learning English history while their own history was lost – and then of course, it was hard to find they were not taken as Englishmen in England. Both were up at Oxford, very bright boys and it seemed a shame that they should find life so difficult. We have found the negros the most intelligent and pleasant group – they never sound off. Most of them are studying in England, on scholarships from their own governments, and most are very well bred. Sam, from Jamaica, is a big cheerful guy – a social worker, for heaven's sake! There is an angelic soul from Ghana, too. The Indians are rather a pain. About 30 countries are represented.

What else, now? Lund is a pretty, peaceful town – 40,000 people of whom 7,000 are students. Red and yellow brick are the great materials, with tile and slate roofs. The 'Nations' – student residences – are beautifully modern. I haven't been in an ordinary house so I don't know what they're like, but I imagine they're pretty grand. Very little *tasteless* material is for sale.

There are lots of handsome women around – big and clear-featured – on the whole they are very good-looking and dress well without fussiness. The men aren't all that handsome.

Later. I finally got a bath and then went over to the 'club' – the conference social room in the Union Bldg. It was a 'drop in' evening but I didn't know whether to or not – when I did I found it lots of fun – danced a lot, talked to an American prof. who is tomorrow's speaker and wound up walking by the seaside in the wind with the course secretary, a sweet young man called Gören, pronounced Urine, meaning George. The beach is only about 8 km from here so it was a nice drive. So what if I have to go to bed for a week after I leave Sweden?

The attractive stains on this page are from the juice of a very large peach, bought to stave off scurvy. It tasted good after that cold wind. The seacoast looking towards Malmö & Copenhagen is low but covered with tall, course grass. Otherwise it looked rather like home.

Well, I must take my swelled head to bed. I am to a certain degree a social success with the right kind of people, which makes me very happy – now I've got rid of the pawing Italians and the prozelytizing Hungarians I am happy. I must look odd wearing sandals with my suit, but for the cobbled streets sandals are the answer – the less shoe the less blistering.

I noticed a 'CAMPING' sign near where we drove tonight! Just waiting for you. Don't worry about me – I'll tell you when to start! Blessings, dears, keep well, and thanks for everything.

Love,
Miggs [M.E.'s family nickname]

To Mr and Mrs F.S. Passmore
Sarnia, Ontario

St Helier
Jersey, Channel Islands

Sunday, 16 October 1960

Dear Ma and Pa,
I am now, for the moment, a retired tourist. Through sheer incompetence, I gave up. I was going to France to stay with Michel and Janine, but as I didn't give them enough notice, and they are moving, they very politely suggested I come later. It was too late to find another place to stay in London so I simply got off the boat here rather than in St Malo and here I am holed up in a bed-and-breakfast with a pile of books and a new bottle of ink, living a very healthy life in spite of my desire to do nothing but sleep 'til doomsday. At breakfast my landlady, who seems to hope I'll some day write commercials for Jersey, suggests a new expedition, and I meekly go off. Today I got rather overenthusiastic and walked 8½ miles and I am now pulling the skin off the bottom of my feet in long shreds and trying to think what you put on blisters.

When I last wrote I have no idea. I simply forget about the time these days. However, Wednesday evening I got back to London and found the Blue Cross letter and your letter from Kingston, plus Michel's and one from a girl I met in Sweden: a nice haul, especially since I won't have mail for another ten days. I should still be in Aix on the 26th but may not. I left England a week early because I wanted to see Mike & J. and because Howie expects me in Paris on the 20th but of course that's all wrong now. Planning never was my forté but I am good at chance, so here I am in this mild, inconsequential place when I could be in Oxford or Paris, and enjoying myself very much. I spent the last of my English money in Bristol on books I thought both Michel and I would like to read – serious things, gaps in my reading, so here I am reading them! It's so long since I've had a good read, and a rest.

Travelling about really is very tiresome. I'm not a very good tourist, you know. For one thing I like comfort too much, for another I'm a simply dreadful coward. I suppose it's being alone that makes me timorous, but I hate going into buildings I don't know, and I'm still shy of going places alone. Well, some places – most restaurants give me fits so I always choose the wrong ones! Still the same idiotic person, but getting used to it. The thing is, on the continent one can do anything because foreigners are excused; here one can do anything because they're fed [up] to the teeth with tourists and hate them, but in England I feel I ought to behave, so the old self-consciousness comes back.

I found England very beautiful and very depressing, and was, on the whole, glad to get away. The English contempt for physical comfort is well-known but the food is on the whole so lousy, the people are so dirty, that it's rather a shock. If I could convince myself that their minds were on Higher Things or that they didn't know any better, I wouldn't mind but they're so damn used to their snivelly noses, raw hands and dirty fingernails that they're anaesthetized. This does not, of course, apply to the top people, obviously, but the top people are being pushed out by the rest, so – oh, dear, poor England. I think it built that Empire on a myth. What a laugh! I suppose I'm very angry because I was brought up thinking England was superior and singing 'There'll always be an England' – but it's really no better than any place else – it just has that sublime confidence. What makes me mad is the talk about the colonies – you hear it everywhere, because of Africa and the terribly superior attitude people have – as if God gave them better souls than the Africans.

Oh well – I'll see another side when I go back – and I went on a bus through the Mendips and saw a Hunt, and I saw gypsies at Evercreech Junction, when I was sneezed at by a cow and fled.[5]

Practical matters: 1) Teeth. London dentist said there was definitely an abscess. It might cure itself, do nothing yet. Charged me two quid. It probably won't go away as it is doing the same old thing, hurting mostly in cold, clear air, but maybe the status quo will hold until I get home. 2) Money. I have spent exactly what I intended to spend and so will be broke when I get to Aix. Never mind. There's Rotary money. But I must get a typewriter if I'm to make any money against next summer. *So* would you kindly arrange for $80 to be sent to me at Aix soon – I suppose a bank draft is the way you do it – for that or about 400 New Francs. 3) Photography – goes on as usual. I hope you get the pictures soon & that they are decent. All taken at appropriate red number and 1/60 of a second. I am now using Ektachrome because you can take pix with much less light. I find this camera very hard to focus so everything is landscape! My Australian friend took some extras in Norway because I was so disappointed about my Scandinavian film. They are dark, but an interesting record. Why he sent me a picture of the Morris being lifted off the ship I don't know. I guess because he's an engineer! I sent him ten shillings in a letter – he will be insulted but won't know how to return it. I hope, by the way, that I haven't written all of this to you before – I do lose track! Tell my dear sister I am neglecting her because mail is expensive (1/3d = 17¢) and I know you'll pass the letters on. An airmail letter takes about 3 days to get to England, sea mail about two weeks, by the way.

---

5 The Mendips, one of five ranges of hills in Somerset; Evercreech Junction, a station on the Somerset and Dorset railway line.

Well – shall I tell you about Jersey? It's very small and very commercialized and very beautiful. I've rented a bicycle but find I see more going on the bus, and then walking. This morning, after a positively resounding breakfast (cereal, bacon, eggs, tomatoes, bread, butter, marmalade, tea) I went down to the beach and walked partway to the castle, but as the causeway is covered at high tide, turned back, walked along and sat against the sea wall on the sand for about an hour. I then proceeded along the shore in my bare feet – it was warm, after all, another couple of miles to St Aubin, where I had a sandwich and set off up a *very* steep road for St Brelade's Bay, where there is a *very* old church. It was 3 when I got there, after getting lost a couple of times. Saw church. Took picture. Tired, but went on dutifully to La Corbière where there's a lighthouse. Thousands of cars on the road. People stared. Very cold at La Corbière. No food. Frightfully tired. Walked *on* and *on*. Blisters. Found bus stop – wrong way – found village, sat on nice cold stone wall and read until the bus came. It took me 22 minutes to go where I had walked in 4 hours – 5 hours, really – but I had smelled the broom,[6] and seen robins, and mooed back at the Jersey cows. They wear blankets. Old, old walls along the road – pink granite. In the country away from the hotel it is very placid and old and hung with ivy. Sun very warm but cold at night. People rather anti-tourist.

Must not use another page. Shall close with love – hope your pictures are good. Take care of your knee Dad. Don't go too hard, you two – think of me, having a holiday from my holiday – to digest the things I've seen.

xx Miggs

Will send a bulletin on roads & car-width soon. Still thinking. (I do not have to send Blue + thing back.)

---

6 A wild shrub, a type of heather.

To Mr and Mrs F.S. Passmore
Sarnia, Ontario

Hotel D'Isly
Paris, France

24 October 1960

Dear folks,
At long last I am back in Paris with a typewriter in my paws again –
guess whose? Howard is back in Paris too and I am up in his room
at the top floor of an old hotel fiddling with the back spacers. If I
chose to look out the window I could see St. Germain des Près on
the left and St. Sulpice on the right and the Pantheon if I stood
on tiptoe but I'll have to get a move on if we're not going to spend
the whole day fiddling around here so I won't look out the
window. I got here yesterday at noon and Howie met the train –
after all the trains I've taken it was a good thing to have a familiar
face at the end of the track! Especially to have him around in
Paris because we eat at good places and go to interesting night
clubs and things. What we are going to do today I don't know yet:
we're waiting to see if someone comes who is driving to Geneva
with someone else, you know how it is.

I spent a few days in Rennes with Michel and Janine, Tante
Rose and Philippe. Tante Rose is J's mother more or less, and
Philippe is the baby who had been sick. They were moving from
one apartment to another, and in a flap most of the time, so it was
a crazy visit. Michel carries a vacuum around himself and he is no
more comfortable to be with, although he is still amusing, than he
ever was and Janine likes fighting with him and Tante Rose puts
her oar in so it is all a mess and they hate Brittany. It was cold and
rainy and Rennes is rather dead, but we had one good dinner
and saw one good movie. They did get moved and I did a lot of

scrubbing and washing at the other flat for them so I wasn't really in the way. Visiting married people is not my favourite thing.

The week in Jersey was rather nice: very calm and flat. There were few places to eat open so that was rather hard but I walked a lot and looked at the sea and the cows and managed to lose my English accent for which thank heavens.

What else is new? I passed Chartres and Versailles on the train; went last night to a bar where there were folk singers and had an excellent supper at a Spanish restaurant: we had mussels in garlic butter: magnifique. They cook the meal specially for one so it was terrific. Had lunch in a Greek place – marvellous shish-kebab and wine with all, naturally. I have become quite a food fancier, the result of eating badly too often and it is terrific to eat well again especially after the garbage one was served with in England. Mixed grills are good there but one never gets good beef. Tante Rose cooked a lovely roast one night in Rennes: it was quite a celebration. So food these days is my main concern. It is hard to hold onto ideas in transit so one thinks mostly about getting fed and clean. I am thinking about shopping for underwear but I am afraid of spending too much money.

Can't concentrate here – will finish this later. Now, next morning, over my coffee – how much better French coffee tastes after England! And Madame makes good coffee, serves excellent croissants with butter and sharp jelly – I am well off. Probably Howie's hotel is better than this but I shall stay here till Friday anyhow. It's a good thing I've done my sightseeing because I haven't done much with him – yesterday we went out for lunch about 2, window-shopped, then took shelter in the rain back at his hotel. We had bought $2 worth of French chocolates so we read and ate chocolate till suppertime, had an apéritif at the Deux Magots and then went to a café for supper – I had snails. We had a carafe of vin ordinaire and rather mediocre food but we stayed till nearly midnight drawing pictures on the table cloth and talking, talking. Howie has been doing some film dubbing and selling a bit of work to the CBC. He may go to London soon but he's still resting up after 4 months of strenuous idling in Ibiza. He lives in a little room at the very top of a nice hotel – nicer than mine – with a slanting ceiling, a good table, dresser and wardrobe, has lots of English-speaking friends and eats as well as he can. We've been to some divine restaurants – the other night we went very late to a place where they make päella – but only on Fri. and Sat. we discovered. But they cooked us up some splendid mussels – about 2 doz. each in garlic sauce, and then we had chops & with new potatoes! I suppose the bill was about $2.25 with coffee and wine. But to-day we economize – no wine, very little coffee. We both have errands to do – I hope we can go to the flea market. And I need a brassiere so that will require research & being measured in centimetres. He has a party to go to tonight & I must meet my Australian girlfriend.

Fran Frazer's sister Renee is in town. Teaching at a Lycée and staying at Howie's hotel. She is very nice and sweet but having a hard time to find a place to stay that she can afford.

I go to Aix on Friday the 28th – hope to find mail etc. It will be *wonderful* to settle down. Then I suppose I'll have to do Xmas shopping – your presents will be *small* and late. I must go out now – it's nearly 10. Excuse the awful writing – hate ball-point pens and this one only works forward! Lots of love to all. Thinking of you.

xxx Miggs

The envelope I addressed in August – forgot to post the letter before I left France for Belgium.

To Mr and Mrs F.S. Passmore
Sarnia, Ontario

17 rue Cardinale
[Aix-en-Provence, France]

9 December 1960

Dear Mum and Dad,
It was so nice to have your letter this foul morning: I had decided
to stay in bed until the mail came and never get up if there was no
letter, but sure enough, it came and your letter was brought to me
by Donna in a blue sweater asking me if I were sick. She has now
gone out into the pouring cold rain to the post office and will
bring me a quiche for my lunch so I shan't have to go out until
four for my class. I presume the rain that has flooded northern
Europe has now reached us. Aix is unpleasant in the rain: the
sidewalks are too narrow to accommodate the pedestrians and
there are too many cars on the road.

I am very glad you have a nice fur coat, maman, and a hat: what
a lady you are getting a chance to be! Lucky it isn't monkey like
madame's house jacket!

This week might as well have not existed for me. I mailed the
play and started another one, and read a couple of books, but
that was about all.[7] Oh yes, I paid the dentist: he felt so sorry that
I couldn't get social security that he only charged ten dollars.
When I opened my wallet to pay him he saw a wad of bills, almost
immediately regretted his decision, but couldn't do anything! I
felt badly because it's a ridiculous price for something that requires surgery and three x-rays! Anyway, I went out in the usual

---

7 Engel's unpublished plays 'The Deception of the Thrush' and 'Beat Up the
  Rain.'

economical fashion and had a skirt made, for I burned a hole in the black one at cooking class and was reduced to my suit skirt – the new one is plain grey flannel, lined in the back and was twelve dollars: they made it to order in one day: it is smart and somehow very French, probably because it is tapered. Most marvellous of all, it is the only skirt that fits perfectly that I have since you stopped making them, mother – except that it is slightly tighter in the waist than I used to be able to wangle from you!

I am very glad you are thinking of sending money for Christmas because between you and me and the gatepost, excluding the Rotary Club, I am going to Italy. I should stay in France but no one has invited me so I don't exactly feel obligated. Sunnier climes are in order and it is only thirty dollars return to Florence, so I'm off in ten days, I hope. I have plenty of money but, you know how it is ... I have not sent you any more Christmas presents as I rather shot my bolt on the Crawfords, but shopping in Italy should be good. I'd love it if Howie would come with me and long to send him a telegram 'Venice anyone?' but he hasn't written yet about my other suggestions so to heck with him; he may be in England by now. Madame has given me some addresses to write to and I hope to be able to find a reasonable kind of accommodation. I suppose I should go to Rome too but I have always wanted to go to Venice so if I go beyond Florence that will be my destination. I adore canals, however smelly! So unless you hear definitely otherwise, think of me in Florence for Christmas, Venice for New Year's: yes, the way to start 1961 is definitely Venice; it will be a marvellous year if it begins there. Holidays start the 21st but apparently everyone leaves before then, so I'll go when the going's good.

My friends have not been too kind as far as the mail is concerned but Christmas is so busy at home; here people have hardly started shopping, thank goodness and there are no lights yet. I must go to Marseille, however, for every day there is a 'foire de santons' – and santons are little figures for creches. Apparently the whole canabière is decorated with booths, for the making of santons is a large Provençal industry.

I didn't go to the Rotary Club this week and by the next time I should go I'll be away, and then reappear after Christmas gay and jolly so everything should be healed up. I don't think they really meant to insult me but it was rather an indication that my company wasn't up to much ... so.[8]

I was very sorry to hear of the Taits' accident: oddly enough I was thinking of them before your letter came.[9] They do have awful luck, don't they? I have sent them a Christmas card but will write a letter tout de suite.

Next time I can corner Félix I'll ask him about the weather in April; I really will, and I did write to Paris about the caravanes.[10]

So, happy holidays and love

Miggs

Went to the movies last night with a very nice French girl & will dine with her Sat. night. Tonight we're giving a bridge party, but a good one, I hope, because some interesting people are coming. French movie programmes are very long. By the time the news & commercials are over my eyes are worn out. Had a very nice letter from Beth, by the way. When you write to Uncle Welles tell him I loved it and will answer after Xmas.

---

8 Surviving letters do not reveal any further information about this incident.
9 Neighbours and friends of the Passmores in Sarnia.
10 Engel uses the French spelling for caravans (trailers) here.

To Mrs D.R. Falconer
[Toronto, Ontario]

17 rue Cardinale
Aix-en-Provence, France

13 January 1961

Dear Auntie Lola –
I very much appreciated both the card from Florida and the package. The latter was forwarded to me in Paris just after Christmas and opened with great glee – the only package that was properly timed. The stockings were a lifesaver – who wants to spend money on stockings in Paris? As for the scarf, it will, as you suggest, make a very nice gift – for a little girl in Marseille who sent me a French one. It is very convenient to have Canadian things to give away. People seem to expect them but one cannot carry very many around.

The holidays were marvellous: I met my friend Howard Engel in Venice, where we spent Christmas, then went to Ravenna with him to see the mosaics. Thence to Paris for New Year's. There were a lot of our friends there so the entire time was spent meeting people in cafés. I did manage to get my hair done once and was very pleased. They spend infinite amounts of time even over very short cuts like mine and it's so luxurious! The clothes in Paris are of course wonderful, but who has money to spend on clothes in Paris? I much prefer to go out in the evenings.

Venice is a dream, as I think you know. It was cold enough but there was no snow. One morning I found St Mark's Square flooded – people were walking about on raised catwalks – they keep the boards & trestles there all the time in winter. I found the huge paintings in the galleries tiresome on the whole. It became a relief to find small Flemish paintings in corners. Ravenna was exquisite.

The mausoleum of Galla Placidia is very small, but the interior above the marble wainscotting is entirely mosaic with 10 alabaster windows.[11] The ceiling decorations are a deep, glowing blue with white & gold flowers & stars, and the pictures of Christ and the apostles, of doves and gazelles, all done in mosaics are beautiful. We took a taxi out to Classe one morning to see the Church of St Appollinaire, which has a wonderful Good Shepherd mosaic, and frescoes. What a place. It was capital of the Holy Roman Empire around 600, is as quiet as Aix now – but full of treasures.

Must close now with many thanks & best wishes to the whole family for 1961.

X Marian

To Ruth Billingsley[12]
Sarnia, Ontario

5 March 1962

Dear Ruth,
Congratulations on winning the Rotary Fellowship! And you're terribly lucky to be going to Dijon ... I was only there on a cold rainy morning but I wanted to go back, to explore, to shelter under those beautiful Burgundian roofs. And how you will eat! Ah. Bourgogne, the province of the Chevaliers de Tas de Vin! I was lucky too, to be in the south (think if it had been Strasbourg), but travelling to and from Paris I longed to stop off around Dijon

---

11 Galla Placidia (386–452), the sister of Honorius, the Roman emperor who moved the capital of the Western Empire from Milan to Ravenna, built the mausoleum around A.D. 425–50.
12 Now Ruth Grogan, professor of English at York University.

and never quite managed to except the once on the way back from Spain, chilled to the bone by a spell of cold weather. You should adopt the country between Dijon and Besançon, and go west into the Ardèche and the Massif Central ... this is, I think, the real France, the heartland, although those from the Midi would argue, and the northerners. So ... France it is, and Dijon, a good university I think, and the only person I know who studied there is in London, Ont., Dr. Lane Heller, whose wife was at McMaster with me. They, lucky things, were married in Paris, and will be full of information. Perhaps, of course, you know Lane from Western already.[13] Their address is 295 Regent Street.

I think the best thing to do about being a Rotary fellow in France is to forget the propaganda about being an 'ambassador' and just be yourself. Lady ambassadors are just not French meat: they are interested in individuals and in seriousness ... the worse thing they can say about you is that you are 'pas serieuse.' Rotary meetings are very different: much less friendly than at home, but once someone takes you up, you are well looked after. French Rotarians tend to be rich, preoccupied, and serious. But they don't listen to the business at meetings ... they are more serious about food. I found that 'how I love France' and 'how I love French cooking' were good subjects of conversation. How you are received will depend on the local club. Several of us in France found ourselves rather strangely treated ... I HAD to go to every meeting, the students in Paris were left absolutely alone, the students in Strasbourg were treated as in England or at home. So the rule is, I suppose, to play it cool and do your own work well. Being a Canadian will be a great help and if you have friends in the F.L.N.[14] don't mention it! (Rotarians are all ultra-conservative in conservative towns, although the Menton club seemed to be

13 The University of Western Ontario.
14 Front de libération nationale, Algerian nationalist group which fought a war of independence against France between 1954 and 1962.

rather left-wing.) Politics is not the subject of conversation this year.

I hope the professor you go to work under is there ... and don't let yourself get put into an Institute for Foreign Students if you don't want to be in one. Get there early, get a good guide book ... as many as you can find, talk as much French as you can and avoid American students until you can really speak French.

Living accommodation? The Cité Universitaire will be much cheaper than a private house, so try to get either the university or the Rotary to get you a room there. I lived with a family, it was lovely to have breakfast in bed, but it cost the earth, my French became very good, my figure spread, my landlady loved me until I had to start doing my laundry myself. I really think a *French* students' residence would be better: luxury is bad for the soul, and remember when you're calculating expenses, the Canadian dollar is between 5 and 6 new francs, 500 to 600 old ones, and the cost of living is high.

Going to France gave me more than anything else a new concept of myself. I realised for good an[d] all that I was a girl! That life could be gracious in the true sense, that seriousness was not allied with slipping feminine standards ... I learned a great deal, lived almost lyrically, and came to understand part at least of the French mentality. The year left me fantastically pro-French, as is my husband, who lived a year and a half in Paris and we're heading back as soon as we can shake London and its smog off our heels. Don't forget that *Elle* and *L'Express* are marvellously balanced to give you a weekly picture of France ... clothes, cookery, books, politics. *L'Express* is left-wing but very fine and true. *Time* I confess I always got, to keep in touch with America. Buy the new books, too, you'll be able to afford it, and go to Paris when you can. If you want to get a fairly cheap hotel room there, go to the Hotel de Nancy, 56, rue Bonaparte, Paris 6. Everyone has his favourite hotel, but if you tell the Janots you're a friend of the Passmores and 'Edouard Engel' (that's Howie ... the J's can't cope with *Howard*) you'll find that although it's not rock bottom cheap it's all right (about $2). Cheaper still but less friendly is the Hotel de Grand Conde, 3 rue Saint Sulpice, but then all your friends will recommend other ones. Don't forget to visit Bourges the (or is it Bourg) loveliest of towns, and meet with the Association d'Anciens Boursiers. Have a good time, come and see us!

Regards,
Marian Engel (Passmore)

Do pardon the typing – I don't try on Sundays!

To Mr and Mrs D.R. Falconer
Toronto, Ontario

64, West End Lane
London, England

Saturday, 29 April [1962]

Dear Auntie Lola, Ray and David,
I've just written to Auntie Jennie, so I'll try not to repeat myself, for I presume you still chat frequently. I am putting in a long and rather lonely day, for Howie is in Paris, but your cheque this morning cheered me considerably! You are very, very generous, and thank you. I haven't any plans for the money. Maybe I'll use it to open a bank account, and keep it as a nest egg, as we aren't planning to buy any more things. Maybe it will have to go, temporarily, for the instalments on the stove and fridge, in which case we'll get something in return for it when we leave the flat. I'm feeling quite bloodthirsty about the people we have sublet from, as they left an inordinate number of creditors ... and about $5

worth of foreign coins in the gas meter! However, we are making no mean use of their furniture, records, etc., and there's a painting I have my eye on, done by the wife, if they leave us in the lurch. Last week the husband wired for money from France: Howard kindly sent him some, which put us in the red and we nearly couldn't go to Dunkirk for Easter. However, the Bank of Montreal is the only English bank that allows overdrafts (my boss was fascinated when I told him about this ... HIS bank won't let him run over) and we went. Had a glorious little trip ... from London Thursday evening. Landed at Dunkirk at 4 a.m., and the only real pain was sitting in that gloomy, badly rebuilt port waiting for the banks to open at 9 so we could change money. Thence to Gravelines, a fishing port on the Aa,[15] where a fair was in progress. We piled off the bus and stocked our basket with cheese, pate de foie gras, apples, tomatoes, French bread and wine; found an old, old, cheap, cheap hotel, picnicked, and slept. Later in the afternoon we explored the town, and walked to two really lovely seaside villages connected by a row-boat ferry. In one of them we ate a supper with four kinds of fish! The next day, on to Calais, which was rather dull: but for the first time this year it was really warm, and we sat without coats on the ramparts watching the beach. Four little girls engaged us in conversation ... Marie-France, Eveline, Annie, and Joselyne ... each about 9 years old, and full of fun! That night we stayed in another of our fourth class special hotels, sans hot water, of course.

We got in from the movies about 11:45 to find it locked up and black as pitch. We thumped, hammered, shivered. No answer. We went looking for a policeman and found a taxi-driver. Hearing our predicament he said, 'Wait 10 minutes.' We waited on the town monument, and were stared at by passers-by, but he came back ... with a skeleton key! He let us in to our hotel and we crept upstairs: smothering our giggles. No one said a word in the

15 A river that runs through Flanders.

morning, when we left for St Omer, about 20 miles inland. It's a very gracious, grown-up sort of town with a good cathedral and museum. In the afternoon we went rowing on the little canals near the town, felt completely submerged in the countryside. It's just like Holland there, and everyone has a black, almost gondola-shaped rowboat. Children play in them, men carry their ploughs from field to field with them! It's market gardening country, and, unlike Holland, cheerfully untidy. It was Easter Sunday, and the riverside inns had just opened; there were a lot of teenagers and family parties rowing up to regale themselves. Then we went to the fair at Cassel, the French WWI headquarters, and saw Marshall Foch's museum and a madly disorganised parade. Thence in a rush down to Dunkirk, where we ran about 2 miles to my boat. I had to get on by climbing a ladder onto the train deck ... but I waved Howie off, and that was really our honeymoon the first time out of England ... practically out of London ... since July. He writes that he's working hard in Paris, and that sitting around isn't fun any more. I found to-day hard to put in and I'll be terribly glad to see him tomorrow, no matter what time he gets in. I've been cleaning this place up, we have hemp carpets which shed like mad, and Marian ex-Passmore who leaves dirty coffee cups and ashtrays around! I bought daffodils and something called 'Cheerfulness' to-day ... at a shilling a dozen! Even at that price we seldom have flowers, as I prefer books and going to the movies, but they make the living room look fresh and spring-like.

Does David graduate this spring ... or horrors, has he? No, it's this spring, and he will just have finished his finals. I don't think he needs to be wished luck or success, because I know he has them already, but we're proud of him for keeping the academic flag flying even if he isn't an Artsman. If this isn't the right year for the B.Sc. we're still proud of him. Tell him he can spend the summer here if he wants, in the bedroom with the leak ... is he good at fixing things? We have some lovely things now, a carving set, your place mats and serviettes and tea towels, a silver serving dish, a sugar spoon, a revolving bookcase (a real find), good sheets ... we're well set-up. Marion Thompson sent money for silver or stainless steel, but I haven't decided what I want yet, probably old silver from the street markets, and will get it later. Howard has bought shirts and shoes, lost his Charlie Chaplin look, a cheque came from the CBC to cover the overdraft; so you have respectable as well as happy relations. And a publisher in New York wants to see part of my novel. Listen for H. on the CBC on May 5th or 7th... a LONG programme on his favourite island in Spain. On *Project 62* I believe.[16] Must close, no space,

thanks,
Marian and Howard

To Mr and Mrs F.S. Passmore
Sarnia, Ontario

64, West End Lane
London, England

20 August 1962

Dear All (7 of you?)
I seem to belong with a large family now – how come 3 children make a family & 4 a very large one? Hello Robert, welcome to the happy circle.[17] Pleased to perform any mad-aunt services! Robert you shall be Spode no more – but it was a lovely name, wasn't it?

---

16 *Project*, a long-running CBC radio series, was called *Venture* during the summer season. Howard's program, 'Return to Ibiza,' was broadcast on *Venture*, 6 May 1962.
17 Robert, Engel's new nephew, son of her sister Helen.

Since I last wrote, life has been overwhelmingly eventful but the 3 of us are getting on very well now & I have been promised 8 hours sleep *every* night.[18] I remember I wrote last Saturday in a fit of ill-humour in a café. That night we went to a party at Jock's & got home about 2 a.m. At 4:15 Romany awoke us with the news that the house was on fire. It was. I phoned the fire [brigade] (forgot about 999 and dialled information). H. grabbed [his] tape recorder & woke other tenants – I *dithered* looking for my typewriter lid, got the passports & was very much last on the scene. Fortunately the fire was confined to one room & no one was hurt. The children were shoved into an ambulance. There were *4* fire engines, police, ambulance & The London Salvage Corps. We sat on the wall and wished for coffee – fire was at the back of the house so we couldn't watch. The room was completely gutted – the *mirrors* melted. The old lady who used to own the house, was a paper saver & used an alcohol stove! She was shocked & singed but ran to the police at once. It was funny to see just how many people live here. Of course we didn't get back to bed before dawn & the house stank & we were all shaky. The following week was pretty upset especially since our finances were in disorder, but on the weekend we had a planning session and decided to leave for *Cyprus* by the end of September. Sunless London is just too much and H. can do a programme. The Cyprus office here is interested, etc. I told Mr Smith today & he's offered to write to his Agents in Nicosia to get me the promise of a job for a working permit! We are trying to work a cheap-fare deal & H. has an income-tax refund due, so it may be possible for me not to work. Anyway I'm quitting here in two weeks to work on my book & sleep in. Glorious developments in our lives, god-willing & we both love adventure & islands. Maybe next year you can come & see us! Plan to be there 6 months to a year. Anyway we'll be here

18 We have been unable to identify 'Romany,' who appears to have been staying with the Engels in London.

for another month & I'll let you know our plans in detail later. Meanwhile thanx for recipes, love to all of you, my sweets –

Miggs

To Mr and Mrs F.S. Passmore, and Mr and Mrs [ ] Engel
Sarnia, Ontario

64, West End Lane
London, England

Sunday, 18 November [1962]

Parents all: –
I'd better announce to the recipients of the top copy first of all that I am using a shady trick – slipping a carbon between two air letters. Think of it as a bond between Sarnia, St. Catharines, and your frustrated offsprings, spending a cold (it's hailing) Sunday waiting for people to arrive for tea, to move in, and to come with trunk keys, three separate lots of people, all late. This makes a nothing day, and us with suitcases, boxes, trunks, and rolling pins all over the living room!

In short, we are leaving this burgh, this island, this Kingdom, this climate. Halleljuh or however you spell it. Our friends seem to be indignant, the Engels have been leaving for so long that they have no right to leave at all! But we have seen everyone and his dog this week and second and third and fourth good-byes are foolish. Solly had a party, Fran and Art Massie took us out to dinner, the Vicherts made a curry, Jane came to stay overnight, and Frankie and Barbara gave a great sendoff last night. So this morning we made out a list – Day 1 – London to Paris. 2&3 – Paris. 4 – Paris-Yugoslavia; 5–6 – Yugoslavia (a stay in Sarajevo?); 7–8 – Yugoslavia-Athens; 9 – Athens; 10 – Athens to Cyprus ...

Since Day One is scheduled to be Wednesday the 21st we should wind up in Nicosia early in December. If you are desperate to contact us before then, try the Canadian Embassy in Athens (Leoforos Vasilissis, Sofias 31, Athens) before December 1st.

On the road again, and isn't it exciting? We can't hang on in this flat indefinitely and as a matter of fact the Millers were supposed to move in with us at 11 a.m. today. They still haven't showed up, nor have our afternoon guests ... we're fit to go to the movies any time.

Are leaving numerous things in London; dishes, tapes, unwanted clothes, much wanted paintings and bookcases, etc. so that we are bound to return. It is a loathsome town as far as climate is concerned but our good friends will be much missed. It is supposed, however, to be very good for a marriage when you go off into the unknown together with nothing but 7 trunks and your portable chess set! I keep making horrible lists in my mind. Shall I take the rolling pin? Shall I leave the coffee pot? We have turned into capitalists after all and are rolling in accessories. I realise you could all have Christmas (wedding anniversary?) presents if we could persuade ourselves to part with the things we have bought but I can't think of Engels or Passmores actually wanting boomerangs, butter paddles, old bits of chain, brass rubbings, battered pewter teapots, or Victorian puppets. I sometimes wonder if we own anything useful, and then I cart it back from the launderette and I know we do.

Our one social engagement before we go, aside from having everyone we know over on Tuesday night, is watching TV at the MacNamaras, as the Behan family will be on 'This is Your Life.' They hauled Brendan back to Dublin from the South of France for it, and he, who had just spent his last £600 on a cure, started to drink in the plane.[19] He's in fine shape now, Scilla MacNamara

---

19 Brendan Behan (1923–64), Irish author and playwright, best known for his dramas *The Quare Fellow* (1956) and *The Hostage* (1958). He died of alcoholism at the age of forty-one.

said, and likely to break up the programme if they put him on the air. He's heading straight for a straight jacket. Dominic and his wife were coming over this week, but we'll have to leave before that date, if we're to get to Cyprus at all.

Mother, did I ask you by the way to phone Mrs. Dr. O'Mahony on Christina street, at least they used to be, and say your youngest's been well-treated by the said MacNamaras, and they send their regards. The O'Mahonys are old friends of Scilla's (if they don't know her by her name, she wrote a book called *The Lincoln Imp*)[20] from Ireland. One day Mae said 'I had a friend once who was an eye ear nose and throat man, went to Canada and settled on the shore of a lake somewhere and did well.' I said 'O'Mahony' at once! Crazy how your friends and neighbours unite. No Irish that we know of in St. Catharines but we had a glorious letter from Milly Heaton, really a fan letter, and thank her very much. We had a good time with her.

I see the air letters are filling up, so I'd better go turn the kettle off. Our friends are obviously never coming. I made scones to use up the flour and the currants. We'll have to stuff ourselves with them. We are rotund, happy, and ON THE MOVE.

And send all our love ...

Miggs

Monday night – Sitting by the fire of blazing boxes, home after an expedition – bought tickets to Athens and DUFFLE COATS & JEANS. We are twins! We are definitely breaking the trip in Yugoslavia. Address in Cyprus: Poste Restante, Nicosia. Can you put up Brendan Behan for a couple of weeks??? Howie.

20 Priscilla Novy, *The Lincoln Imp: A Novel for Children* (London: Pilot Press, 1948).

To Mr and Mrs F.S. Passmore
Sarnia, Ontario

6 Vasilios Voulgaroktonous St., Flat 1
Nicosia, Cyprus

Ye 25 December 1962

Dear Mum and Dad,
Merry Christmas! I don't know whether or not you are at home, but if not, there will be word from us to welcome you and let you know we are thinking of you on the other side of the world. We can't boast of being outside in shirt sleeves today, but it was warm enough to go happily without gloves and with our overcoats open.

So Christmas has turned real at last. The week before I thought I just wouldn't bother with it, the weather was wrong and who cared ... but yesterday we caught its spirit at last and dashed about hunting for presents and paper and ribbon, and a good thing too, for we were invited out last night by our Santa Claus landlord ... we went with the 4 members of the family (he and his wife are called Zoe and Achilles; the boys are Constantine (in London) Jacobus (Jack to us, Gobus in the family) and Michael); another friend-tenant, an Englishwoman; all in two cars to the Hawaii restaurant which is run by another tenant ... lovely turkey dinner, with quiet merriment. H. bought Mr. Z. a bottle of liqueur and I found a mini-stapler for Jack; we also wrapped up a little bag of nuts and candies for the others ... all in red and white checked shelf paper, as I couldn't find any decent Xmas stuff.

A few days ago I bought a little tree, a kind of cedar, I guess, about 3 feet high: we decorated it with cutouts from our toy theatre. It is Howard's first tree and he is pleased with it. It sits propped up by books, wrapped in two orange place mats, in my big Cypriot cooking pot on the hall table: our first Christmas married. Howie has bought great bowls of nuts, (almonds, Cyprus peanuts (delicious!) and walnuts), I bought sugared almonds ... we feel ready for anyone who may drop in. Except of course Costas, our policeman, who came at 9:30 (a.m!) this morning and has come at 9:30 every other morning. We are having to be a bit formal to discourage his early hours.

Anyhoo, at midnight last night we opened our presents, just little things: the biggest surprise was a lamp H. made from an amphora, made of beige local clay, and a good-looking shade he searched all Nicosia for. Then I found 3 neatly-wrapped packages of cigarettes, two pairs of beautiful stockings, the kind that make legs look thin and elegant, and bath salts ... and an aluminium tin exactly the right size for Banana Cake. All I need now is a measuring cup. I gave him a little tool-set – pliers, awl, screwdrivers, rather poor quality (where's the SNAP ON tool man?)[21] but useful, and the only book I could find, a history of the 30 Years War. The poor guy is trying to plough through it now.

Today, though, was the best day ... we went to Lyssiotis' at 12:30 and found the whole family there, from Baby Xanthos up, including 2 grandmothers, grandpa (a well known poet), and great-grandma, young uncle (Kyriakos, 15), Reno and Mara, and Miss Davies, who runs Reno's beauty business. It was like being back at grandma's, but from the outside ... we had turkey, with delicious pine nuts and raisins in the stuffing, roast potatoes, salad, cannelonis (H's favourite thing ... pasta stuffed with meat), jellied pork, olives and pickles. Yes, ham too, in neat little rolls. For dessert there was a kind of mousse with nuts in it, and Greek almond cookies rolled in icing sugar. Wine with and turkish coffee after ... then presents – breakfast mugs, the angels supplied! After we left ours in London! We gave them a bottle of Cyprus brandy and one of our Pollocks play sheets, framed, for

21 Snap-on, a well-known manufacturer of hand and power tools, established in Wisconsin, U.S.A., in 1920.

the baby's room. We talked til 5 after dinner ... Reno and Howie are both interested in magic, and it turns out that Reno partly supported himself by magic shows when he was in London, even to sawing a lady in half. The baby Xanthos was passed around, and was as good as gold ... no wonder with so many grandparents around him.

So that was our Christmas, and we are home, a little sleepy, too well fed to want supper, drinking coffee out of our new mugs, thinking of you all at Helen's, putting Robert to bed ... And now a word from my sponsor ...

Hello. I'd like to associate myself with the seasonal remarks of my better half. I hope your Christmas has been as much fun as ours has. Today we found that Greek Uncles, too, doze after turkey with their big hands spread across watch chains stretched to the breaking point. Greek babies are admired no less than Canadian bairns. We were surprised to see that the Christmas tree had survived the political troubles the Cypriots have had with the British. And speaking of trees, Miggs has just written a letter to my folks in which, for some reason, there is no reference to our tree. I can't account for it.

Well, I'd better get back to the wars, Piccolimini, Wallenstein, and my new book.[22] I wouldn't want to make my wife think that I was unappreciative. Love to all from the Engels, on the very brink of their first wedding anniversary. Why, in a few weeks we will be giving advice to other young people!

Miggs and Howard

---

22 Ottavio Piccolimini (1599–1656), military leader in the Thirty Years War. Albrecht von Wallenstein (1583–1634), commander of the forces of the Emperor Ferdinand II in the Thirty Years War.

To Mr and Mrs F.S. Passmore
Sarnia, Ontario

Voulgaroktonous 6
Nicosia, Cyprus

12 February 1963

Dear Mum and Dad,
Just a hurried line before I run off to work; Mrs. Demetriou picks
me up at Reno's office and drops me at the Pallas Cinema, which
adds an extra half hour to my time.

So sorry I haven't been very faithful writing, and also if my
letter to Mrs. Mills wasn't written: I'm sure I answered hers, and
also Molly's, but I guess I didn't. I suspect mail to Canada is still
being held up in English snowstorms.

We've been madly busy lately. I think I told you about cycling to
Pera on the 3rd. Well, this Sunday – but wait, I didn't tell you we
have a houseguest, a young American we met on the boat coming
over, staying with us: Stephen is the son of an American psycholo-
gist, went to Colombia, and has spent the past few years working
as a woodcarver and poet in Denmark. Not very remunerative,
but it makes him a pleasant person to know and his pa seems to
subsidize him from time to time. He spent about 6 weeks in Israel
and was for a while a carpenter in Nazareth! He's staying with us
for a couple of weeks, until the next boat to Rhodes, and the
Cypriots are particularly fond of him as he lives in Denmark and
Constantine of Greece has just got engaged to a Danish princess.

So anyhow Stephen came last week, and we had a string of
invitations, including a cocktail party in Kyrenia, where we met
the director of the Peace Corps, whose last post was, guess where,
Missoula, Montana! They're about our age and lots of fun. We'll
be seeing more of them.

Then on Sunday Mammas the tailor down the street took us to his village, for the feast day of Ayios Charalambous (ears and eyes!). The village he comes from, Larnaka Tis Lapithous, is perched on the mountainside and St. Charalambous' church was in one slightly higher up – up a goat trail only thousands of rickety buses were making their way. We walked part way, thank heavens, as eight in a rented car going up a goat trail is a bit worrisome. In the church everyone was kissing icons like mad, and the priests held St. C's picture up while everyone walked under it, assuring themselves of good ears and eyes for the coming year. At the fair they sold sweets, nuts and a few handicraft things, e.g. goats' wool pullovers. Afterwards we drove across the hills to an abandoned monastery ... that is, some of us drove: there were nine in the car so finally the parents and the two little boys walked, as the car wouldn't pass over the humps between the ruts! It was a rented car, and Soterias drove it like a jeep, over anything. No wonder Cypriot cars rattle! I can't describe those rutted trails: white stone on the mountainside. But the wild anemones are out: large, but pale mauve and white, the blood of Adonis, wept over by Venus. So were the enormous almond blossoms: pink and white like apple, but larger, lusher. At the monastery small kids and lambs were penned in the monks' quarters: what a cry they set up when they saw us: 'Mama, Mama!' The shepherds send them out in the fields after a few weeks so these must have been brand new. There were several busloads of picnickers, and we went into the monastery church, a very old byzantine structure, with stone and wood carvings well before AD 1000 in style. We lit some candles with the best of them and watched them tie silver offerings on the icon of St. Mary. Then a picnic, and Mammas and Howie and Stephen singing and dancing. Mrs. Mammas, who is about 45, ran a footrace with the boys, and won! Her sons are matinee-idol handsome, big lads with brown faces and clean-cut features. Mammas is short and stout, but the new generation is Hollywood-looking.

Other things here: a nice letter from Helen promising a pie plate; a filthy letter from the CBC claiming that H. had misrepresented himself as a staff member here, which took many telegrams and a phone call to Toronto to clear up – what a crisis. The London office sent a par-excellence scolding, and H. is still *persona non*[23] but he says it will blow over. It's very complicated and depressing but fortunately H. has copies of all the letters pertaining to the Cyprus visit and will be able to clear the matter up with help from Harry.[24] Then yesterday Stephen found a cheap editing tape recorder which he is helping us buy, good lad, in return for the use of Howard's portable here. The thing is, Howie can't get the use of machines at the Cyprus Broadcasting Corporation, thus can't edit tape and send it off, so we've had to sink every cent into this other machine. I hope the job they offered him at the Forces Broadcasting Co. comes off.

I am on the second last chapter of my book, which is why letter-writing has fallen off, for I find my chronicles to my friends sop up my need to write.

I'm doing a washing, so the morning is cluttered. We've run out of butane so there'll be no proper lunch, which is a help!

Serendipity: just as we were wondering how we'd eat after buying the tape recorder, Howard finds in his wallet an uncashed cheque for £5! I'm so ruddy glad he's being forced to buy this machine, because without an extra one he's always dependent on companies and kindnesses. Of course it will mean porters at railway stations from now on, but it's only $80 and if it goes at all we're all set up as professionals! Love to Uncle W [elles] when he comes, and to youse.

Miggs

---

23 *persona non grata*
24 Harry Boyle (1915–), Canadian journalist and broadcaster. He started working for CBC Radio in 1942.

P.S. H. says I am to quit Mrs. Demetriou: she makes me too cross! Reno is going to Israel on a business trip and I'm going to take charge of his office while he's away. XX Miggs.

P.S. 2. Pictures taken at Pera were wonderful – will send. Have you read *Bitter Lemons?*[25] Please do – it's so good.

To Mr and Mrs F.S. Passmore
Sarnia, Ontario

Sunday, 10 May 1963

Dear Mother and Dad,
It is Sunday and by virtue of my throwing really sensational fits of temperament, threatening to jump off balconies, cut my throat, etc., we are at home, Howard having explained to everyone that his wife was too unstable to attend flower festivals in Limassol. I am henceforth to be treated with great gentleness, consideration and blagh [*sic*].

The inevitable has you may gather happened: Mr. Zavallis has given us a young English couple to live with us. They're quite nice if you like young English couples living with you, they've even asked H. to be their best man, but they stick, cling, need us. He is working as a draftsman, she as a secretary. The man is a big booby addicted to appearing untidily in our bedroom doorway in his pyjamas, and telling the uninteresting story of his unfascinating life to our friends, who are beginning to think twice before dropping in ... I try to preach the virtues of being independent and finding one's own friends, but he likes ours just fine!

Well, they're supposed to be moving upstairs to another flat on the first of June.

25 Lawrence Durrell, *Bitter Lemons* (London: Faber and Faber, 1957).

Steve's wife has come back from France,[26] so we are not in Famagusta, though the Armstrongs invited us to stay with them; but I must send a copy of my book to London, make beds, etc., hunt for air letters ...

They have at last received my book in New York (the acknowledging letter was addressed to us in Nicosia *Crete*), think it touch and go with selling it, but are going to try, bless their hearts. I have not, however, got the London copy ready yet, so that's on the agenda today.

I was talking to Squadron Leader all yesterday and found I shan't be paid until June 1st, but I'll try to look into the dresser scarf business soon and send a little parcel through RAF post, which is cheap and quick.

School is going along very well, with Howie's very creative ideas. I haven't done as much preparation as I might, but find that I can do a lot in my spares, and keep up with the children well enough. The staff I like better than I did at first, though there are a number of timeservers we'd be better without ... Mr. Southcombe was nothing on them![27] Teaching Saturday is not, however, very nice at all.

H. has made us a very nice bedroom lampshade and now I'm supposed to be making him a bathrobe, but it isn't progressing very quickly. It's from the same pattern as my Norwegian robe, looks simple, but has to be worked on on a cleared table with no one around: that doesn't exist!

We have had two or three hailstorms already: the other day there was a real cloudburst which filled up parts of the moat. I thought you'd like the enclosed of a stranded donkey. Fortunately the storms were spotty so not all the crops are ruined: they are just cutting the wheat now, and some of them thresh it with a kind of stone boat dragged by oxen while others have combines just across the road. Friday afternoon we visited a cheese factory

26 Steve and Christiane Caramondanis became close friends of the Engels.
27 We have not been able to identify Mr Southcombe.

where Steve was adjusting the freezing machinery for ice-cream, and watched them transferring cheese mixtures from huge modern vats into grass baskets to drain: they can't sell cheese that's drained in any other shape of mold.

It's very hot when it isn't stormy. We long to live by the sea and may be able to arrange it in the summer, as the RAF is trying to get me a contract which will entitle me to a cost of living allowance, and other perks. It will take two months to come through, but a nice lump at the beginning of July would set us up for the summer.

I'm so glad Welles is with you, and that Maude is coming ... a sort of family reunion which will make you happy.

Well I must leave you, do some work in time to catch the Kyrenia bus and roll over this painted landscape for a swim ... we are not so devoted to Nicosia that we give up our free day completely to work!

Lots of love,
Miggs

Same day but later:
Hopped on a bus (well, waited 1¼ hours in a bar with Peter Helier for a bus to appear) and rattled across the Mesaoria to Kyrenia & then Karavas, a village wreathed in flowers. Walked to the sea & found a monastery, the ruins of an ancient city, and a hermit's cave! All this for a 45¢ bus ride! It was hot & sunny & the sea shore was covered with blue everlastings – I've picked some to dry & decorate the house with. A really magic afternoon, far better than staying in Kyrenia with thousands of people (the Greeks are still in winter clothes & make us hot) and a band concert. I came home & slept – just awoke to hear Peter & Valerie tell about their flower festival & now I'm back to bed.

Can't find the donkey picture – sorry.

Much love again,
Miggs

To Mr and Mrs F.S. Passmore
Sarnia, Ontario

Voulgaroktonous 6
Nicosia, Cyprus

31 August 1963 – 18 years and 3 days ago we moved to SARNIA.

Dear Ma and Pa:
Howie has gone out so I can work on my new book,[28] but I just
found your letter in the mailbox and thought how nice to answer
it. I am so seldom alone in the house I feel rather sneaky about
not working, but honestly I must have some life of my own or I'll
start wanting to steal it.

I was interested to hear you wanted to go out west: do have a
nice trip, and let me know when you're going so I can perhaps
write to Auntie Maude instead, and she can pass the letters on.
What's her address?

This is the first day it has been reasonably cool, only 93. I don't
care about your friend's 135 in Turkey either! I'm hot enough
here. I've been terrible about housework and entertaining, but I
am also trying to toughen myself up and not care what other
people think, and I do quite enough work in the heat for me,
thanks.

The two days with S.'s kids passed off reasonably well ... much
drama, but of a very unreal kind. C. phoned to ask if I could keep
them overnight, at least that's what I thought she meant, until
next morning she phoned, very confused. I thought she was tight,
and instead of trying to locate S., who was working in town, waited
until he came at noon to take the kids to the beach. He spoke one

---

28 Probably 'Death Comes for the Yaya,' an unpublished mystery novel.

word to her, phoned the doctor, had her taken to clinic and her stomach pumped. But we still went to the beach! I was on pins and needles all afternoon but he resolutely waited until five to telephone and announced that she was having tea. All this while trying to keep children's minds on other things. I keep wondering what kind of weekend they are having. We both absolutely adore S. because he's the kind of resolute person we should like to be but I hope he keeps tab on the kind of pills that enter the house ... She's on a month's probation now, poor lamb. The guy she was having an affair with we knew fairly well; he has no chin, no character, a bitchy wife, neurotic kids and ... charm. But I suppose after 11 years with a man with too much character, in a foreign country, you want something soft. Cyprus, too, is a good place for ruining marriages. In some way it has no resources, and perhaps only the old fashioned arranged marriage works. Why? It's too small, and too hot, and too isolated. I bet Montana was like this, but I saw another side.[29] Anyhow, I think he's got to forgive her her obsession, because he can't be easy to live with and the children are too beautiful to be dispossessed of their mother. Cl. is eight, and a full-fledged person. The little boy is three and as tough as they come. That's the way to make kids.

About our plans for coming home. H's programme is scheduled for 8th December, we're supposed to be out of the flat by 15th September, but Zavvo[30] has gone to England so the inferiors probably won't evict us. So far we're undecided about when exactly to leave Cyprus, but it will probably be about Oct. 1st. Then there's the problem of H's editing and writing. He doesn't think he can get any perspective on the island until he leaves, and we're thinking seriously of spending a month in some industrial town in Italy, where the cost of living is low. By that time the off-season fares will be on, and we'll head to Paris and London,

29 Engel taught at the University of Montana for a year, 1957–8.
30 Mr Zavallis, the landlord.

collect our goods, and sail home. He'll ask Harry Boyle for a job, I'll try to get on at Dun and Bradstreet[31] (I can bluster now, about being a credit underwriter) and we'll see whether we can settle down uncomplainingly in Toronto. I hope to heaven he can get a job without much trouble, because my being the mainstay (financial only: Howard has the staying power, tact etc.)[32] has been very hard on both of us. I think the long sieges of no work have been good for him, though: we're both lazy as coons but he's sick of captivity. The Forces job here has been a godsend, though. And I've never known anyone with such guts: already he wants me to apply to the CBC for a job, though he knows I'd wind up, with his help, with a better one than he'd get, because of race, creed and outlook. It's really fantastic how that guy has survived with a wife like a snowplough, a tottering career (on the UP again, thank heavens) and an offbeat sense of humour. Well, here I come with my miracle man but I must warn you that Christmas is his parents' wedding anniversary. He's really petrified of Passmores and we must bring him round gently because underneath the shell he's a fantastically good person, and he gives, gives and gives.

Oh, philosophy. You don't want to hear all that. My flu went away, by the way, but my pot came back when I started eating again so I am sleek with a bump as usual. The kitten is recovering from the children and cuts his teeth on one's feet, so he has to be spanked, which I hate doing. Howard's brother advises me not to have any teeth work done until we come home, but send x-rays, as the ones that were taken here showed the situation not to be as dark as the doctor said. I can still inhale a cigarette, so I guess he's right.

Have a nice trip and love to Auntie Maude.

xxxx Miggs

---

31 Dun and Bradstreet, an international credit information company.
32 Parenthetical note added by hand in the margin of this typed letter.

To Diarmuid Russell[33]
Russell and Volkening
New York, U.S.A.

London

17 September 1964

Dear Mr. Russell: –
Howard is delighted with this piece and suggests I send it to you. I am less pleased, but it is one thing less to pack.

We are returning to Toronto next week, where I hope to find a letter from you. Don't suppose anything happened to the Cyprus book. I didn't bring a copy here as that English agent never wrote, but the Irish Contingent has promised to flog it for me if I send the MS from Canada.

It has been a sad summer here: the ghost of Louis MacNeice everywhere, and Brendan Behan, and Gaynor-the-Ginger-Man.[34] Desmond MacNamara busy making death masks all year.[35] I am working on two novels: one bosh about how deeply one can hate Toronto, another possibly quite good, remittance people on an island. This last will be quickly written, and sent to you before next year, I hope.[36]

---

33 See note 8, p. xxiv.
34 Louis MacNeice (1907–63), Irish poet, critic, and author. He worked for the BBC from 1941 to 1961. Gaynor-the-Ginger-Man possibly refers to J.P. Donleavy's *The Ginger Man*. The first UK unexpurgated edition appeared in 1963 (London: Corgi).
35 Desmond MacNamara (1918–), Irish novelist, biographer, and critic.
36 Parenthetical note added by hand to Engel's carbon copy of the typed letter: 'Try the short stories – maybe one about a garland of flowers & thyme.'

2

Waiting for *Honeyman*, 1965–1970

Marian Engel was a prolific correspondent during her travels and time abroad. This productivity slowed down in the immediate period following her return to Toronto, as the more modest number of letters in this chapter suggests. A major development contributed to the decrease in Engel's letter writing. Twins Charlotte and William were born 30 April 1965. Surviving letters to Engel significantly outnumber those written by her during the latter half of the 1960s, which are dominated by the two concerns of writing and domesticity – now with the added dimension of motherhood.

Leaving Cyprus, Engel had expressed high hopes for a quick completion of one of two novels she was working on (17 September 1964). Half a year later, she revised her expectations: 'I was hoping to finish a novel before B-day but had not realized that pregnancy reduces one to a state of mental moo; there is also a horrifying possibility that I shall have to take another name and write cosy articles about raising twins, so let's try to get as much travel work in as possible so I can buy a big fat machine mother wolf and get on with the work' (16 April 1965).

Engel is amusing and forthright on the subject of raising twins and the constraints of domesticity. A witty letter to the Toronto Public Library's chief librarian rebuked the library for insensitive fines handed out to young mothers too busy to get books back on time, and for its outdated selection of books on pregnancy, parenting, and domesticity: 'Sooner or later all of us become involved in it and what a sneaky, shamefaced section you have just by the exit!' she admonished (24 September 1965). A letter to family friend Mrs Mills is matter-of-fact on the trials of travelling with two-year-olds. It was 1967, the year of Expo, and along with thousands of Canadians, the Engels travelled to Montreal for the international fair in celebration of Canada's one hundredth year as a nation. Difficult though it was to travel with the twins, the trip nevertheless invigorated Marian: '... when I came back I realized that I had stopped at last wanting to be dead when I went to sleep. So now we are having reforms. I chase my scamps with a large wooden spoon. I forget about house cleaning and great big dinners and just try to enjoy the children' (10 August 1967).

The Expo '67 world's fair coincided with the culmination of post-war Canadian national sentiment in the political and cultural domains alike. The year marked the establishment of several notable cultural institutions and organizations, such as the Canadian Artists Representation (CAR), influential in the emergence of artist-run centres and galleries across the country, Toronto's Rochdale College, an experiment in education supported by many of the city's artists, writers,[1] and intellectuals, and the Canadian Film Development Corporation (CFDC), precursor to Telefilm Canada, which helped launch Canada's feature film industry and supplemented the country's already renowned historical documentary tradition. By 1967, as Canadian Studies scholar John Wadland points out, the NFB (National Film Board), the CBC, the New Canadian Library, and the Canadian Centenary Series had enormous cultural weight.[2] Trudeaumania was about to explode in 1968, the same year that the Broadcasting Act, which created the Canadian Radio-Television Commission (subsequently the Canadian Radio-Television and Telecommunications Commission, or CRTC), introduced Canadian content quotas. The next year, 1969, the Independent Publishers Association (forerunner of the Canadian Publishers Association) was founded to represent the interests of small regional presses.

Two other such developments particularly stand out in the story of Canadian cultural history, and both took place in Toronto, where Engel made her home: the establishment of Coach House Press in 1965, with Stan Bevington at the helm, and of House of Anansi Press, founded in 1967 by David Godfrey and Dennis Lee. A young Douglas Fetherling became Anansi's first full-time employee. The press had just received its first Canada Council grant, enabling it to add four titles to its still small list. Two were poetry, a collection by George Jonas, *The Absolute Smile*, and *The Circle Game* by the then still relatively unknown Margaret Atwood. 'George Woodcock was right,' Fetherling recalls, 'when he wrote in a letter to Dennis [Lee] that "something unprecedented happened to Canadian publishing and even to Canadian writing when Anansi came on the scene."'[3] Fetherling went on to explain that 'Anansi was at the forefront of a movement that it both helped to create and then gave voice to. There were many other little presses, of course ... Anansi was different. It was out to change writing by displacing the old generation with the new.'[4] Anansi introduced a generation of new, young writers to Canadian readers, including Marian Engel, whose second novel, *The Honeyman Festival*, it published in 1970. Its list of authors featured such notables as Atwood, Al Purdy, Michael Ondaatje, and George Grant, under whom Dennis Lee had studied.

Whereas Anansi focused on mass market publishing, Coach House concentrated on fine printing, producing the work of a handful of friends, Fetherling recalls. Coach House also claimed an important influence on literary studies by 'making what was previously unappreciated the standard curriculum.'[5] Through Stan Bevington, Coach House had links with Toronto's Rochdale College, an alternative school modelled on A.E. Neill's Summerhill in England.[6] Fetherling described the Rochdale experiment as 'a college within the university where students would live and work independently of the normal university structure ... no faculty, no grades, none of the oppressive infrastructure of the old way.'[7] These were the revolutionary 1960s, a decade of almost unfathomable change, the years of 'the Cultural Revolution in China, the war in Vietnam ... *les événments* in Paris, the Soviet invasion of Czechoslovakia, Woodstock, Neil Armstrong's stroll on the moon, and the Arab-Israeli War.'[8] In Quebec, a 'quiet revolution' was taking place, and in Toronto, amidst an active cultural scene and between her newborn babies, Marian Engel was writing.

Of the two manuscripts that Engel was working on in the early 1960s, she expected the story about remittance people on an island to be most quickly completed. Ironically, it proved to be one of her most demanding and drawn-out efforts, eventually becoming her third book, *Monodromos*. Instead, it was her 'bosh' book about Toronto that turned out to be Engel's literary breakthrough. *Sarah Bastard's Notebook*, first published under the tamer title *No Clouds of Glory*, came off the press in early 1968. The story of a bright, bold, and unconventional young woman, the novel received glowing responses from readers, made the best-seller list, and generated celebratory letters from fellow writers Austin Clarke (3 March 1968) and Hugh MacLennan (26 February 1968). MacLennan had 'nothing but compliments and admiration for the book,' though her former professor could not resist a few suggestions regarding Engel's future efforts: 'I believe in your next book you can afford to be far less defensive, totally forgetful of critics and academics and relax a little more inside the sentences and paragraphs.' Engel's mother, for her part, was evasive in her letter of congratulations (8 February 1968). She had 'read the book aloud to dad' and then 'loaned it to Maude,' whose eyes were bothering her. A direct comment on the gutsy Sarah Bastard might have been too much to manage, though Mrs Passmore clearly was enjoying her own newfound celebrity in Sarnia as mother of a local author.

Engel's success put her in a good position to receive a Canada Council grant, for which MacLennan wrote her a strong reference. She was delighted when news of the award arrived. She was hard at work on her next novel, 'The Silent Companions,' an early version of *The Honeyman Festival.* Protagonist Minn Burge is vastly pregnant with her fourth child. Former mistress of film magnate Honeyman, whose work is being celebrated by a festival, Minn is now awash in a world of 'women's stuff.' This was a world that Dan Wickenden of Harcourt, Brace,[9] like other male readers of the work at the time, found unsettling. 'What the book has most vividly left with me,' he wrote to Engel 16 December 1968, 'is an impression of the more disgusting aspects of infancy and of the domestic life in general. I wonder if it isn't to some extent a personal purging, something you had to get down on paper and out of your system before you could go on to write a book of more general interest' (16 December 1968). Wickenden's response provides a measure of the attitudes faced by women writers of Engel's generation. In response to another unfavourable assessment of the book, Engel's reply (2 February 1970) was brief: 'I'm sorry about *The Silent Companions.* I wish most of all that it were a better book. Some day, perhaps, it will be.' It was. The manuscript came together and appeared in 1970 under the title *The Honeyman Festival.*

Engel's Canada Council funds were quickly depleted, and soon she was pressed for money again. 'I am also virtually unemployed at the moment,' she wrote Mr McVey at Macmillan. 'If there are any small literate jobs at your esteemed establishment you might keep me in mind. I spent a year and a half in England turning German financial reports into beautiful English English, which is still, I think, within my grasp' (2 February 1970). Meanwhile, book reviews paid small fees. *Globe and Mail* book review editor William French assigned her a challenging novel by the elusive Québécois author Réjean Ducharme (2 April 1968).[10] With her knowledge of the French language and experience living in Montreal, Engel was a good choice for the task. Engel also joined Robert Weaver's roster of short story writers for the CBC,[11] and she would eventually publish two collections of stories, *Inside the*

Easter Egg (1975) and *The Tattooed Woman* (1985). As the 1960s drew to a close, Engel's contacts in the Canadian literary world had expanded considerably, and the new decade began promisingly with the appearance of *The Honeyman Festival* – Engel's second published novel.

Notes

1 See below, note 6.
2 John Wadland, 'Voices in Search of a Conversation: An Unfinished Project,' *Journal of Canadian Studies* 35.1 (Spring 2000): 59.
3 Fetherling, *Travels by Night: A Memoir of the Sixties*, 108.
4 Ibid., 108–9. Fetherling (110) cites as comparable to Anansi the Vancouver presses Talonbooks and Very Stone House. The latter was founded in 1966 by poets Patrick Lane and Seymour Mayne.
5 Ibid., 114.
6 Bevington was Rochdale's official publisher and printer (Cohen, *Typing: A Life in Twenty-Six Keys*, 86). Anansi's Dennis Lee was also involved with the Rochdale experiment, and with the related magazine *This Magazine Is about Schools*, which evolved into *This Magazine*.
7 Fetherling, *Travels by Night*, 132.
8 Wadland, 'Voices in Search of a Conversation,' 59–60.
9 (Leonard) Daniel Wickenden (1913–89), novelist and editor, joined Harcourt, Brace in 1953.
10 William French (1926–), literary editor of the *Globe and Mail*, 1960–90; Réjean Ducharme (1941–), novelist and dramatist, whose insistence upon anonymity has captured the public imagination. Ducharme's first published novel, *L'avalée des avalés* (1966; trans. *The Swallower Swallowed*, 1968), won the Governor General's Award and was followed by an active but determinedly anonymous artistic production in the fields of literature, visual art, film, and music.
11 See note 9, p. xxiv.

To Diarmuid Russell
Russell and Volkening
New York, U.S.A.

116 Pembroke Street
Toronto, Ontario

16 April 1965

Dear Mr. Russell:
First of all, I received my detective novel and article last week; thanks for returning them.[1] It's a pity I didn't put the Cyprus material to better use, but my husband, who likes puzzles, says that he wants to have a crack at re-writing the thriller, so you may see it some time again, if you can bear it, in a revised form that includes, I am sternly told, a plot.[2]

The good news from Arnold Ehrlich came as we were reading *Only you, Dick Daring,* which made it doubly pleasing that he was impressed.[3] I certainly will dope out another article, but since I am vastly pregnant, it will have, I fear, to be on Toronto. This is not such a bad idea, as there's never been anything good written about it yet and I can flesh the text out with comments from a humourless and inaccurate ancestor whose house-hunting experience here has been roughly parallel to mine.

---

1 The manuscript of Engel's unpublished detective novel, 'Death Comes for the Yaya,' can be found in the Marian Engel Archive, McMaster University, box 4, file 18.
2 Howard Engel's own first work of detective fiction, *The Suicide Murders,* was to appear in 1980 (New York: St Martin's Press).
3 Arnold B. Ehrlich (1848–1919), founder of a British publishing house; Merle Miller and Evan Rhodes, *Only You, Dick Daring! Or, How to Write One Television Script and Make $50,000,000, a True-Life Adventure* (New York: W. Sloane Associates, 1964).

I was hoping to finish a novel before B-day but had not realised that pregnancy reduces one to a state of mental moo; there is also a horrifying possibility that I shall have to take another name and write cosy articles about raising twins, so let's try to get as much travel work in as possible so I can buy a big fat machine mother wolf and get on with the work.[4] Shall I contact Ehrlich or will you? Thanks for everything.

To Chief Librarian, Toronto Public Library
Toronto, Ontario

16 Clarence Square
Toronto, Ontario

24 September 1965

Dear Sir:
Baby-sitter: 75¢
Bus fare: 35¢
Fine: $3.50
   $4.60

There are times, you know, when systems break down. Husbands are kept late at work, babysitters disappear into some underworld only they know about, babies get sick. One hesitates to send the books back in a taxi because maybe tomorrow something cheaper can be arranged. A telephone call to a librarian elicits the information that one's books can be returned by mail – but a trip to the post office is almost as far and just as impossible. Central Circulating says, 'You know, the people at the desk are human ...'

---

4 Engel's twins, William and Charlotte, were born 30 April 1965.

Alas, the people at the desk may be human, but when the day of library and liberation arrives, the traditional grim gorgon is there, cheerfully extracting three-fifty for SIN. Dirty slogans to write on walls rise to the mind. After all, two weeks is not eternity and it's not worth the trip to take out less than five books.

I'm one of your amateur authorities on libraries, having been first plunked in the Galt Public at three in front of *Johnny Crow's Garden*,[5] gone to and taught in a few universities and patronised everything from the Montreal Mechanics' Institute to the British Council in Nicosia. And I've never minded parting with a few shillings or francs or nickels to the worthy cause of staying out of the rain on due day. But your present fine set-up makes it awfully easy to rationalise dishonesty.

I know also that you don't take inventory, it's cheaper to re-place lost books; that you probably won't prosecute; that I could keep the books out until I was 95 for another buck and a half; that I could re-join under an assumed name at another branch and get away scot-free. Why should I be a sucker before Mr. Carnegie's miracle?[6]

Well, you've got your three-fifty and I need you more than you need me. So please use it to decide whether you're a good library or not and review your prejudices against:

1. American novelists – very incomplete.

2. Detective novelists – you seem here really to want a section labelled 'crap' but to be too ladylike, so restrict yourself to ordering four copies of one pot-boiler every year and then shilly-shallying as if waiting for dear uncle Henry James to write one.[7] There are some good detective novelists. Get your buyer to read

5 L. Leslie Brooke, *Johnny Crow's Garden: A Picture Book* (London: Frederick Warne, 1935).

6 Andrew Carnegie (1835–1919), Scottish-born American industrialist and philanthropist, financed the building of thousands of libraries.

7 Henry James (1843–1916), American author, among whose best-known novels are *Daisy Miller* (1879), *Portrait of a Lady* (1881), and *The Bostonians* (1888).

Julian Symons in the *Observer* to discover them.[8] In these and several other departments there is evidence of a strong moral bias towards the useful as opposed to the enjoyable, and a confusion of aims. One wonders if your librarians are ordering for a completely imaginary public, one which should be reading Virginia Woolf and is reading Mickey Spillane.[9]

3. Domesticity: Sooner or later all of us become involved in it and what a sneaky, shamefaced section you have just by the exit! Lots of us learned to cook from Elizabeth David borrowed from any library but yours. You ought to have *all* the good *cookbooks* in French and English and all the useful ones – just paperbacks, like Katharine Whitehorn's *Cooking in a Bedsitter* and Peg Bracken's *I Hate To Cook Book* – surely these would be extremely useful to your lonelier clients.[10] Your books on *restaurants* are delightful and might be added to. I know a lot of people who love reading about eating! In addition, I have lately become a user of the *pregnant-and-childraising section*. Perhaps because many librarians are single, they seem to have no idea what is useful. Books published in 1928 tend *not* to be. Spock is, though you get a copy from Heinz and Curity in the hospital.[11] What one wants is something reasonably scientific about pregnancy (there is a paperback by a Dr. Guttmacher of the Mount Sinai Hospital, New York, which helps

8 Julian Symons (1912–), English mystery writer and critic, author of more than twenty novels, including *A Reasonable Doubt* (1960) and *The Colour of Murder* (1978).

9 Virginia Woolf (1882–1941), English novelist and essayist, whose *Room of One's Own* (1929) is considered a classic of the feminist movement; Mickey Spillane (1918–), American writer of popular mysteries, many featuring the unconventional detective Mike Hammer.

10 Katharine Whitehorn, *Cooking in a Bedsitter* (Harmondsworth, England: Penguin, 1961); Peg Bracken, *The I Hate to Cook Book* (New York: Harcourt, Brace, 1960).

11 Benjamin Spock's books on baby and child care have been frequently reissued. Engel may be referring to *Baby and Child Care* (New York: Meredith Press, 1946). Heinz and Curity are manufacturers of baby food and baby supplies respectively.

tide one over), Gray's *Anatomy* (because you suddenly discover you don't know quite what you contain) and all those vastly comforting natural childbirth books – including, of course, Dick-Read which you have.[12] Pregnancy makes one self-centred and curious and catering to this interest can raise the level from old-wives'-tale to intelligent. Throw out that ghastly book on twins: it's cute and all it tells you is that you'll be enormously tired (which you know) and that you need to hire servants (which you don't). Nonsense, nonsense, nonsense. There MUST be better books than this. Victor Gollancz, by the way, has several good childbirth books on his list, and you have a copy of *Babies are Human Beings* which is excellent.[13] *Interior Decoration:* Here's your chance to join the anti-uglies. There are excellent and gloriously expensive books on furniture and architecture which if propagated might promote a modicum of purism in this country – all those Spanish-style bedroom suites! Probably they're tucked away in your art library. Forget Dewey and haul them out.[14] These are not women's subjects – they are subjects for decent people who care about their environment.

4. Literature: here again, confusion of aims. I think you really should have, if not a crap section, a light-reading section, so that you can sort out your aims and then acquire the *complete works* of the important writers, at least insofar as they're in print. Your Balzac is maddening, both in French and in English, Henry James

---

12 Alan Frank Guttmacher, *Pregnancy and Birth: A Book for Expectant Parents* (New York: Viking Press, 1957); Henry Gray (1825–61), whose classic *Anatomy* is available in many editions; Grantly Dick-Read, *Childbirth without Fear: The Principles and Practice of Natural Childbirth* (New York: Harper, 1953).
13 Victor Gollancz (1893–1967), English publisher, socialist, and social activist; Charles Anderson Aldrich and Mary M. Aldrich, *Babies Are Human Beings* (New York: Macmillan, 1954).
14 John Dewey (1859–1952), American philosopher and creator of the Dewey decimal classification system for libraries.

needs at least sorting out, your Americans are weak, and even mediocre libraries have all of Arnold Bennett.[15] You're probably the biggest public library in Canada and a lot of us don't have access to U. of T. so we need your literary section to be at least as scholarly as your public affairs section. I should think, if you want to speak of numbers, that more people would read Dickens and Thackeray than those turgid volumes, new as they are, on African politics.[16]

I guess this is my three-fifty worth. I like your library, and most of the people in it. But of course like anything else it can be improved, if not according to my ideas, according to someone else's. And, please, do let us renew books by telephone otherwise one will have to go into bankruptcy through Britnell's.[17]

Yours sincerely,
Marian Engel

---

15 Honoré de Balzac (1799–1850), French realist novelist, author of the great series of interconnected novels *La Comédie Humaine*; Arnold Bennett (1867–1931), English author of thirty novels, including *The Old Wives' Tale* (1908), the best-known of which are set in the Potteries, the Staffordshire of his childhood.

16 Charles Dickens (1812–70), one of England's best-known and best-loved novelists, whose works include *A Christmas Carol* (1843), *David Copperfield* (1850), and *A Tale of Two Cities* (1859); William Makepeace Thackeray (1811–63), English journalist and novelist, remembered for his 1848 novel *Vanity Fair*.

17 A well-known bookstore in Toronto, which has since closed.

To Mrs [A.W.] Mills[18]
Sarnia, Ontario

16 Clarence Square
Toronto, Ontario

10 August 1967

Dear Mrs. Mills,

Oh, I'm so sorry I haven't written since you went to the hospital. I thought I'd have all the time in the world in Montreal, but of course I was in a strange house and my time got frittered away.

We came back entirely restored, probably because the 'maid' there was so difficult it was wonderful to be alone again. She was a French girl, very tidy and intelligent, but lazy, and since I decided not to exhaust myself pushing her, and Howard disapproves of my not managing her better, and the twins misbehaved in every possible way, life was difficult. However, we both had a rest – I suppose worrying about *different* things is a rest – and when I came back I realized that I had stopped at last wanting to be dead when I went to sleep.

So now we are having reforms. I chase my scamps with a large wooden spoon. I forget about house cleaning and great big dinners and just try to enjoy the children.

Two-year-olds are pretty hard to enjoy, though, aren't they? Ours seethe around the house destroying things – turn your back and the vacuum cleaner has lost its bag *again*. On the other hand, they are learning more and more words and more and more things to do with their bodies. They need a yard, but it's impossible to find them one this year in Toronto. Howard has fenced

18 Mrs Mills, friend of the Engel family from Sarnia, and mother of former Lieutenant-Governor Pauline McGibbon.

the roof beautifully and built a sandbox so we go up there for a while every day.

Our best man, Frank Herrmann, was over from England in July and took some beautiful photographs of them. I will forward copies when I get them made up. I don't think they're really that good looking but I don't mind seeing my children look like movie stars! Charlotte has a brown gingham smock which makes her look like a million dollars.

Mum and Dad really enjoyed Expo.[19] I wish I had their strength! But then, they weren't changing William all day. I loved the little trains and boats. We intended to eat there a lot, but even though we're extravagant about food, the restaurants were mostly out of our range so we found places in town.

The whole fair has a wonderfully international flavour, and, as you have no doubt heard, Ontario does itself proud.

I still think about Sarnia more than I see it. Jan Fowlie was over the other day and we gossiped a bit – about the Cases and the Hawleys and the Grays. We'd like to come up but after the Montreal trip we haven't the courage. Maybe late in the summer. We enjoyed ourselves last year.

My book isn't coming out until next February now.[20] I guess we haggled about the contract too long. It's a good thing, because by then I'll have got over my feelings of self-importance.

Well, I must go. I hear from Pauline that you're not very well. I'll try to send a line once in a while to cheer you up – but if you don't hear it means I've been impaled by a safety pin!

Much love,
Marian

19 Expo '67, the world's fair, held in Montreal in 1967.
20 *Sarah Bastard's Notebook / No Clouds of Glory.*

From Hugh MacLennan[21]
McGill University
Montreal, Quebec

2 October 1967

Dear Marian:

I have written you as strong a recommendation as I can under the circumstances and told them I was writing to you to suggest that you submit a set of galleys of your new novel. In cases of this sort, the work speaks much more strongly than any words from a referee. Congratulations on having finished a novel and on getting it published, for never was it harder in a free country to get a novel accepted than now. I'd like to read it, but I'm a full professor now, classes are enormous and I can hardly keep up with my work in this fall session, when I have 9 hours in the lecture room and so much paper work to handle I nearly go around the bend. I'll read your book when it comes out, when the pressure will be a little less.

It will probably be a while before anyone in this country will be able to read my last book as a novel.[22] It is getting the best treatment I ever had in the States, considering the generally negative attitude to fiction these days, but was hatcheted in Toronto. Partially this was malice, but it was also an incapacity to understand that a novel can deal with a contemporary, living situation of enormous social importance and still be a novel. A combination of the shibboleths of the higher criticism and an understandable belief on the part of journalists that I was dealing with 'news.'

The situation in Quebec was terrible about ten days ago, but

21 See note 5, p. xxiii.
22 *Return of the Sphinx* (New York: Scribner's, 1967).

now I think it will hold together.[23] The crunch is on, and it is at the moment a financial crunch. I expect some violence again, but that is infinitely preferable to the cheap conspiracy of the clique who were mixing racism with blackmail and Gaullist power politics. Thank God the Tories got rid of Dief.[24] He paralysed Ottawa for six years.

Good luck with your new novel, good luck with the children, the Canada Council and life.

Sincerely,
Hugh

From Mrs F.S. Passmore
Sarnia, Ontario

8 February 1968

Dear Miggs and Howard,
Your letter has just come in with the clipping and the account by Fulford,[25] which we greatly enjoyed. We would like to have this picture of you if you can get another for yourselves. I am enclos-

23 In 1968 the FLQ (Front de libération du Québec) intensified its campaign for an independent, socialist Quebec. Beginning in 1963, the FLQ placed bombs in Montreal mailboxes. Its actions culminated in the 1970 October Crisis, when the FLQ kidnapped British diplomat James Cross and Quebec labour and immigration minister Pierre Laporte. The federal government, under Prime Minister Pierre Elliott Trudeau, invoked the War Measures Act (16 October 1970). Montrealers suspected of being FLQ members were arrested in large numbers. Laporte was found murdered, and Cross was released in exchange for his kidnappers' safe passage to Cuba.
24 John George Diefenbaker (1895–1979), Canada's thirteenth prime minister, replaced as Conservative party leader by Robert Stanfield in September 1967.
25 Robert Fulford (1932–), Canadian journalist and author. The article was 'A War inside Sarah's Head,' *Toronto Daily Star*, 6 February 1968, p. 23.

ing the *Observer* account and the photo which we liked even better than the one on the jacket of your book. The article in the *Observer* was signed M.B. so I assume it was written by Marcella, but there might be another MB on their Staff. I did not think it too critical, do you? I read the book aloud to dad and then have loaned it to Maude. Her eyes have been bothering her, so she may take a bit of time to finish it. We still have the Taits' copy here. Incidentally they have invited us to have dinner with them somewhere on Saturday night. We have had this bit of stomach upset for a few days and I hope we will be over it and fit to eat a good dinner by Saturday evening.

There is a Kiwanian[26] film Saturday night on Pakistan, but we prefer to attend the next one which is on Australia. We buy one ticket and it entitles us to have 3 pictures, so we choose those we like best. We used to attend all six, but they became rather tiring and the same outline. Marg Watson (Principal's wife) invited us to come in for coffee after the Travelogue, so it never rains but it pours and going out with Taits will be enough for the one evening.

Miss Lucas called to ask about you: Minna Mann called and we had a long chat and she was so interested and wished me to give her kindest regards to you. Her daughter taught in the same school as Anne Marie, but discipline upset her, so she is taking a course to enable her to teach something else. Minna veered away from the subject of her husband's health, but he is back at work again.

Other people wish to congratulate you and Helen Archibald, who was Pres. of our Univ. Club was interested. You would not know her!

When dad and I were coming home from the store yesterday afternoon, we noticed a big brown cat – dead at the foot of McLeod's retaining wall. It may have been struck by a car on

---

26 Kiwanis International is a philanthropic organization with clubs in many communities in Canada and throughout the world.

Colborne and just crawled there to expire. I phoned them about it and Odette said 'Ugh' so she phoned the Humane Society to ask if they would remove it. I would think that the City Sanitation Dept would be the logical ones.

Love to all,
Mother

Manley's are advertising your book in their sale column – I think for either four or five-fifty and they state that 'Marian Engel is known here as Marian Passmore'!

From Hugh MacLennan
McGill University
Montreal, Quebec

26 February 1968

Dear Marian:
As I told you, I was swamped, pretty well as usual, when your book arrived and had to get out from under enough stuff to read it properly and think about.

Well, there's no question about your talent, none at all. You have a lightning mind, behind every paragraph is a tough and powerful personality, and you can write sentences like daggers. There is a strong vein of modern poetry in the work, quick darts aside and then back again, and the reader has to concentrate to keep up, a little as he does even in the early chapters of *Ulysses*.[27] Nothing but compliments and admiration for the book as you have written it.

Naturally I'm thinking about what you will do after this, and it

27 Novel by Irish writer James Joyce (1882–1941).

may be impertinent for me to make any suggestions whatever. God knows I wouldn't dream of suggesting that I could teach or even help anyone else to write anything. So all I'm doing is thinking aloud.

I believe in your next book you can afford to be far less defensive, totally forgetful of critics and academics and relax a little more inside the sentences and paragraphs. By which I mean specifically that you can stay with a scene or an idea a little longer if for no other reason than to allow the reader to catch up with you. A story is a story is a story. You will never be long-winded, so you can afford to expand if you feel like it. And let the reader continue to see and hear the characters. The critics today tend to condemn this, but the readers do not.

I was delighted to see that it entered the best-seller list of the *Montreal Star* last Saturday, though I don't know what that means in sales. Normally this would go straight into a paper back, and for all I know it already has done so. *The Sphinx* has not because, so Scribner's tell me, the U.S. paper back trade has at the moment saturated the market and oversold itself, and is pulling in its horns. But I hope you have made it, or soon will, for the trouble with fiction now is that hard backs are so damned expensive. When I started writing, they sold for $2.50 to $3.60 and were much better printed and bound, and in those days a book like yours would have picked up anything from 4,000 to 6,000 sales automatically in the Canadian-American lending library trade, where it would have been read (each volume by anything from 30 to 100 people), and so you would have got more widely known. The paperback revolution killed the lending library and fiction has been in market trouble ever since. *The Sphinx* so far has sold 11,000 in Canada and 16,000 in the States, which shows what little difference reviews make these days.

Good luck, Marian, and again my congratulations, and I'm sorry I couldn't get to Toronto for your *lancement.*[28] DuBarry

28 Book launch.

Campau telephoned me about you from Toronto and liked both you and the book[29] –

Best wishes, as ever,
Hugh

I've stupidly lost your letter & must send this c/o your publisher.[30]

From Austin Clarke[31]
Yale University
New Haven, Connecticut
Guest Suite

3 March 1968

Comradess Mariannovich Engelofsky
CONGRATUFUCKINGLATIONS! as Sarah Whatshername in NO CLOUD OF GORY GORE would say.

But how come you so smart to get a Canada Council so soon?

It looks as if I will be back here next year, for a year, as writer in residence; plus doing something such as a fellow-research-something. But I can't take two fellowships so I shall probably postpone the Yale deal until after the expirations of the Canada Council bread.

From the Number Two best novelist in our screwed-up country to the Number One woman (you didn't think I was going to say Number One Novelist, did you?) novelist in our virginal country.

---

29 DuBarry Campau wrote for the *Toronto Telegram*.
30 In *Dear Marian, Dear Hugh*, Verduyn notes the disparity in numbers of letters from MacLennan to Engel, whose papers contain a rich MacLennan correspondence, and letters from Engel to MacLennan, whose papers include very few Engel letters (20). This comment by MacLennan offers an explanation.
31 See note 13, p. xxiv.

Greetings, salutations, libations, congratulations, re-evaluations, alcholambulations ... keep a drink for me; make Howard buy the scotch and bring it to the CBC Project Office. I going buy you a draft in the Red Lion, and you buy me a double champagne in the Four Seasons.

(Incidentally, what is your home address? I feel absolutely stupid addressing these letters Mrs Engel, c/o Mr Engel ...)

Salaam, HOYTY-TOITY FELLOW, etc., Raider-in-Residence,

Austin

From William French[32]
Globe and Mail
Toronto

EDITORIAL DEPARTMENT

2 April 1968

Dear Marian:
Thanks for the fast job on Ducharme.[33] It arrived in time for me to get it into the issue of April 20, and also in time for your payment to be included in the March cheque-list.

I changed it around a bit. Your version violated French's First Law: Never start a review with a direct quotation from the book. It's invariably too confusing for the reader. If the quote is essential, it can usually be fitted in right near the top, after a brief

---

32 See note 10, p. 55.
33 Engel reviewed Réjean Ducharme's *The Swallower Swallowed* (London: Hamilton, 1968). The review was published in the *Globe Magazine*, 27 April 1968. The original version can be found in the Marian Engel Archive, McMaster University, box 24, file 30.

explanatory introduction as to what the quote is all about. In your review, I didn't think the quote was essential; it wasn't really all that illuminating as to style or content. So I took it out.

In rewriting the first page, I tried to set the stage for the reader giving him perspective and background so that he can better understand the detailed discussion of the book. I've tried as far as possible to keep your own words and phrases.

I'm sending you a carbon of the rewrite. After the paragraph at the top of the second page, it just continues with your review, with the appropriate deletions to avoid repetition. I hope you approve of the changes; if you don't, call me and we'll talk about it.

Incidentally, French's Second Law is that the reviewer should give an adequate summary of the book's contents; a plot synopsis, if the book is a novel, or highlights, if non-fiction. You were marginal on this score; I would have liked to know a little more about Bernice, what happened to her and her family, but I decided that since plot is secondary to style in *Swallower*, I'd let it pass.

And French's Third Law of reviewing is that the reviewer must express an opinion on the book's merits or lack of them, pass some kind of judgment, however qualified. Too many reviews leave the reader wondering just what the hell the reviewer thought of the book, whether he liked it or not and why. No problem here with your review. You made your opinion very clear.

There's just one more rule: under certain circumstances, all three of French's Laws can be broken. But rarely.

Best regards,
Bill

From Dan Wickenden[34]
Harcourt, Brace and World
New York

16 December 1968

Dear Marian:

It's a mean and painful thing to have to do at any time, and an especially mean and painful one just before Christmas, but the bad news must be broken sooner or later; and there's no point in waiting until 1969 to tell you that, with the utmost regret, we have decided not to publish *The Silent Companions*.[35]

Your talent and originality are as manifest on every page as they were on every page of *Sarah Bastard's Notebook*, as I keep on calling it in my own mind, but this time they haven't, to our way of thinking, produced a novel. It is, as you wrote to me when you shipped the MS off to Diarmuid, horribly short, an awkward length in the best of circumstances; but if it had seemed successful to us we could have overcome that problem. I wonder, though, if it didn't turn out a great deal shorter than you yourself had expected, and if you didn't somehow begin to lose faith or interest in it somewhere along the way. Or is it just that we are being particularly obtuse?

Diarmuid finds it powerful, he tells me – it's odd, he says, but it carries one on. Alas, it didn't really work as well as that for anybody here; certainly it didn't for me or for at least one other particular admirer of *Sarah*. Neither of us became really involved with, engaged by, Sam, Jane-Regina, Alice and Gertrude, and so on – or quite understood about the Silent Companions themselves. (I found I didn't believe in the Silent Companions, didn't

---

34 See note 9, p. 55.
35 Early working title for *The Honeyman Festival* (Toronto: Anansi, 1970).

believe Minn would have lent herself to such a game.) And Minn herself – try as I would, I could not work up much sympathy for her. What the book has most vividly left with me is an impression of the more disgusting aspects of infancy and of the domestic life in general.

I wonder if it isn't to some extent a personal purging, something you had to get down on paper and out of your system before you could go on to write a book of more general interest. What that other Sarah fan and I think most interesting potentially is Minn's relationship with the hippies, and the hippies themselves. You don't show us enough of them for us to be sure, but maybe something good might be made of them and their similarities to and differences from Minn.

I hate having to say all this about a manuscript on which I know you have worked very hard. But we are puzzled because the result looks almost like a series of random jottings, fragments never really developed, never fused into an organic whole.

Enough, enough. I'm sending a copy of this letter to Diarmuid, and returning the manuscript to him, and I hope he's right and we're wrong. But, you do have a very considerable bunch of fans here, and we dare to think that maybe, if you eventually decide that *The Silent Companions* is not for publication, we can go on being your U.S. publisher. I hope I have not broken a heart this Christmas, and I send you, as always, my very best wishes, along with my regrets.[36]

Yours,
Dan

cc: Diarmuid Russell

---

36 Engel was to use this phrase for a short story, 'Break No Hearts This Christmas,' which appeared in *Inside the Easter Egg* (Toronto: Anansi, 1975), 91–8.

To Dr K.A. McVey, Executive Editor
Macmillan Company of Canada
[Toronto, Ontario]

503 Merton Street
Toronto

2 February 1970

Dear Mr. McVey,
Thank you for your letter of 30th January.

I'm sorry about *The Silent Companions*. I wish most of all that it were a better book. Some day, perhaps, it will be.

The new book went off to New York early in January.[37] It is only at Longmans' here unofficially. I owe them some money for books and was trying to talk Curly Hunter into a reading job and got talked into letting him see it. But as far as I'm concerned Diarmuid Russell decides its fate. He is much better at this sort of thing than I am.

I was very happy, though, when Hugh Kane expressed interest in *The Silent Companions*.[38] I have every respect for Mac as a publishing house, and the offer to look at the book came at a time when I needed encouragement – any kind of encouragement. I do not know whom Diarmuid plans to send the new book out to in New York. Certainly, we are quite free of any claim at the moment and if you are interested in seeing it, get in touch with him at 551 Fifth Avenue. He says it's better than *The Silent Companions* but needs editorial work. I wanted it out of the house so I could think more comfortably about it.

I am also virtually unemployed at the moment. If there are any

37 *Monodromos* (Toronto: Anansi, 1973).
38 Hugh Kane (1911–84), president and general manager of Macmillan Company of Canada, 1969–72.

small literate jobs at your esteemed establishment you might keep me in mind. I spent a year and a half in England turning German financial reports into beautiful English English, which is still, I think, within my grasp.

Yours very sincerely,
Marian Engel

To Robert Weaver
[CBC,
Toronto, Ontario]

503 Merton Street
Toronto

21 June 1970

Dear Bob,
Pardon the holograph but there is a novel in my typewriter.

I intended to have 2 short stories for you – but Anansi leapt in, so nothing will be done until the book is ready for the printer.[39]

What I wanted to say is that I have read your memo to Peter Meggs.[40] It is one of the best things on the literature of this country I have read. Take that from a Canlit graduate.

I don't know what to say about the 'New Wave of Nationalism' stuff. My spirit is eternally partisan but I've never found the WASP world worth being partisan about, so remain suspended. But one night at the Family Compact I was interviewed (by a young man

39 Presumably Engel's book of short stories, *Inside the Easter Egg*.
40 Peter Meggs, a CBC radio producer, co-authored a report with Douglas Ward in 1970 on the state of radio in English Canada: *CBC English Radio Report* (Toronto: CBC, 1970).

who did not know how to wield a tape recorder) for an Ontario Govt. sound project. He said, 'But isn't it true, in 10 years, it will be the new London, the new Paris? What do you find wonderful about Toronto?' Given my allegiance to a dying world, I gulped & said, 'The truss stores.' I hope I did right, Pa.

The other thing: have you glanced at Butor's *Niagara?*[41] In his effort to create a *really* new novel he has created the radio programme. One could air it in French but the American Negroes are too, too bad in English.

So the pregnant novel comes out in October.[42] Owing to the faith & perspicacity of Dennis Lee, it is no longer a scrambled egg. I don't think you'll like it, but a lot of women will.

I have not shown your memo to any other Canajun Authors – but I still find it splendid. Hope one is allowed to read one's husband's papers.

Thanks,
[Marian][43]

From Douglas Fetherling[44]
London, England

23 September 1970

Dear Pass:
Many thanks for your aerogramme, received to-day. Sounds as if you're writing a lot. I, for a change, am too. About a week back I finished my 100–page novel (*Boreal Baby*) which I'll give to Dennis

41 Michel Butor, *Niagara: A Novel* (Chicago: H. Regnery Co., 1969).
42 *The Honeyman Festival.*
43 There is no signature on Engel's carbon copy of this letter.
44 Douglas (now George) Fetherling (1949–), Canadian writer and artist; he has published over fifty books, including works of poetry, social history, cultural analysis, and biography.

[Lee] to look over, I suppose.[45] I'm satisfied with it, though it's nothing great. Its main value is a personal one; it proves to me that if I can write a big piece of fiction I surely can write one twice as big and twice as good by putting in double the time and double the juice. I'd like to show it to you when I return (maybe you can give me a blurb?); it's about a real bastard who's a bastard in self-defence and who always has to force himself into shallow water because by instinct he lives the way a drowning man tries to swim. I'm eager and anxious to start another one, about a broken-down old mobster I knew in my newspaper days. But first I'm trying to finish a book of poems (my best to date, for what that's worth) by the end of next month. May or may not make it.

In all my considerable bookstore browsing I have yet to find any Cyprus stuff for you. I've been looking, believe me. In Charing Cross, however, there is an antiquarian Greek bookshop but the selection is in Greek itself and therefore all Greek to me. I even went to the Cypriot travel centre but they have only propaganda booklets, more or less the opposite numbers of Canada House's. All that's come my way has been the enclosed review from one of the papers, which may or may not be of some small use or interest. Sounds like an okay book. But I'll be here until October tenth or fifteenth before either going to Paris or coming straight home and if in that time I see anything it will be yours as fast as Her Majesty's mails can carry it.

Whether or not I get to Paris depends upon how much political trouble I reckon I'm in. Looks bad at the moment. Besides, my body has stopped working and I ought to come back to Yonge Street to die. My nerves are very bad. Yesterday I held up traffic for about five minutes in Shaftesbury Avenue trying to give an address verbally to a cabby. It's no fun being a grown freak. Though if at all possible I shall go over briefly. I'm always reminded of that line of W.C. Fields's. He's in a cell, with his hands on the bars, about to be taken to the gallows or something, and

---

45 Apparently unpublished.

says: 'I'd like to see Paris before I die ... but at the moment I'll settle for Philadelphia.' Tell Howie I still have his map. Pardon, montrez-moi le wimpy.

I'll get in touch when I get back (won't be at this address long enough for you to reply) whereupon I hope I can come up with some wine one night. God I need a drink. Take care and thank you for your letter, hullo to Howard and regards to the kids.

Cymru Am Byth,[46]
Doug

---

46 Gaelic for 'Wales forever!'

3

Growing Up at Forty, 1971–1975[1]

The 1970s opened on an auspicious professional note for Marian Engel with the publication of her second novel, *The Honeyman Festival.* During the next few years, Engel's literary life expanded to include a generous measure of activism on behalf of Canadian writers like herself. She was closely involved with the formation of the Writers' Union of Canada and instrumental in the establishment of Public Lending Right for authors.

Officially established in 1973, the Writers' Union of Canada was a response to the increased production and professionalization of Canadian writing in the 1960s. Poets in Canada had been provided with the assistance of the League of Canadian Poets since its formation in 1966. The aim of the League was to 'enhance the status of poets and nurture a professional poetic community, to facilitate the teaching of Canadian poetry at all levels of education and to develop the audience for poetry by encouraging publication, performance and recognition of Canadian poetry nationally and internationally.'[2] Like the League, the Canadian Authors Association, founded in 1921, advised members on issues of copyright, contract, government legislation, and freedom of expression. However, it welcomed unpublished as well as published authors, and as a result many professional writers believed that the Association could not adequately represent their concerns. There was clearly room for another organization, and in early 1970s Toronto there was a move to unite to serve the needs of those who were primarily fiction writers.

Early meetings of the fledgling Writers' Union took place in the living room of the Engels' house on Brunswick Avenue. 'In those early days of the Writers' Union,' Matt Cohen recalled, 'issues of professionalism and constant discussion about writing itself had no trouble co-existing.'[3] This would have suited Engel. Correspondence from the 1970s reflects her growing professional activism and the ever increasing number of writers with whom she was in contact. Hugh MacLennan displayed initial reservations about the Union. His letter of 26 January 1974 explains why and provides valuable evidence of the publishing challenges faced by Canadian writers of the day. A few months later, however, MacLennan revised his views and joined the union, crediting 'two women like you [Engel] and Margaret [Laurence]' for bringing sense and sensibility to the undertaking (9 May 1974). Joining Engel and Laurence in the effort were Margaret Atwood, Fred Bodsworth, June Callwood, Austin Clarke, Graeme Gibson, and Farley Mowat, among others.

In 1973 Engel agreed to take on the task of chairing the newly formed Union, a decision prompted in part by the members' view that the position was best held by a writer who had recently finished a major work. This was precisely Engel's situation. Her third novel, *Monodromos*, long in gestation, had just come out with Anansi.[4] There were numerous practical and business matters to consider in the initial stages of the organization's development, as Graeme Gibson's letter of 20 December 1973 indicates. Engel also confronted some ethical considerations. As Chair of the Writers' Union, she felt she could not accept an Ontario Arts Council grant, even though the funds would have eased financial pressures for her. 'I don't want anyone to say that I was in it for myself,' she wrote firmly to Ron Evans on 16 February 1974.

Engel's duties as Chair of the Writers' Union of Canada extended beyond her own country. On 25 June 1974 she wrote a blunt response to an optimistic, aspiring American writer: 'I find your faith in Canada touching, but I think I ought to tell you that the writing situation here is not prosperous. Those few magazines we have seem to be lowering their rates and though Canadians seem to read a lot they have a nefarious habit of getting their books from public libraries. Our nationally owned publishers are few and trembling before the paper shortage; branch houses of U.S. and British publishers publish a few original titles every year. These are the books that get into the stores. So the situation here isn't marvellous for Canadians.' A letter to the Irish novelist Brigid Brophy enclosed ammunition for a copyright fight in which Brophy was engaged,[5] a case that Engel described as 'another loathsome American Imperialist deal' (10 February 1975).

In fact, notwithstanding the national optimism of 1967 and the explosion in cultural activity and Canadian literature, literary magazines, and periodicals of the late 1960s and the first half of the 1970s,[6] the future was far from assured in the cultural arenas of the country. John Wadland recalls:

The American book giant McGraw-Hill purchased Ryerson Press in 1970. Shortly after, in 1971, McClelland and Stewart announced that it was up for sale. Public concern was expressed through the Ontario Royal Commission on Book Publishing which reported (regrettably, without much effect on government) in 1973. In 1975, following the apparent collapse of the venerable *Saturday Night* magazine, a group of civic-minded magazine publishers combined to create the Canadian Periodicial Publishers Association (CPPA) to lobby for conditions more favourable to the protection of Canadian-owned publications.[7]

Incredible though it seemed so soon after the country's spirited centennial celebrations, Canadians still appeared to need 'to know ourselves.' This was the title of the report of the Commission on Canadian Studies, which had been established in 1970 by the Association of Universities and Colleges of Canada.[8] Chaired by then president of Trent University, Thomas H.B. Symons, after whom the commission's findings were named, the Symons Report was in part a response to a growing sense that insufficient attention was being paid to Canadian issues, themes, and approaches in Canada's educational and cultural institutions. The Report stated that 'an alarming number of students were graduating from our universities lacking even basic knowledge about the culture, history, government, geography, science and social dynamics of their homeland.'[9] A proper understanding of Canada must begin with a thorough knowledge of the country's history, its peoples, and their daily lives. Countervailing arguments maintained that 'there was no cause for alarm because knowledge is universal and therefore could not or should not be fostered in any particular national context.'[10] Debates about the national versus the universal would soon be complicated by theories of postmodernism and postcolonialism about to unfold within critical and cultural circles. Setting the stage in Canada, the federal policy of multiculturalism, introduced by the Trudeau government in 1971, contributed to and gained insight from new work investigating issues of race and ethnicity within cultural and academic communities alike.

Engel was not immune to the nationalist sentiments expressed in various Canadian cultural communities, including pockets of the writing community. 'Pessimists have been crying for years that Canada is turning [in]to another U.S.,' she mused on 25 June 1974.[11] 'Probably that is true but I personally cling to the fact that it isn't yet, and may never be.' Then with her characteristic humour, Engel queried, 'I mean, who'd want us, with our enormous problems? Would the U.S. have time?' Yet, just as often, it was more immediate local and personal issues that raised her ire. Engel wrote indignantly to Jean Wright, managing editor of *Chatelaine* magazine, about the ways in which publications take advantage of Canadian writers. 'I am returning your cheque and stub for the McGibbon article, which I enjoyed doing immensely, because "first world serial rights French and English" is really too much! ... *Nobody*, not even housewives, should sell world rights. And if you want French rights you should negotiate them with authors' (26 June 1974).[12]

Engel's work as first Chair of the Writers' Union of Canada came close to convincing her that 'there isn't a goddam reason in the world why anyone should write books anymore,' as she complained to Robert Weaver on 8 March 1974. 'Publishers expect you to do everything but turn the crank on the press, readers expect masterpieces, and NOTHING will ever get you out of scrubbing the pots and pans.' Nevertheless, not only did Engel persist in her lobbying efforts, she also continued to write, albeit 'with the worst kind of cranky, selfish stubbornness,' she warned Weaver, 'because if you can't have money you should have your own way' (8 March 1974).

Engel's literary activism continued after her term as Chair of the Writers' Union ended. She served on the board of the Toronto Public Library (1975–8), and she carried out important foundational work on the question of royalties for authors, the issue which later became established as Public Lending Right or PLR. Both sets of activities were vital endeavours. Public libraries were sites of heightened national consciousness during the 1960s when increased funding enabled public and academic libraries alike to develop or strengthen a Canadiana research collection. The Toronto Public Library had previously published *The Canadian Catalogue of Books, 1921–49*, and in the financial boom of the postwar years, it secured its pre-eminent position among Canadian libraries. Engel's experience as a library board member provided her with helpful insights in her pursuit of lending rights for authors. The establishment of public lending rights for Canadian writers was her 'baby,' Engel proudly told the secretary of state in a letter of 1 April 1982, and the eventual success of PLR owes much to Engel's early lobbying efforts (8 March 1974 and 10 February 1975). Officially established as a federal program in 1986, a year after Engel's death, PLR pays Canadian authors for the availability of their books in Canadian libraries. Operating within the Canada Council, the program's founding Chair was Andreas Schroeder, who had added his efforts to those of Engel in the formative early years. MacLennan gave a nod of approval (26 January 1974), and Lovat Dickson[13] was full of praise: 'All that you are doing is first-class, particularly with a Lending Right Agreement,' Dickson wrote, 'and I wish you the greatest possible success' (20 February 1974).

Union work was not without impact on Engel's writing. '[M]y thinking time has got absorbed by Public Life,' she acknowledged in reply to a letter from Robert Weaver expressing his regret at returning stories she had recently submitted, 'and my rhetoric is used up mostly writing long letters to people like the Bureau of Intellectual Property, so it will be some time before I get down to serious work again' (15 July 1974). Nonetheless, the period was hardly unproductive for Engel. She worked on several projects simultaneously. The real-life story of William Kingdom Rains inspired a script for a play (8 March 1974).[14] The CBC had commissioned *Joanne*, a short novel for radio,[15] and characters Ziggy and Ruth inspired new short stories.[16] Engel also continued to review books for newspapers and magazines, garnering warm letters of thanks from writers such as Irving Layton (15 March 1973), Ernest Buckler, who praised Engel's writing as 'searching, nimble and dexterous' (1 January 1974), and the influential English biographer and critic V.S. Pritchett.[17] Pritchett admired *Monodromos* for its economy, the vividness of its allusive method, and its 'astonishing later pages' (17 December 1973). It was, he observed, 'original in approach and matter and in amount of courage as well as intelligence.' Hugh MacLennan lauded the novel's 'tight, allusive and excellent writing' (10 February 1974), and Margaret Laurence praised its 'sense of Exile': 'All the terrific things about another culture – and you, in that novel, get across so many of them – and yet the sense one is left with, I think, is that one has to come home again' (6 September 1974). Engel had indeed come home again: *Monodromos* would be her only novel set outside Canada, and her next work was to be deeply rooted in the Canadian scene.

As her professional literary life shifted into high gear and her Governor General's Award–winning novel *Bear* (1976) was gestating, her personal life was becoming more difficult. The Engel marriage was in trouble, as is revealed in the letters to Margaret Laurence and from Hugh MacLennan toward the end of this chapter. By November 1974, Engel had made the difficult decision to separate from Howard. As the chapter begins, however, the Engels appear affectionate, charmingly awkward, and almost shy with one another in a rare letter exchange (18 March 1971 and 31 March 1971).

In March 1971, Marian had the opportunity to make a return trip to Cyprus. *Maclean's* magazine had commissioned an article, and, travelling on a Canadian Air Force flight, Engel was able to revisit the island where she had lived a decade earlier. With the twins now nearly six years old, the assignment undoubtedly presented a welcome break from domestic routine. As well, the island was the setting of Engel's novel *Monodromos*, the novel she was still struggling to complete. Finally, the assignment provided some modest income. These benefits notwithstanding, Engel felt guilty about travelling alone, as she wrote to Howard from Nicosia on 18 March 1971. The very same day, on the other side of the ocean, Howard was writing to her. Their letters crossed in the mails. Engel was about to take the donkey ride so graphically fictionalized in *Monodromos,* published two years later in 1973. That was also the year Engel turned forty and, as she wryly observed, growing up began in earnest.

Notes

1 'Growing Up at Forty: Or the Real Joanne' was the title of an article Engel prepared for *Chatelaine*. See the Marian Engel Archive, McMaster University, box 26, file 13.

2 From the mission statement of the League of Canadian Poets: http://www.poets.ca/linktext/about.htm

3 Cohen, *Typing: A Life in Twenty-Six Keys*, 181.

4 Margaret Laurence was in the finishing stages of *The Diviners*, which appeared in 1974.

5 Brigid Brophy (1929–95), Irish novelist, playwright, and social activist whose works include *Flesh* (1962) and *In Transit* (1969).

6 Even a brief inventory is impressive: *La Barre du jour* (1965), *Open Letter* (1965), *University of Windsor Review* (1965), *West Coast Review* (1966), *Wascana Review* (1966), *Mosaic* (1967), *Malahat* (1967), *Herbes rouges* (1968), *Ellipse* (1969), *Antigonish Review* (1970), *Descant* (1970), *Canadian Fiction Magazine* (1971), *Event* (1971), *Journal of Canadian Fiction* (1972), *Exile* (1972), *Grain* (1973), *Essays on Canadian Writing* (1974), *Ontario Review* (1974), *Voix et images du pays* (1975), *Estuaire* (1976), *Studies in Canadian Literature* (1976), *Lettres québécoises* (1976), *Jeu* (1976), *Canadian Poetry* (1977), *Brick* (1977) (Wadland, 'Voices in Search of a Conversation,' 61). In the domain of the visual and performing arts, new publications included *Cinema Canada* (1967), *art magazine* (1969), *Dance in Canada* (1973), *Journal of Canadian Art History* (1974), *Canadian Theatre Review* (1974), *Canadian Drama* (1975), *Parachute* (1975) and *artsatlantic* (1978). The social sciences saw the creation of *Histoire sociale / Social History* (1968), *Labour / Le Travail* (1976), *Canadian Journal of Political and Social Theory* (1976), and *Canadian Public Policy* (1976). Publications featuring feminist perspectives included *Québécoises deboutte!* (1971–5), *Kinesis* (1974), *Atlantis* (1975), *Room of One's Own* (1975), *Les Têtes de pioche* (1976–9), *Fireweed* (1978), and *Canadian Woman Studies* (1978). For more detail, see Wadland, 'Voices in Search of a Conversation: An Unfinished Project.'

7 Ibid., 61–2.

8 T.H.B. Symons, *To Know Ourselves: The Report of the Commission on Canadian Studies*, 2 vols (Ottawa: Association of Universities and Colleges of Canada, 1975).

9 Ibid., 2.

10 Ibid.

11 The letter is addressed to an otherwise unidentified Mr Beatty.

12 The dispute with the magazine was apparently resolved; the article appeared in the October 1974 issue of *Chatelaine*, pp. 46–7, 88–91.

13 Lovat Dickson (1902–87), Canadian writer, biographer, and general editor and director of Macmillan & Co., London.

14 William Kingdom Rains (1789–1874), an early Ontario settler.

15 Letter from MacLennan, 9 May 1974.

16 Letter to Bob Weaver, 8 March 1974.

17 Irving Layton (1912–), Montreal-based Canadian poet, author of over forty volumes of poetry, short stories, and essays (his collection *A Red Carpet for the Sun* won the 1960 Governor General's Award for poetry); Ernest Buckler (1908–84), Canadian novelist, whose 1952 *The Mountain and the Valley* is a Canadian classic; V.S. Pritchett (1900–97), English author of forty books of fiction, biography, memoirs, and criticism.

To Howard Engel
[Toronto, Ontario]

Ledra Palace
Nicosia, Cyprus

Thursday, 18 March [1971]

Papali! O andros mon –
So – the old Yukon[1] finally gets here, much aided by masking tape – there is sun & a big wind – a smart new airport & the usual old women digging. Gord Hilchie, the information officer, to meet me. At once to sit by the pool at the Ledra Palace & drink brandy. Then to HQ for briefing.

I had forgotten that this place is heaven. The palm trees & the big villas, the yellow stone. It is a good thing I came back – I had missed so much.

I am booked in here and will stay a few days because it is next to HQ at Wolsey barracks. Warn P. Newman he will have to pay![2] Steve is disgusted.[3]

We are all just the same! Mark is 11 – a very clever eleven. Christiane came for me at six – very smart, green suede coat – Claudine a big graceful girl in *blue-jeans*. The Indian things a smashing success. Mark tore around playing Indian. They live in a dower house – very lush – but not private. We had a drink & I ate with the kids – they went out & I came back here to sleep.

1 The 'Yukon' (CC-106) was introduced into service by the Royal Canadian Air Force in 1961. The largest aircraft yet to be built in Canada, it was retired from service in 1971.
2 Peter Newman (1929–), editor of *Maclean's* magazine, who had commissioned Engel to write an article. 'Travel in Cyprus' appeared in the December 1972 issue, pp. 77–8.
3 Probably Steve Caramondanis, an old Cyprus friend of the Engels.

We were 2 days at Lahr the Princess Pats & I.[4] None of the officers spoke but I got on with the Sergeants! I bought a big Vitabath for $10 – heavy as lead, dammit.

I overlook a bastion.

It is so selfish of me to come alone – but it was impossible for all of us, so here I am & I can't feel it is entirely wrong.

I see my hand is still shaky from the big trip. The extra day at Lahr was a bore but I got to know what your ordinary soldier thinks of this posting – grrr. That sounds like her ladyship doesn't it? I spread the word about Regaena St. Really –

My window overlooks Victoria Street. A woman is hanging washing out on one of the bastions. The almond blossoms are out though there was snow last week.

It is 8:30 a.m. The Greek HQ is across the Rd. Canadian HQ is in Kutchuk's old house. Now I will go out & get [lens paper[5]] – before I see Hilchie at 9:30. He thinks I am very vague – and not militarily knowledgeable. Mastering Effective Militarese is the next course I take.

I hear Ronah has been ill. I will phone her to-day.

I am writing in Christiane's English, I can tell. Odd blanks in communication. It is amazing how none of us have changed. They still have the same things. To-night I will have more to report. Steve still seems vastly intelligent – no wonder we liked him. The wind is cool – but the sun! All my love and I hope you are managing. I am mean to come without you!

xxxxxx Pass [M.E. nickname]

---

4 The Princess Patricia's Canadian Light Infantry regiment had a base in Lahr, Germany.

5 Engel's handwriting is difficult to decipher here; lens paper is used for cleaning optical lenses – perhaps for Engel's camera.

From Howard Engel
Toronto, Ontario

%)#C START AGAIN
%)# ONCE MORE

18 March 1971

Dear Pass, (I already feel awkward writing you)
Greetings from the land where we stand on guard. Greetings to those who happen to live in places where we send left-over standers to keep the peace.

Mrs. Faull hasn't broken her hip yet,[6] but I've looked up the number of the orthopaedic hospital and have kept the stair-rods in and the sidewalk ice chipped. She is frail, but we are managing, now that the mysteries of the stove and the can opener have been revealed to her. William is having the hard time you probably imagined he would have at first, but Charlotte is very accommodating. I've had her pick them up at school since Tuesday when Will decided to go home with Robbie without mentioning it. I came home from the office only long enough to paddle him and trot him off to bed. She is endlessly kind to them, but credulous, and at her age it's probably too late to start using your eyes independently. Anyway, we manage, and it's even fun. Mrs. Faull has lovely eyes, and knows many tricks which she learned on the islands. I admire her sweet calm, her small feet, and quiet ways. I have to watch myself.

I went to Ivan's for a haircut. I didn't see much hair on the floor afterwards, but what remained on my head stood upright when I read the bill. But it was worth it: one should do some things once in a lifetime.

---

6 Mrs Faull, housekeeper hired by the Engels during Marian's absence.

Letters: Jane on the postal strike, changes on Oxford Street, and your little place on Charlotte Street, which seems to have survived Mod-With-It-London; an invitation to Ted Phillips' vernissage tomorrow; a catalogue from L.L. Bean that I ordered for you and then forgot about, featuring all the clothes you'll need for your expedition into darkest Karpassia; an admiring note from the young author of the critique in *Le Soleil* – he wishes that Minn would be unfaithful with him in her dreams, but goes on to mention that the stain in the upper corner was caused by his kid's orange juice;[7] a copy of a note from Weaver about putting 'Sublet' on CBC Tuesday Night during Easter Week; a contract for the latter; and a few High Barnet things.

The phone doesn't ring. One has peace. I have cleaned your '0.'[8] I have been to the movies, I have cooked, and I have been offered all kinds of help.

This letter, with the bank draught, will probably cross with your 'I arrived safely but travel-worn' letter, so I'll shut up for now. No, I haven't finished the play yet. There's lots of time, and I haven't dug the gunk out of your 'e' yet. Yet. Take the draught to a Barclay's Bank, and they should recognize its substance.

Much love and squalor,
XX Me

---

7 Robert Dickson wrote an enthusiastic review of *The Honeyman Festival* for the Quebec newspaper *Le Soleil* (27 February 1971), as well as a personal letter to Engel admiring her work.

8 The letter *O* on Engel's typewriter.

To Howard Engel
[Toronto, Ontario]

Cyprus

31 March 1971

Howie mon –
Steve just came with your letter – at first I was frightened – it seemed so soon after the other – something might have been wrong. But I gather that things are Faulling[9] into place as well as usual & 'cool it' is a useful remark.

My donkey and I rendezvous at Reno's tomorrow at 8:30 p.m.[10] Where the hell he spends the night I do not know. I would ask Steve but he is doing commissions for Christiane, who is not in a good mood about moving to the new flats. I have Marc busy working out a route for me now. I have been here a week & we are all a bit tired of each other. Only a bit, I hope.

This week has been fabulous. I could have come home today, but at the last minute Reno challenged me to do the donkey thing & arranged the donkey. Today I bought a car rug & cut a hole in it for a poncho!! I'll need it. Spent the a.m. hunting for shoes – remembrances of Europe – & wound up with Elegant Spanish ones like huaraches. God help us if the donkey just goes back to his village.

Zavro was so pleased with his money he ordered me an *Excerpta Cypria* – a reprint which I paid roughly the price of a *Britannica* for![11] But it really is superb. Last night I was to see the painter who has Chris's things – quite a good chap – good talk about donkeys & Spanish wine which really is nutty.

9 Reference to Mrs Faull.
10 Engel's journey on the donkey was to be vividly captured in *Monodromos*, which appeared two years later.
11 C.D. Cobham, ed. and trans., *Excerpta Cypria* (1908; repr. Cambridge, 1969).

Mammas's family gave me a party last Sat night. Dino was there with his *frail blonde brittle English* wife – very upper class. It was most unrelaxed until Sotiris burst in. A big man, Sotiris.

Gosh, it's hard to write to you. When your letter came I was so lonesome for you.

I spent a week at the Ledra & have been a week here. If I stay I'll go off on a donkey or a bicycle, *really* because I have this passion to know villages.

Christiane is getting worried about boxes for moving. The new flat on Limassol Road is smashing but apparently they have to move by themselves. Wow – now she has a lot of things to say! I must retreat – perhaps I'd better go tomorrow! Anyway I'll post this. Letters take 12 days.

Much love – to all,
Pass

From Mrs F.S. Passmore
Sarnia, Ontario

26 December 1971

My dear Miggs & Howard,
I have just finished a letter to Martha thanking her for her card and magnificent poinsettia. It has several blooms on it and should last for sometime. It was good to get your letter and also THE phone call! Thank you very much and I am sure your goose would be done just right, if you poured off the grease as it cooked. I have not done one for years – not since Welles bought one for us when visiting down here with us. Our turkey was good and I think cooked properly. I followed directions, but our oven must be hotter than most for the meat was done early and we just left it sitting in

the oven. Maude is here to-day, Sunday, and she is now lying on the chesterfield resting for her side and back pains her so much. It is such a pity that she must suffer so much from that untoward accident of falling over her mat. I am going to take her home soon for the weather promises to be rain and maybe freezing.

As I mentioned over the telephone, we tasted that good raspberry jam in the fancy jar; also the little pots of honey from Cookes and you and the Crawfs could not send us anything more acceptable. Dad was showing films – *Bird Watching* which is good and he has revised it, also the *Niagara Parkway in Autumn* which is my favourite and the Millers liked both films very much.[12] I suggested that we put on the bird singing tape as our guests were coming in and you should have seen the look of bafflement and puzzlement! Charlotte looked all around for our 'new bird' and was so surprised when she found it was a tape. I suggested that Logan be my bus boy and carry out the dishes from the diningroom table and he was very good and took orders without saucing me back! I did not want Maude to attempt it for she was not up to it. We are invited up there for afternoon tea on Tuesday and to Littles for dinner on Wednesday. I am leaving our dining table set up and must invite [the] Evans[es] in soon for they have been so good to us. They had Ted's family there for Christmas Eve dinner and it left them free to go to Westovers' for Christmas day. Molly also invited Katie Turner and Margaret for dinner for they are mighty lonely at this time – not having relatives in this country. Katie teaches all the Annear children music and she must be good for the children are good musicians.

[The] Taits invited us out to dinner at the Laurentien which is opposite the Sahara. It was such a pleasant surprise and we had a delicious roast beef dinner which is my choice always. I really splurged and ate things 'i shouldn't otter' but everything seemed

---

12 We have not attempted to identify the many Sarnia friends and neighbours mentioned in Mary Passmore's letter.

to agree with me. Then Herb took us down the River to see the lights which are very modest this year compared to former years. I hinted that I wanted to go, so Herb rose to the occasion. Edith was poorly that night and I nearly lost my balance when assisting her to the washroom. Poor dear – it is such an affliction and Dr. Carruther's son, who is also a doctor is confined to a wheeled chair now with the same complaint. Maude said she was talking to all her grandchildren and Nancy [the] night before Christmas. Helen has phoned and said they could not get any of the circuits on Christmas Day and Howard told her that you folks had also tried several times before reaching us. Mrs. Crawford and Ethel are having such a good time and I am sure the others will be enjoying their company too. Don and Helen are driving the women back to St. Catharines to-morrow for the bus service is rather slow and tiring for Mrs. C. Shelley gave Tom a dart game which was being put to good use. She and Fred Fitz are driving Gay back to Montreal to-morrow, so all the Crawfs are going their separate ways. Fred does not go with Rita now apparently and is staying free.

You should have seen us craning our necks and trying to get a look at the twins on that TV!![13] I was sure it was Charlotte and there was a fair little boy beside her, but it was exasperating because the photographer just whizzed the camera back and forth so fast and it would not rest on any of the children for any length of time. I made my shortbread from two new recipes and never again for they were not nearly as good as we had hoped for, as my old recipe brought out the taste.

With love and thanks again for your most generous parcel and stay healthy and have a satisfying 1972.

Mum & Dad

13 We have been unable to discover why the twins appeared on television.

To Diarmuid Russell[14]
Russell and Volkening
New York

503 Merton Street
Toronto

27 March 1972

Dear Diarmuid,
Thanks for your kind words.

The country is still in a fever of nationalism and one's dearest friends continue to insist that it is somehow morally superior to be published in Canada by nationalists for little return than to deal with the Wicked Yank. At the same time they see no reason to fail to take their cut. And would be hurt if one pointed out their inconsistency. And would be shocked if one pointed out that since people find it almost absurd to buy novels in this country ...

14 This letter appears not to have been completed. It was probably replaced by the one which follows.

To Diarmuid Russell
Russell and Volkening
New York

Toronto, Ontario

[27 March 1972]

Dear Diarmuid,
Thank you for your kind words.

I remember years ago you said authors usually enjoyed living in the country away from the literary feuds and now I know why. Instead, since we have to leave this house, we're moving deeper into the forest – so that if I have to go downtown it doesn't take all day – and just trying to ride out the New Nationalism, the New Puritanism, etc.

I would be delighted to send you the MS but not quite yet as talking with [Dennis] Lee enabled me to clarify my own feeling that I was doing certain narrative things that led the reader astray – in other words I needed a feeling that there WAS a reader, and now that I have that I want to make a few changes before the MS is seen. As Lee says it is not yet obvious that the book fails to develop in an ordinary way on purpose, and I think this can be fixed by eliminating about six sentences.

As for the business side, thank heavens for you. I feel I owe something to Anansi in a vague moral sort of way but I think because many of their writers are shareholders they think they ought to own foreign rights themselves.[15] But they seem to be 'above' reading contracts and accounting, etc. I got the feeling that Lee thought I was exploiting him. I think author-publisher relationships are terribly prone to paranoia, and I know I was

15 Anansi had published Engel's *Honeyman Festival* in 1970.

'using' him asking him to read the MS – but it seems to me that when one is desperately short of thinking time, this is valid.

I have the last typing-paper box in the world in my grip and am saving it to send the book to you.

[Marian]

To Catherine Macdonald
Canada Council
Ottawa, Ontario

503 Merton Street
Toronto, Ontario

6 April [1972]

Dear Mrs Macdonald,
Thank you for your notification of my Arts Award which I received today.

Though I have some qualms about accepting unearned income I now feel saved from making speeches at libraries about how Canadians don't buy books and rescued from having to make rude remarks like 'Why?' about Canadian Nationalism. Having a full-fledged career that causes one's husband's outgo to exceed his income has been humiliating.

I am enclosing the appropriate forms with many thanks.

Yours sincerely,
Marian Engel

From Irving Layton[16]
York University
Toronto, Ontario

15 March 1973

My dear Marian,
Considering what you thought I'd said about women, your review was a gratifying miracle of kindness. I loved every word of it.
May a Greek sun always shine for you.

Yours,
Irving

To Robert Weaver
[CBC,
Toronto, Ontario]

2 August 1973

Dear Bob,
I *did* sell 'Bicycle Story' to *Chatelaine*.[17] Re-wrote it slightly. Solves my tax problem. Now if I can just sell one to you we can get a bathtub in here ... or will some horrid fiscal emergency crop up?

16 See note 17, p. 87. We are unsure to which review Layton was referring, but the *Canadian Forum*, in an introduction to selections from Layton's collection of poems *The Pole Vaulter*, reproduces Engel's observation that 'the man who took the underpants off Canadian poetry sings an unfashionable tune. But it's a good one and he sings it well' (*Canadian Forum*, October 1974, p. 30).

17 There is a typescript draft of this story in the Marian Engel Archive, McMaster University, box 20, file 19. It was to appear in *Inside the Easter Egg* (Toronto: Anansi, 1975), 163–72.

I'd love to have lunch with you when I emerge from rural obscurity, which is okay when the weather's fine but fairly sordid in times like this as clothes don't dry and the flies bite.[18] However, one gets a good deal more time to mooch and think up here and I think it's good for us. I also get time to write letters, therefore feel virtuous.

I see there's to be a homage to your 25th anniversary with the CBC. Do you feel like St. George or the Dragon? I wasn't asked to contribute but you know I feel hommagey anyway ... that's all I'll say.

I'm having a funny literary summer writing back and forth to New York explaining House of Anansi and Clarke Irwin (for a children's story)[19] contracts to my old agent's new staff, as he has retired. They have found all sorts of clever little inserts that tie me down in unaccustomed ways. All of $250 advance on one book and none (but a good percentage) on the other. I am not convinced that a Writers' Union is a bad idea, and I'm really sorry to be missing tonight's meeting with Margaret Laurence. However the bus goes just too late and I've discovered it would cost us $8 return! So that's out. Pity they didn't tell me about it before. Fetherling isn't doing such a bad job on the *Star*, is he?[20] We have lots to gossip about. I must think about where to find a dress and ask you out!

Yours sincerely,
Marian Engel

---

18 For a brief period of time, the Engels had a summer home in Holstein, Ontario.

19 The story appeared as *Adventure at Moon Bay Towers* (Toronto: Clarke, Irwin, 1974).

20 Douglas (now George) Fetherling was literary editor of the *Toronto Star*. See also note 44, p. 76.

From Robert Harlow[21]
West Vancouver
British Columbia

3 December 1973

Dear Marian,

Those were good meetings we had, and if everything turns out well we should gain a pretty loud and perhaps even powerful voice in the community. My belief that you are the right person to head us up at this time has been further strengthened by the weekend.

Monodromos, which I've bought and read, is a good good book, one you should be proud of. Get on the air, on TV and into the papers and magazines full force. It's the kind of book that also should earn its keep.

And, finally and most importantly, I want to thank you and Howard for putting me up. Putting up with me. Also your daughter who moved out of her room. And William whose home was taken over partially for those two days. Bless you all.

Cheers,
Bob Harlow

---

21 Robert Harlow (1923–), Canadian writer, radio producer, and academic, author of seven books of travel and fiction, including *Scann* (1972).

From V.S. Pritchett[22]
London, England

17 December 1973

Dear Mrs Engels,[23]
Thanks indeed for sending me your review of Balzac, a very
flattering and interesting one.[24] You have been very generous. I
wish the book could have had more critical material, but I would
have had to double its length – and that was not possible in the
format. Anyway, it is a *Life* and Balzac was one of the few authors
who have had a life as remarkable, in its way, as the works.

I am so glad you have found a very good publisher for
Monodromos which increasingly gripped me as I read on to its
astonishing later pages. I was much struck by the vividness of your
allusive method and I liked its economy. The homosexual seduc-
tion scene is very well managed. There is always something harsh
about the Mediterranean which the beguiled traveller or foreign
resident tries not to see. Your book is, in the very best sense,
original in approach and matter and in amount of courage as well
as intelligence.

The glimpses of Louis MacN[eice] are tantalizing. He was a
strange, aloof man yet always somehow very near and whole – his
end was deplorably careless. He was such a mixture of the simple,
affectionate, complex, gregarious and solitary.

Thank you for the book and again for the review. A happy
Christmas and New Year to you from Dorothy and me,

Victor Pritchett

22 See note 17, p. 87. This letter is published by permission of PFD on behalf of
   the estate of Dorothy Rudge Pritchett.
23 Misspelled in original.
24 The first American edition of Pritchett's biography of Balzac appeared in
   1973 (New York: Knopf). Engel's review, for CBC Radio, was broadcast on *The
   Arts in Review*, 13 October 1973.

From Graeme Gibson[25]
Mansfield, Ontario

20 December 1973

Marian,

I've been thinking some more about the mechanics of Alma's job and it occurs to me that the next few months are important because they will see the job defined in specific ways.[26]

As I said to you yesterday we must remember it is a well paying job for what it'll probably involve. Furthermore, it has chances of being an interesting one. So we needn't feel apologetic to Alma, or whoever, for insisting that it be done well.

Anyway, I have a number of suggestions. 1) we must draw together a reasonably detailed 'job description.' It should include, not only the day by day responsibilities, but also the annual ones (arranging general meetings etc.). It should set down such things as holidays, benefits ... all that crap. I suggest that Alma, on the basis of what she knows so far, might pull together a suggested 'description' and that the executive take it from there. *I believe this should be done before the job defines itself without our realizing what is happening.* 2) we must sort out with Alma whether she was paid 'reasonably' for her work during the past year, and how much time she's been able to spend on Union business since the last conference, since the national council meeting, in order to determine when she's to go on salary. The chaos of her move has made it impossible for her to concentrate on the job so possibly we won't pay her full salary until whatever point she's become, or becomes full time. Let me emphasize (although I'm sure it's

---

25 Graeme Gibson (1934–), Canadian writer and cultural activist, and one of the founding members of the Writers' Union. He served as its Chair during 1974–5.

26 Alma Lee, the first paid staff member of the Writers' Union.

unnecessary) that we'll not short change her in any way ... only that very soon we must establish the job, its definition, in a very professional way. Because we will be spending tax payers' money, as well as the dues from our members, to maintain the office so we must be bloody minded.

Until all this is sorted out I feel you should insist upon some routine such as we discussed last night. If you get a taxi charge account and visit the office once a week, get Alma to handle all correspondence and have it ready for you to sign, plus let the officers of the union know that Alma is there to do Union work for them as well, then I expect we'll have a pretty good idea of what the job entails by the time we negotiate with Alma in three months.

Also (with emphasis) the reason we've always insisted the Union needs an executive secretary/director is our recognition that the chairman and other officers cannot be expected to do a whole pile of paper work. You must not let yourself get trapped into doing anything that Alma can do as well.

Obviously we're at a disadvantage because we don't now know exactly what's involved with the job. But we can expect a full week's work. That should easily include correspondence, newsletter, memberships as well as research and bookkeeping ...

Anyway. All of this isn't something for you to worry about alone. I suggest we have a meeting with David (newsletter) and someone else from the council or executive, and set up ways of ensuring the job works best for Alma and for the Union ...

Graeme

From Ernest Buckler[27]
Bridgetown, Nova Scotia

1 January 1974

Dear Marian Engel,
As I'd told Margaret, I was in a Slough of Despond that would make Bunyan's look like a pot-hole.[28] Christmas had tended to melancholize me, and I was severely afflicted by the writer's occupational disease: galloping anomie. So what a tonic your letter was! And how extraordinarily kind it was of you to take the trouble to send me those real nuggets of encouragement.

Myself, I'm not much of a Buckler fan; but I take great heart from your endorsement of my work. Particularly because it comes from one whose own pen is so searching, nimble and dexterous. Thank you. And thank you.

I don't need to tell you how much your gift of praise to *The Mountain and the Valley* moved me. Bless you for assuring me that the people in it are real. That, of course, is the prime compliment. Doing it again, I guess I'd pare David's introspection down a bit. (Good novels should breathe out, not in.) But then it *was* largely autobiographical – and I suppose that every writer is, in the last analysis, always sort of birdwatching his or her *self,* right?

HAPPY NEW YEAR – and again I owe you gratitude to a degree beyond the 'n'th. Love,

Ernie

27 See note 17, p. 87. Buckler's *The Mountain and the Valley* was first published in 1952 (New York: Holt). Its first Canadian edition was in 1961, and it was reissued by McClelland and Stewart in 1970.
28 Buckler's reference is to John Bunyan's (1628–88) *Pilgrim's Progress.*

From Margaret Laurence[29]
Trent University
Peterborough, Ontario

25 January 1974

Dear Marion[30] –
How goes the battle (query). (This typewriter has a lot of fancy signs such as ñ ç © ¶ § ¨ ˆ etc, but no question mark!) I wonder how the membership brochure is coming along (query). I haven't heard from John Metcalf for awhile,[31] so assume he was getting an okay on it from other Membership Committee people.

I was really glad to hear that you feel a bit more cheery about things. Nonsense ... of course you'd have got through it without me, but thanks all the same – I really am glad if I was any help at all. Well, it's a two way street, kid – we help one another, to coin a phrase. I happen to be in fairly good shape (mentally speaking, not physically!) at the moment, but without dear friends there would have been many times when the passage would have been much rougher. I feel pretty good about the fact that the novel is totally off my mind, and I have no further responsibility towards it.[32] The dust-jacket arrived the other day – a pull of it, I mean – and it is beautiful. Simple elegant print in scarlet and black, and a marbled background in bluegrey that looks like the swirling waters of a river, very suitable as the river is the central image in the book. This was Knopf's second try at a jacket – for the first time ever, I was consulted about my feelings, and I absolutely detested

---

29 Margaret Laurence (1926–87), one of Canada's most widely read novelists. She was writer-in-residence at Trent University in 1974 and settled in nearby Lakefield the same year, residing there until her death in 1987.
30 Misspelled throughout this letter.
31 John Metcalfe (1938–), Canadian writer and editor.
32 *The Diviners* (New York: Knopf, 1974).

the first one – it looked like *Ladies Home Journal*, quite pretty but all wrong.

Peggy Atwood has done a v. good article on me for *Maclean's*.[33] It will come out in April. She very kindly phoned and read it to me, to check various things and said was there anything I hated in it (there wasn't). The other day a girl from *Saturday Night* arrived – she is going to do an article for Fulford, on me.[34] Her name is Valerie Miner Johnson ... do you know her (query). She is a nice young woman, but alas, seems determined to interpret *The Diviners* as being totally autobiographical. She had a tape recorder, into which I talked at some length, trying to explain, really, the nature of fiction. Can one really explain to someone who does not already know (query). I think perhaps not. I kept trying to say that of course certain things are drawn from life – geography, even some events, but this does not make the novel autobiographical. Morag Gunn in the book is both me and not me – we're related. I felt the same about Stacey, and even Rachel.[35] But I don't think Valerie really got the point, so I fear the article may be embarrassing to me and painful to my ex-inlaws. Valerie is coming back again in a few weeks, so maybe I can try to explain a bit more. But one has the feeling that the more one tries to explain something really subtle like that, the more other people (if they are not themselves writers of fiction) will just think – aha, methinks the lady doth protest too much. I feel kind of depressed about this and don't quite know what to do. She kept saying things like 'Well, you have a daughter, too, don't you,' and then I would say 'Yeh, but she isn't the illegitimate child of a Manitoba Métis.' Then she would say (she read the novel, see, having got

33 Margaret Atwood, 'Face to Face: Margaret Laurence As Seen by Margaret Atwood,' *Maclean's*, May 1974, pp. 38–49.
34 Valerie Miner Johnson, 'Matriarch of Manawaka,' *Saturday Night*, May 1974, pp. 17–20.
35 Protagonists of *The Fire Dwellers* (New York: Knopf, 1969) and *A Jest of God* (New York: Knopf, 1966) respectively.

page proofs from M & S), 'Well, you lived in England – did you make the same kind of pilgrimage to your ancestral home in Scotland,' and I would say 'Yeh, but my people were Lowlanders from Fifeshire, not Highlanders from Sutherland, like Morag's,' which, when I said it, did seem to be a kind of mock-up of a reason, but it wasn't, Marion, it wasn't!

Finally she said (you see, Morag does get divorced in the book, after 12 yrs marriage ... not 22, like me), 'Now, can I ask you about your own marriage and divorce,' and I simply said, 'No. You can't.' Marion dear, it was actually pretty ghastly, and God knows what will come of the article – I anticipate disaster. She tried to get me to define 'the Black Celt,' a state of mind, asking if I, too, ever felt anything like that (well, she knew damn well I'd used the expression of myself, in various printed interviews!), and adding that *her* family was Scots but *she* didn't have any such mental state. Oh hell. I lay awake half the night, firing off furious mental letters, but have decided that it would be the wrong approach. My one consolation is that Peggy's article is so damn perceptive, about everything, including the nature of fiction. Anyway, if Valerie happens to be your bosom friend, I'm sorry – I should have enquired first! I didn't dislike her – I just felt I wasn't getting through to her. She also refused to let me see the article before it goes to press, saying it would be unprofessional. Well, maybe it would, but Peggy didn't think so. Sorry to go on and on about this, but I do feel very vulnerable about this novel. I knew, of course, that some critics are bound to interpret it as straight autobiography, thinly disguised, which it isn't. I guess I had better get used to the fact that some, indeed, will do this. Well, never mind, I can bear anything, as long as Barry Callaghan doesn't give it a good review![36]

36 Barry Callaghan (1937–), Canadian writer and professor at York University since 1966. From 1966 to 1971 he was literary editor of the *Toronto Telegram*. See also note 15, p. 167.

I have a huge 2-bedroom apartment here – quite ridiculous, but rather splendid. My office is attached, which is very convenient. I have my little cat Amber back with me now – she was looked after by the people at the farm near my shack, while I was at Western.

I have discovered a hilarious fact – my Lakefield house used to be a Funeral Home! I went up a week ago, and was driven there by Mrs. Brethauer, whose husband Elwood owns Elwood's Lakefield Taxi. As we drew up to my house, Mrs. Brethauer was heard to remark, 'Oh, I see you've bought the Old Anderson Place.' Not adding what Mr. Anderson's occupation was. Then my young tenants, whilst I was going around with my tape measure (I want to begin looking for furniture, and had to do some measuring) accompanied me and finally said, very tentatively, 'Don't know if we should tell you or not, but we hear that this house used to be a Funeral Home.' I fell about with laughter, and they gave me strange glances. I did not explain that the Funeral Home figures largely in everything I've written about Manawaka, so in some way it seemed a good omen, and I was not at all bothered by the thought of the departed forefathers of the hamlet. Some days later, I went out to talk with a Canlit class of Grade 12 and 13 kids at the Grove School (posh boys' school), and an elderly Maths teacher came up and said 'I live across the street from where you'll be living – I knew within 2 hours of your signing the deal last August that you'd bought the old Anderson Place.' I asked him if it had been a Funeral Home, and he said 'Oh yes. The Andersons kept it real nice. That big upstairs bedroom – they used to use it as a sittingroom when the downstairs was .. er .. um .. busy.'

Must go. God bless, and take care.

Love, Margaret

From Hugh MacLennan
McGill University
Montreal, Quebec

26 January 1974

My Dear Marian:
I was so glad to get your letter, if only to find an address where I could write you. For a long time I've wanted to do that – to congratulate you on how well you have done and to find out how you are. Your letter told me much.

My chief reasons for not joining the union were simple enough – I'm too old for it and I've been through much of it before and some of the literature I received from them did not seem too realistic. A standard contract put forward by the Canadian Authors Association by Gwethalyn Graham and my first wife Dorothy (in the late 1940s)[37] contained pretty well everything that could reasonably be expected, though the present paperback situation may require re-definition. Rod Kennedy[38] and I were responsible for the Income Tax laws which now exist. We went up to Ottawa and got the law passed by Ken Eaton, then Deputy Minister of Finance to Ilsley.[39]

Four years later persistent haggling and heckling by extremely minor and self-important people in the CAA so annoyed the bureaucrats that they refused to honour their previous agreement. In short, they told me I could not spread the income from

37 Gwethalyn Graham (1913–65), Canadian novelist, author of the best-selling *Earth and High Heaven* (1944), a novel about anti-Semitism. MacLennan married Dorothy Duncan in 1936. She died in 1957.
38 Roderick Stuart Kennedy (1889–1953), Canadian writer and editor, past president of the Canadian Authors Association.
39 James Lorimer Ilsley (1894–1967), minister of finance, 1940–6; Albert Kenneth Eaton (1894–1965), assistant deputy minister of finance until 1958.

Each Man's Son (at a time when I was desperate for money and had no other job save writing) over a three year period.[40] This time I went to my lawyer, who got the Deputy Minister on the phone (whom we both knew) and told him if he didn't write the agreement into the jurisprudence, I and every other writer in the country would be after him in the press and the magazines personally. Of course he knew nothing about what had happened below him, but he did write it into the jurisprudence.

The public lending right is a good idea if it can be worked. But what I'd like to see above all is a better distribution of good Canadian paperbacks on the news stands in airports, drug stores etc, across the country.

You probably know that situation; in case you don't, these seem to be the facts. For years the American News Company controlled every paperback rack in the country. It used to do a little better than lately; in short, you could once find quite a number of good books on their racks, though none from Canada. Then it appears it was taken over by the Mafia who has always been interested in pornography. (At the time I appeared as a defence witness for *Lady Chatterley* I had mixed feelings.[41] I really was defending Lawrence. But the blunt truth is that the *Chatterley* decisions in England, Canada and the USA have virtually ruined current fiction by making it possible to swamp it in a sea of pornography.) Just before Christmas, Jack McClelland[42] told me that MacLean-Hunter had taken over the American News Company in Canada, but this, apparently, has made no difference so far. The junk on

40 *Each Man's Son*, MacLennan's fourth novel, published in 1951 (Boston: Little, Brown).
41 The unexpurgated version of D.H. Lawrence's novel *Lady Chatterley's Lover* was banned in the United States until 1959, and in Britain and Canada until 1960. For Canada, see '*Regina versus Penguin Books Ltd*,' *Criminal Law Review* (1961): 176–80; and Charles D.L. Clark, 'Obscenity, the Law and Lady Chatterley,' *Criminal Law Review* (1961), pp. 156–63, 224–34.
42 J.G. (Jack) McClelland (1922–), Canadian publisher and former owner of McClelland and Stewart Publishing.

the racks comes from the same U.S. writing factories and almost never do you see a Canadian novel among them.

Distribution really is the most important thing for the writer, as I'm sure you'd agree. I think you would also agree that there's nothing a writers' union can do about taste, but I also believe that any writer should have some kind of say in jacket design. Generally, I've been very fortunate here. With no say from me at all, my American publishers have always turned out superb jackets, though Heinemann in England put one on *Each Man's Son* which could have been guaranteed to ruin it.[43] The paperback of my *Return of the Sphinx* appeared with a jacket so appalling I wonder a single copy of it was sold.[44] And one of yours had, at least in my opinion, a ruinous cover.

Turning to personal things – I think it wonderful that you have been able to accomplish so much, because bringing up young children is a double career in itself and makes concentration on other things almost impossible. Yet I would think it is amply worth it.

For myself, I've one more year to go before I will have to leave McGill at the age of 67. I'll miss it, because I like this young generation more and more. There were few stimulating students in the Fifties (you were a great exception to the rule). For much of the Sixties they were conned by real pros into all those demonstrations, which were abetted unconsciously by the small-l liberals who ran the administrations. All is quiet now and they're on the whole the most stimulating, intelligent and attractive young or old crowd I've ever met – at least the ones I have.

I took a year off fiction and re-did and enormously enlarged and deepened my old book on Canadian Rivers.[45] It will appear

---

43 *Each Man's Son* (London: Heinemann, 1952).
44 *Return of the Sphinx* first appeared in 1967 (Toronto: Macmillan; New York: Scribner's).
45 Originally published in 1961, the revised *Seven Rivers of Canada* appeared in 1974 (Toronto: Macmillan).

next fall (I'm afraid at a big price) with 112,000 words of my text and about 150 coloured photographs by John de Visser. They've just finished processing them in Verona. It was a fine change to try to think like a river and I covered the country from Cape Breton over Labrador to the Columbia System in B.C., even spending 12 hours in helicopters studying the Hamilton and that amazing wilderness of lakes knitted together by the Churchill Falls people. Now I'm trying once more to see if I can write one more novel at least – difficult in an age where all normal perspectives have disappeared.

I've also developed a cervical disk and am getting my neck stretched daily. It's been nerve-wracking these past six weeks. And the whole thing developed out of a bizarre accident the year before. Down with London flu the Christmas before last at a sister-in-law's in Toronto, I was given muscle-relaxing pills. When I was doped up, a two and a half inch upholsterer's needle from the cushion slid into my neck without my knowing it and I carried it around for three months before an x-ray showed it. This meant surgery, and the whole thing didn't do my neck any good at all.

Bless you,
Hugh

From Mrs F.S. Passmore
Sarnia, Ontario

27 January 1974

My dear Miggs & Howard,
This is your wedding anniversary and is it the 11th or the 10th? Anyway many happy returns for a long and satisfying life! We received your welcome letter, Miggs, and also we have been watch-

ing for your story and on Saturday dad found it in Matthews in the February number of *Chatelaine*.[46] I read it to him and it is so good and we do enjoy your short stories so much. We especially enjoyed the little deaf girl who lip read her grandmother's mumbling and found out all her secrets. You are capitalizing on my bad habits!! Never mind Mr. Boyd confessed that he talks to himself and his secretary never knows if he is alone in his office or if he has a visitor! All good people talk to themselves!

I am also further along in *Monodromos* and enjoying it more but I like to have time to digest it as I go along and do not like to hurry with the descriptions and story.

We have invited [the] Doug Turners and also Elders in to see some films this evening and dad does most of the fixing of the cheese, pickles and cracker plates. I baked a chocolate cake this morning before church (mix) and hope it is good. Those mixes do not keep fresh like the butter cakes do, but are nice if eaten fresh and I put mocha icing on the top, flavoured with almond. Do you remember the Elders? Winnifred is a cousin of the Stevensons we knew at Delta United Church in Hamilton. The girl was about the same age as Elizabeth Preston and she had long very fair hair. Gerald is assistant personnel manager at Imperial. Turners have come back from ten days in Florida and they took his daughter Beverley with them. The two girls seem to get along so well with their stepmother and they have a jolly time of it, I often wonder if the first wife feels jealous of all these trips and also that Doug gets along so well with Sarah. She is tall, large and very good natured in manner and talks with quite a midwest accent of U.S. She was originally from the southern states but worked in the Mayo clinic.

The Crawfs got back without incident last Monday and picked Fred Fitz up in Toronto at 9:30 a.m. so got home in time for Helen and Don to go to work and Robert to attend school, but I

46 'Girl in a Blue Shirtwaist,' *Chatelaine*, February 1974, pp. 34–5, 59–62.

guess they were all very tired by Monday night. I think Helen is dreading moving to a very cold city like Montreal. Don was pre-occupied when here and he was concerned with starting in on a new job and also tying up loose ends of the present one in Kingston. These moves must be such a headache to these men and their families, in spite of the promotions they receive. Tom had TV dinners to cook for himself when his folks were away but the oven would not work so he had to fry eggs and I guess he was glad when his people arrived home.

Edith Tait is in hospital and she has not been well for sometime and took a stroke in hospital last Tuesday during the night. It is St. Joseph's and if you have a minute could you send her a card and Herb could read it to her? It does not need to be anything but a card for she is poorly and lying flat on her back – paralysed on her left side.

Dad and I went out to Woolco to get him a pair of everyday shoes and we had our lunch there – fish and chips. The fish was in a very heavy batter and mostly batter and everything greasy and the cole slaw was very sour. It made both of us really sick afterward and no more fish and chips for me! I had bought steak for Herb and ourselves, but pop and I could not eat ours but I cooked up one for him. I told him 'if he had the nerve to sit and eat steak while we ate baked potatoes, we would be shocked.' He ate every-thing as he always does and enjoyed it after relaxing with us and talking quietly for a couple of hours. He has surely had things very very hard the past few years and so has poor Edith. Dr. Annear wants Edith to go into a nursing home but both Herb and Edith do not want it and I can quite understand for it would be breaking up their home and what enjoyment they do have in this life. His ulcer is some better but he looks pale and wan and is so worried about how things will turn out with his Edith who is all he has!

We had a card from Lola from Mexico and they are having nice weather and good guides as well as interesting scenery. She is worried about being so far away from Jennie, who is getting along well after her operation, she tells us. Lola says she received the thank you letters from the twins.

I believe the Crawfs are going on the school break down to Cozumel for a week. It is off the tip of the Yucatan Peninsula I believe and it must be near where the Falconers have been. There is scuba diving which will interest Thomas.

With love,
Mum & Dad

From Hugh MacLennan
McGill University
Montreal, Quebec

10 February 1974

Dear Marian:
Thank you so much for *Monodromos*; I'm touched that you should have sent me a copy. I've had so much work piled up – mostly students' papers – that I have so far had time only to read half of it. It's very tight, allusive and excellent writing, and I think much the best thing you've done so far. I'll write you later on when I've finished it.

You always were a very determined person, and to have written three novels while raising a family is another proof of it. Your story about 'You're a cook' is lapidary.

What you told me about New Press is shocking, but no surprise. So that's why the Writer's Union is needed. I have a high regard for Jim Bacque,[47] but I've suspected that there was a little holier

47 James Bacque (1929–), Canadian novelist (*The Lonely Ones*, 1969) and historian (*Other Losses*, 1969; *Just Raoul*, 1990).

than thou attitude about some of these new, smaller houses. What you want in a publisher is a combination of a discriminating editor and a first class business organization. You seldom get it. You came close to getting it in Macmillan's (Toronto) while John Gray was in charge.[48] You absolutely get it with Scribner's. But those royalty rates you quoted me from New Press are utterly scandalous.

Don't get me wrong about the CAA.[49] I left it ages ago. I joined it only in a moment when they had a competent man as president. Shortly afterwards it went down the hill again. As for McClelland and Stewart, they at least had a long experience of book selling, mostly as agents for foreign books, before Jack took over and went to town. He was supposed to have been reckless in business, and disorganized, but Pierre Berton is now a member of his firm and whatever else he may be, he's a dynamo of energy and a superb organizer.[50] At present he's virtually his own publisher. How other writers fare with that firm I don't know. I think I was responsible for Jack [McClelland] being called a National Asset, for I used that phrase before the Ontario Royal Commission on publishing about two years ago. His chief contribution has been the New Canadian Library. Without it almost all Canadian novels would have disappeared. Without it there could be no Canadian literature in the schools.

The flu returned about ten days ago and has left me washed out, though finally it's about gone. It was a vile infection.

All the best,
Hugh

---

48 John Morgan Gray (1907–78), president of the Macmillan Company of Canada.
49 Canadian Authors Association.
50 Pierre Berton (1920–), Canadian journalist, historian, and author, whose popular explorations of Canadian history have attracted a wide readership. Berton has received numerous awards for such works as *The Mysterious North* (1956), *Klondike* (1958), and *The Last Spike* (1971), among many others.

P.S. In thinking back over this matter of royalty rates paid by these new and weaker firms, the situation seems to me to be the familiar one that haunts the non-academic book publishing business. The cost of paper, covers and general organization has become astronomic. These firms tend to publish a good many books that may be excellent, but don't get by their very nature a large market. If they are unable to make a profit under current conditions, will they be able to pay more royalties?

Jack McClelland went broke because he issued a large number of titles which didn't sell. He was bailed out by the government and the success of his three top writers, above all Berton. Ever since the soft covers took over, the publishing business has been confused everywhere. E.g. when my *Each Man's Son* appeared in 1951, the enormous review coverage it received in the States (Little, Brown was good then) would have guaranteed a sale of 90,000 copies under conditions prevailing only three years earlier. But the soft cover had just arrived and was taking over and (N.B.) the cost price of the novel in hard back was only $3.00. Also at that time the lending libraries still offered a back log of a certain 2500 copies. Two years previously, Jonathan Cape[51] came over to try to talk sense to the N.Y. publishers. They were in such clover they expected it to go on forever. He warned them about rising paper and production costs but above all about the soft cover competition. Well, *Each Man's Son* sold only 12,000 hard covers in the States and never did go into paper there. And as you know, a normal soft cover now costs as much as a hard cover did 25 to 30 years ago.

The Quebec Government has a scheme of underwriting publishers' losses. It's led to the publication of a relatively enormous number of books, but of very few good books or even popular ones, as I knew anyway and as Roger Lemelin was pointing out

51 (Herbert) Jonathan Cape (1879–1960), head of the English publishing house which bears his name.

only last week.[52] But I repeat: sound professional distribution is the main thing, and these small firms just don't have it. I couldn't get *Monodromos* in Montreal last fall, though it might have been in a few stores. A year or two earlier Ronald Sutherland's excellent *Double Image* (New Press)[53] was unheard of by Classic Book Shops.

H.

To Jack Stoddart[54]
General Publishing Co.
Toronto, Ontario

16 February [1974]

Dear Jack,
Thank you for phoning the other day.

I'm glad you're interested in the rights to *Honeyman Festival* and talked to Mrs. Gibson.[55] It would be nice to come out in a uniform edition. Let my agent know what kind of offer you can make.

Thank you for offering to get me an Arts Council grant. I do not think, however, that it would be ethical for the Chairman of the Writers' Union to accept a grant, in view of the fact that I was

---

52 Roger Lemelin (1919–92), Quebec novelist, journalist, and dramatist, best known for his second novel, *Les Plouffe* (1948), which inspired the 1950s CBC television series and Gilles Carles's 1980 feature film of the same name.

53 MacLennan is referring to Ronald Sutherland's *Second Image: Comparative Studies in Québec/Canadian Literature* (Don Mills, ON: Newpress, 1971).

54 Jack Stoddart, Sr, purchased General Publishing in 1957. His son, Jack Stoddart, Jr, ran the company from the late 1970s until it declared bankruptcy in 2002.

55 Shirley Gibson (1927–97) joined House of Anansi Press in 1969.

one of the agitators who got Ron to double them.[56] I'm full of self-interest but I'd like to stay clear of it for just one year. I will write to Ron and explain my reasons. There are many other subjects I have to discuss with him and I'd like to be free of obligation. And I guess it doesn't really matter where one lives, if one buys a house, etc. We have always been screwed in our housing deals because we're that kind of people. So let us. We can't have everything.

I'll be interested to see the new jacket. Nice to think of good old *No Clouds of Glory* coming out, because I liked that book.

Yours with thanks,
Marian Engel

To Ron Evans
Arts Council of Ontario
Toronto, Ontario

338 Brunswick Ave
Toronto, Ontario

16 February 1974

Dear Ron,
Last week our landlady offered us the chance of buying our house – at an arm and a leg.

I told this to both Shirley Gibson & Jack Stoddart, who publish my books. Both of them offered me not a better deal with them, but money from you.

This is their right but I think that as Chairman of the Writers'

56 Ron Evans – see the letter which follows.

Union I had better not accept. I hope you understand that it's not that I disapprove of POCA (or OAC, I guess, but that still means Guelph to me!)[57] but that I think you and I are probably going to talk about increasing writers' possibilities again before 1974 is out and I don't want anyone to say that I was in it for myself.

So if they write and ask you to allocate grants to me, please take it with a grain of salt. I find integrity very difficult to work up where money is concerned but think it's necessary this year. Besides, if they want me, they should be prepared to fork out.

Hope everything is going very well for you. You are doing some good things. I think in the future I will advise writers to press publishers to match sums your organisation puts forward, or try to. Otherwise you are being used.

Yours with great respect,
Marian Engel

From Lovat Dickson[58]
Toronto, Ontario

20 February 1974

Dear Marian Engel,
Thank you for your letter of February 1st. I am most interested to hear of all you are doing. You have certainly got some good names, and certainly what we want is a standard contract. I recently settled with the CBC for what they called a 'buy-out' of a script I wrote for them, and thought myself quite well-rewarded

57 Ontario Arts Council. 'Guelph' refers to the Ontario Agricultural College, now part of the University of Guelph.
58 See note 13, p. 87. This letter is published by permission of the estate of Lovat Dickson.

when they agreed to pay the same fee again as they had originally paid – only to be told since by an old hand, that they usually pay three times the original fee. We need to be protected from our green-ness.

The great danger is that most writers' quarrels are not with their publishers, but with other writers. I am feeling sore because Berton did a program on Grey Owl, which couldn't have been done without the research, expensive research, which was in my book, and which used at least one photo which is my property (but of course not my copyright) with only the most niggardly acknowledgement, about 14th out of a list of fifteen at the end of the program, and without any mention of my book.[59] The trough isn't big enough in Canada for too many to feed at it. Also I thought Farley Mowat's letter in the *Globe & Mail* this morning would have been better not written.[60] When a writer of his modest achievements dismisses Solzhenitsyn as a mediocre writer, we see that what we have to strive against in Canada is not our enemies but our friends. So it is a good thing that there won't be a social side to the Writers' Union, or there would be blood on the floor. All that you are doing is first-class, particularly with a Lending Right Agreement, and I wish you the greatest possible success. I am going to be in London for three weeks in April. Let me know if I can do anything there for you in this regard. I shall be glad to help, and I look forward very much to meeting you. I don't know whether you live in town or the country. If you are here, let me

59 Dickson's book was *Wilderness Man: The Strange Story of Grey Owl* (Toronto: Macmillan of Canada, 1973). Dickson had long been interested in Grey Owl's life; his first book, *Half-Breed: The Story of Grey Owl*, appeared in 1939 (London: P. Davies).

60 Farley Mowat (1921–), a prolific and widely read Canadian writer, author of the popular *Lost in the Barrens* (1956), which garnered a Governor General's Award, and numerous other narratives set in Canada's North. The letter, headed 'Russian Writers,' gave Mowat's frank opinion of the literary abilities of Aleksandr Solzhenitsyn.

know if you would lunch with me one day before I leave. It would give me great pleasure.

Yours sincerely,
Lovat Dickson

From Margaret Laurence
Trent University
Peterborough, Ontario

27 February 1974

Dearest Marion[61] –
Thanks much for your good letter. Massive relief that you liked *The Diviners!* Hope the *Chatelaine* piece wasn't too difficult to do.[62] I find book reviews hell to do, quite frankly – I sweat blood.

I'm enclosing the letter I received this morning from Fraser Sutherland.[63] I've read it to Peggy over the phone. The bit about Peggy's lawyer demanding recall of all copies of N.J.3 is nonsense – apparently the law requires at least some token attempt to recall copies, altho it is quite obvious that not all copies could be recalled, nor was Peggy's lawyer suggesting that.[64] However, in a

61 Misspelled throughout in the original.
62 Engel's review of Laurence's *The Diviners*, 'Margaret Laurence: Her New Book Divines Women's Truths,' appeared in *Chatelaine*, May 1974, p. 25.
63 Fraser Sutherland (1946–), Canadian writer, and editor of *Northern Journey* and, later, *Books in Canada*.
64 The journal was *Northern Journey*. In issue number 3 (1973), a story called 'Slow Burn,' by Wil Wigle, included a reference to a claim by John Glassco that he had 'a great big erection' at one of Margaret Atwood's poetry readings. In an editorial note in the next issue of the journal (number 4, 1974), the editors refer to an 'attack' on the story by Atwood's lawyer, Rosalie Abella, and the Writers' Union of Canada. The editorial states that Engel, as Chair of the Writers' Union, had recommended a boycott of the magazine in the membership newsletter. The editors refused to withdraw copies of *Northern Journey* or to publish an apology.

more recent letter, which Peggy read me over the phone, her lawyer simply asks for a printed apology in the next issue. If Sutherland is willing to admit he was wrong, and can bring himself to do this printed apology, no more need be said, and the journal need not be ostracized by any of us. But if he will not – well, I personally could not ever have anything printed in it, thereby giving tacit approval to the policy of the journal, and I would guess that most of us would agree. Your letter to Sutherland was very very good.

Re: Andreas – no doubts about his talent as a writer etc etc. I have just obtained *The Late Man* (stories)[65] plus 2 books of poems of his. Have read some of the poems and about half the stories, which to my mind are brilliant, and now realize I read the title story in *Fourteen Stories High*,[66] and just hadn't remembered that it was by him – it's an unforgettable story. My letter got there too late to be used in court, but apparently he had lots of letters. I feel fine now about having said he was a talented young writer – if I'd remembered *The Late Man* was by him, I'd have put it in much stronger terms. Have written to tell him I've got his books, and to communicate just something – well, what can you say except *hang on, kid.* Don't think there is any doubt that he pushed quite a lot of hash. To buy writing time, I think was his belief. Better he should've dug ditches, and I doubt much that he'll do any pushing again. I'm not going into the morality or otherwise – my point of view in matters like this is that if he had pushed heroin, I would think it morally evil and would not lift one finger to help him. With pot and hash, I do not at all have the same certainty, and as a smoker of tobacco and a drinker of alcohol, I do not feel I have the right to make judgements about hash, which I would suspect is probably a lot less lethal than scotch. However, my view also is

65 Andreas Schroeder, *The Late Man* (Port Clements, BC: Sono Nis Press, 1972 [c. 1971]).
66 David Helwig and Tom Marshall, eds, *Fourteen Stories High* (Ottawa: Oberon Press, 1971).

that if it is at present illegal, you are pretty damn dumb to be caught in a public place with the stuff on you and even dumber to push it. There are other ways of earning a living, as those of us who have sweated blood over book reviews, publishers' reading, articles, readings and other things, know. (I always say to young writers who ask me how they can get a grant immediately from the Can Council, 'Al Purdy worked 7 years in a mattress factory.')[67] (I think it was more like 4 years, actually, and I don't recommend work in a mattress factory, but he did it, damn it, and wrote all the while.) (One could, of course, also say – Marion Engel and M. Laurence have scrubbed many a floor and washed many a diaper and made many a meal, whilst also doing book-reviewing, articles, etc. etc., and have gone on writing.)

The Trent U's Writers Weekend looms, with readings and seminar sessions with me, Al Purdy, Alice Munro, W.O. Mitchell, Tom Marshall, A.J.M. Smith, John Newlove, Robert Finch, Graeme Gibson, Richard Wright, Rob Davies, George Johnson. Oh heavens I feel we will all be exhausted, but at least I have managed to keep Sunday free, so writers can gather here, unmolested, in my apartment, and exchange news. Let us hope it all goes okay. Will report (unofficially) when it's all over. I dread the reading I have to do – I wish I could get through that sort of thing without being so damn nervous. But can't.

My REAL concerns of the moment are all connected with the Lakefield house, so I feel a bit of a traitor here – I'm spending a lot of time lining up paperhangers and painters and carpenters, and buying old furniture. A hell of a lot of fun! I really love putting a home together – it's one of my 2 talents! I now have some really lovely pieces of old furniture, and am organizing the

---

67 Al (Alfred Wellington) Purdy (1918–2000), Canadian poet and Governor General's Award winner who mapped 'the country north of Belleville' (Ontario) in his work. His correspondence with Margaret Laurence was edited by John Lennox: *Margaret Laurence – Al Purdy, a Friendship in Letters: Selected Correspondence* (Toronto: McClelland and Stewart, 1993).

whole thing like A CAMPAIGN. I get possession of the house on March 17th. On March 18th, the paperhanger/painter, the carpenter, Bell Tel,[68] the carpet co., and so on, move in, IN FORCE. At least, that is how it is lined up now. It will work out. I have luck in two areas, my house and my work.

Re: 'Witchers' ... yes, this is an alternate way of describing the person who divines the well. It might have been more accurate, idiomatically, but I couldn't use it, because of the verbal connotations. 'Witcher' to me has good connotations, but 'witch' to some has the (for my purposes) wrong connotations. 'Diviner' has the right connotations, and is also the word that came to my mind when I thought of it. Well, it's Royland's word and Morag's,[69] and let us hope it is acceptable. But no, Marion, you aren't right in your affectionate and much-appreciated reassurance – Royland doesn't recover his powers; the whole point is that they are at some point withdrawn, to be given to other and younger diviners, and *that* is the wisdom or answer or whatever that Morag has sought from him for years. So far from being pessimistic, that concept to me is enormously hopeful and connects the generations.

God bless and love,
Margaret

---

68 Bell Telephone Company.
69 Characters in Laurence's novel *The Diviners.*

To Robert Weaver
[CBC,
Toronto, Ontario]

338 Brunswick
Toronto, Ontario

8 March [1974]

Dear Bob,

I'm sorry I missed your lunch this morning but I was politicking with a librarian about PLR. Such is life these days.

I don't know whether I'm frittering a book away with Ruth stories, but I've been writing a lot of them and this is a Ruth & Ziggy story.[70] Ziggy will make a book one day. I thought of another one in the bathtub a couple of nights ago but it's almost left me; Ziggy and naked ladies at the YMHA.[71] Trite?

The librarian at the Soo has been sending me fascinating material about Rains.[72] There were *23* children. I wrote to the Soo Star and they published my letter. A woman wrote and said she had Rains books! Howie points out that if we can get on the Tobermory ferry the Sault isn't far from Holstein so I hope we can go up this summer. What I think I'll do is re-write the play, trying to do the dialogue really, really well, and simplifying the line. *Then* go and see if there's enough material for a book in it. The U of Soo Mich

---

70 Ruth and Ziggy stories figure prominently in Engel's short story collection *Inside the Easter Egg* (Anansi, 1975): 'Amaryllis' (42–50), 'Home Thoughts from Abroad' (63–74), 'Sublet' (75–83), 'What Do Lovers Do?' (84–90), 'Break No Hearts This Christmas' (91–8), 'Nationalism' (99–104), and 'Marshallene on Rape' (105–10).

71 Young Men's Hebrew Association.

72 Sault Ste Marie, Ontario, close to Saint Joseph Island, where Major William Rains settled and established a sawmill. Engel's research on Rains was later woven into her novel *Bear.*

has his papers, apparently, or at least his granddaughter's.[73] It's gorgeous fun. I used to love doing *Letters and Journals* for you.

I regret staff hassles lately. The talent obviously wasn't turned in the right direction. Still, it's a good mind lost to the department. Trouble is what one needed was a good body to lug a tape recorder. I think academics are awfully spoiled. They don't. Enough said. Friend, I guess, lost. Can't remember liking someone's company that much for years.[74]

Must go up and be militant with the children. They were just settling as two streakers streaked down the street yelling TODAY BRUNSWICK TOMORROW THE WORLD!

The Union stuff has convinced me there isn't a goddam reason in the world why anyone should write books anymore. Publishers expect you to do everything but turn the crank on the press, readers expect masterpieces, and NOTHING will ever get you out of scrubbing the pots and pans. So I shall go on writing but with the worst kind of cranky, selfish stubbornness because if you can't have money you should have your own way. Findley has done a beautiful presentation to CBC about a book TV programme, though. Life & hope etc.

Cheers,
Marian

---

73 We have been unable to trace this reference; there are no Rains papers at the University of Michigan or at Lake Superior State University.
74 We have been unable to identify this reference.

From Hugh MacLennan
McGill University
Montreal, Quebec

9 May 1974

My Dear Marian:

Thank you for sending me your newsletter from the Writers' Union. It's well done, interesting and to the point. In fact, it decided me to apply for membership in the Union if you'll take me and I enclose a cheque for the admission fee. My memory may be faulty, and if this is more or less than the regular fee, do return the cheque and I'll send you another in the right amount. Frankly, I was put off in the beginning by a somewhat frenetic tone in the handouts from the union promoters. It probably needed two women like you and Margaret to make some sense in it. I've been through most of the turnstiles before, almost always alone, with no support anywhere, and was fed up.

Good luck with *Joanne,* and may it have better direction than did the original CBC dramas.[75] Like all bureaucracies, the CBC is inefficient, full of in-fighters and it was Pierre Berton's sheer size, I'd guess, that was able to push through *The National Dream.* But I fear the old legacy of the NFB documentary still hangs heavy in Canada. With works of the imagination they are still very backward.

Another McGill season, my next to last, ends this week. I've never seen students so uniformly excellent as this year, and I said the same after last year.

All the best,
affectionately,
Hugh

75 *Joanne: The Last Days of a Modern Marriage* (Don Mills, ON: General Publishing, 1975), first commissioned for CBC radio.

To Hon. Pauline McGibbon
Lieutenant Governor of Ontario
Queen's Park, Toronto

338 Brunswick Ave
Toronto

5 June 1974

Dear Pauline,
I am enclosing the *Chatelaine* piece.[76] Doris Anderson would have a fit if she knew,[77] but since I have put words into your mouth it is only proper to let you know what I have made you say. As I was not using a tape recorder I may well have forgotten some details.

What I'd like to have them use for an illustration is a collage – your official photo but also perhaps the wedding picture, the bas-relief, your mother etc. That will depend on them and on you. Might take too much time to dig things out.

I've really enjoyed doing this. It's a challenge to write down an old friend in a way that communicates. It's also important to let people know that women are formed as well as men – have histories, families. I find *Chatelaine* a superb channel for this kind of information.

I wonder if I told you the Union is setting up a Foundation. I've been rooting around in my mind for the names of people who would make directors. It occurs to me that you might have more information about this than I do! Pierre Berton wants somewhere to leave his money; Harry Boyle wants a kind of McDowell Colony

76 The article, entitled 'Pauline McGibbon,' appeared in the October 1974 issue of *Chatelaine*, pp. 46–7, 88–91.
77 Doris H. Anderson (1925–), Canadian journalist, women's rights activist, and editor of *Chatelaine* magazine, 1957–77.

place for writers to go;[78] the Union would like the interest from some kind of fund as its income. These interests might be combined by a skillful person.[79] The Canada Council is splendid but of course it can't do all that needs to be done to keep writers going. Perhaps some day when you are freer we might chat about this. If it's done just right it can be a tremendous force for good. The buying public is never, after all, going to be able to support all the good writers we are throwing up now.

Pauline, I have the very highest admiration for you and thank you for a good afternoon.

Yours sincerely,
Marian

To 'Mr Beatty'[80]
[U.S.A.]

25 June 1974

Dear Mr Beatty,
Thank you for your letter of June 10th.

I find your faith in Canada touching, but I think I ought to tell you that the writing situation here is not prosperous. Those few magazines we have seem to be lowering their rates and though Canadians seem to read a lot, they have a nefarious habit of getting their books from public libraries. Our nationally owned

78 In 1896, Edward MacDowell and his wife, Marian, established a colony for American artists in Peterborough, New Hampshire.
79 Pierre Berton donated funds for the purchase of his boyhood home in Dawson City, Yukon, to the Yukon Arts Council in 1989. The Berton Home hosts Canadian authors for residencies of up to three months per year.
80 The correspondent is not further identified.

publishers are few and trembling before the paper shortage; branch houses of U.S. and British publishers publish a few original titles every year. These are the books that get into the stores.

So the situation here isn't marvellous for Canadians. It might be better for immigrant Americans. In fact, several have produced books here but only time will tell whether they are literary stayers.

One simply can't foretell the future. Books are selling better than ever before – where they are available – but mostly as paperbacks and remainders. Canadian authors are reaching their own peoples to a degree and for the first time. Critics still proclaim loudly that they are provincial. Some even go so far as to envy the U.S. its seething condition. Even decay gives off energy. A peculiar quiet that is not to everyone's taste reigns here. We love it, some do not.

Pessimists have been crying for years that Canada is turning to another U.S. Probably that is true but I personally cling to the fact that it isn't yet, and may never be. I mean, who'd want us, with our enormous problems? Would the U.S. have time?

Your own writing is yours; wherever you do it [it] will continue to be yours. I know of no markets for the kind of writing you suggest except little magazines which pay abominably. Come up if you wish, but do not expect to make a million a year from writing. Lots of us have trouble making a thousand. What we like about it is that it's our own place and we therefore have a say in its organization, a stake in our own fate. You would lose that if you came here, and perhaps part of your audience. Hope I don't sound pessimistic because I liked your letter, and thanks for writing.

Yours sincerely,
Marian Engel, Chairman

To Jean Wright
Managing Editor
Chatelaine magazine
Toronto, Ontario

338 Brunswick Ave
Toronto, Ontario

26 June 1974

Dear Jean,

I am returning your cheque and stub for the McGibbon article, which I enjoyed doing immensely, because 'first world serial rights French and English' is really too much!

I realise that these words reflect a general change in MacLean-Hunter policy. It is not, to my mind, a healthy one. It is pleasant that your rates are going up (to a thousand, I heard the other day – people are beginning to tell and it's healthy) while *Maclean's* are going down. I know you want French rights because of French *Chatelaine,* but to have the world bit slipped in on the cheque stub is too much to stomach.

You force me back on a funny proud position. I don't make enough money writing not to care if I lose some; still, I won't work on terms I consider unfair. After all, I could be making dresses or a garden or being a good mum instead of a tired one. The most galling thing of all is to make a sale to a good outfit like yours and find it to be on twisted terms.

I don't of course consider you and Doris [Anderson] and the girls responsible in all this. It's clearly company policy. Would you let the Company know how I stand? *Nobody*, not even housewives, should sell world rights. And if you want French rights you should negotiate them with authors.

Yours very sincerely – and it was good to see you Monday night!
Marian Engel

cc Alma Lee, Writers' Union
T. Seldes, New York

To Robert Weaver
[CBC
Toronto, Ontario]

338 Brunswick Ave
Toronto, Ontario

15 July 1974

Dear Bob,
Ouch.

Your letter followed one from my agent who said books of short stories (The Ziggies) were just slightly easier to sell than long narrative poems!

Anyway: I reserve the right to reserve you the right to buy what you want. If you don't like 'em, don't buy. Who else in this country has both money & integrity? However, I like 'Marshallene on Rape' better than anything I've done lately and may press it on you if I have nothing else.[81]

Right now I'm rewriting the famous radio serial *Joanne* for PaperJacks under Colleen Dimson who is a treat to work for,[82]

---

81 The story was eventually included in *Inside the Easter Egg*, 105–10.
82 Colleen Dimson, Canadian editor and later faculty member in the publishing program of Centennial College. PaperJacks was a mass market imprint founded by Jack Stoddart, Sr.

and also getting things together to go up to the Rains country in August to interview hordes of surviving Rainses. Howard will be working closely with me on this as he discovered the fellow and has friends who own Rains Lake. I won't be able to finish the Bush & Salon thing until after that piece of work is done. Or should I bother finishing it now the series is canned? I went over the script and found it very bad.

I appreciate the commission. I really want to do a good serious story for you. Remember, Gandy Dancers was a commission and came out a meaty one?[83] However, my thinking time has got absorbed by Public Life and my rhetoric is used up mostly writing long letters to people like the Bureau of Intellectual Property, so it will be some time before I get down to serious work again. It's enough to drive a person back to church to sing hymns of Courage, Conflict and Victory.

Meanwhile the U of Ottawa press is starting a series of short-story books and wants one from me and I think I'll give them to them if they use our Standard Contract. Leo and John Nause trumped this [on] us. Their design is awful, circulation small, etc but it doesn't hurt to have more books out and they're mostly Anthology stories.

Gosh, though, I wish I could get down to writing-as-writing. Oddly enough there's even less time with 9 year olds around than there was with smaller ones as they didn't stay up so late then. Or is that just boon-doggle excuse-making from a head that's gone soft?

And at my back I hear, I hear/ Time's winged chariot etc.[84]

I'd love to see you in the fall. Coffee time or any other. I think I used to see you more often before. I miss your gossip! My political

---

83 'Tents for the Gandy Dancers' also appeared in *Inside the Easter Egg*, 146–66.
84 The reference is to English metaphysical poet Andrew Marvell's (1620–78) poem 'To His Coy Mistress.' The poem reads: 'But at my back I always hear / Time's winged chariot drawing near.'

career will be over late in October.[85] Won't be able to persecute magazines little or big any more. But it's more important to write before one's era is inevitably over. I'm doing one last Ziggy to have enough for a set called Ziggy & Co. and then the sky's the limit.

Must stop boring you. I've needed to write to you for a while. Cheers,

Marian

From Margaret Laurence
Lakefield, Ontario

6 September 1974

Dearest Marion[86] –
This is almost an apologetic letter, for not having said before what should have been said about *Monodromos*. I read it last winter, when my mind was not free. I have recently re-read it, when my mind was really quite free, at the shack, with the river and the trees around, in an atmosphere which strikes me so deeply and so incredibly – i.e. home.

Because I re-read it now, when I am home, I saw things in it I didn't see before. Like your amazing sense of Exile. I guess I felt rather strongly about that, because for many years I lived in Africa, and I loved it, I really *did*. But I was in exile, all the same. All the terrific things about another culture – and you, in that novel, get across so many of them – and yet the sense one is left with, I think, is that one has to come home again. The cooking

---

85 Engel's term as Chair of the Writers' Union was drawing to an end.
86 Misspelled throughout in the original.

may be great in distant parts; the sex may be something, but never really acceptable somehow, because altho we hate our puritanism, it is part of us, ho ho, so what we *really* want (as women) is a relationship which is committed and which knows where we come from. One gets tired of telling lies, as Laddie constantly tells lies and as Audrey can't and won't, and yet, in the long run, it seems to me that the false relationship which they have, brother & sister, is really what they *are.* They *are* brother & sister, aren't they? The thing, to me, in all this seems to be that out of the same background, a man and a woman can be brother & sister, but not man and wife. I find that sad. I also find it true.

The sense of place is something else, Marion. With Cyprus now doing what it is doing, I read your book last week and thought – oh hell, it is all there, all the predictions. You knew. You also had a sense of what I think I had in my time in Somaliland, with *The Prophet's Camel Bell*[87] – the knowledge of being an outsider, describing a land and a people with help from the guidebooks, accurately, with a real sense of the details, the smells and touch and sights, but always from the stance of Another. The chapter about taking the cat to the vet, with the old/not-old crazy was superb – I doubt if anyone here will see it; maybe one has to have been in another land at some point to know what that means. I know. I played nurse to some really sick men in our camp in Somaliland, and finally came to see how idiotic this was. Also, I played nurse to some women who asked me, and I was speaking very haltingly their language, how they could get relief from their menstrual pains and how they could cope with clitoridectomy ... they had their clitoris cut off at puberty; it was done, there. Yeh, it breaks your heart, but the thing is really, I guess, to come home. I felt so sad about Laddie, who could not realize that his home was where his heart was, even though he'd been played up by it. But

---

87 Margaret Laurence, *The Prophet's Camel Bell* (Toronto: McClelland and Stewart, 1963).

Audrey, I felt, would come through. She hasn't yet, not in the end of the book, but she – or some other protagonist – will, I think. She's strong – and that is okay. I sense in the novel a beginning of another novel. I hope I'm right – it's a novel we need.

Much love,
Margaret

ps. what really makes me incredibly angry is that the book was reviewed with so little understanding. I would like to write an article on it for *Canadian Literature*[88] and maybe if I get strong enough I will.

To Ron Evans
Arts Council of Ontario
Toronto, Ontario

338 Brunswick Ave
Toronto

9 September 1974

Dear Ron,
Some time ago you offered me a grant; I didn't want to take it while I was chairman of the Writers' Union and I also thought I'd do better negotiating with publishers if I refused.

My negotiating is done, I'll be out of the Union job at the end of October and I've a feeling I'll be skint. Could I therefore ask for a grant after that time? Stoddart said he'd allocate the money.

Of course, if it isn't available, I'll also understand.

---

88 *Canadian Literature / Littérature canadienne: A Quarterly of Criticism and Review* (University of British Columbia, Vancouver), established in 1959.

I shouldn't change my mind this way but you know how it goes – one wants to be proud and independent but there's also the landlady always threatening to sell us the house if we don't pay the repairs and the novel not written etc.

Let me know if this seems craven, will you?

Marian Engel

To Margaret Laurence
[Lakefield, Ontario]

338 Brunswick Ave
Toronto

7 November 1974

Dear, dear Margaret,
Actually the kids conned me into taking them to the movie of *The Bears and I* and it was awful. We stood an hour and a half in a cold wind to be insulted by Chief Dan George doing phoney incantations over a sick bear.[89]

The book is quite wonderful and just right for my story, of which I am tempted to send you a carbon – though I'll resist for the moment. It does seem that a bear is the only animal with whom these semi-human relationships are possible, although my new black puppy seems anxious to have a relationship of a very friendly sort! Not, I think, legendary, more puppyish, however.

Anyway, I've just read it and been moved. Thank you VERY much because, put off by Disney's maladroit treatment, I wouldn't have bought it.

---

89 This 1974 film is based on Robert Franklin Leslie's book *The Bears and I: Raising Three Cubs in the North Woods* (New York: Dutton, 1968).

Things here are up and down. By day, I often have a bad conscience. But on a quiet evening like this I feel very good. Howard and I are beginning to be friends in the right way but I can't persuade him that he can't have me the way he wants to because he doesn't really want a wife and family the way he thinks he does. I have given up confiding marriage-tales however: they all sound too sordid.

It would be so nice to get together again, rework things, make our lives more practical, but it strikes me that the real problem would still be there.

And what is that? Interesting session with John Rich[90] about it this week – strong feeling the lid of Pandora's Box (what an unfortunate expression!) is about to be opened, strong happy feeling. Rapunzel let out of her tower into the world, the Lady of Shalott (did you grow up on the long fields of barley and of rye too?) sprung through her mirror miraculously unwounded.[91] Perhaps it won't happen any more than the bear novel will happen but the mere prospect makes me happy.

Word from Cyprus that virgins are being exported, children sent to English boarding schools – children of people who hated England. My particular friends lodged themselves in their boat which they had had to anchor on the south coast during a storm and never got around to picking up. Now my Stavro has gone to the Persian Gulf to work on British Army electrical contracts – to pay the boarding school bills.[92] His family have fled the Turks so many times. The last time I saw him I noticed his neck was getting old. With all this, his beard will be white. He will stay in Cyprus whatever his wife and children do. There are his mother and brother and Ahhhnty Nina to look after. It seems romantic and sordid and far away.

It is good to be able to think of private things again. I am going

90 Engel's psychotherapist during the 1970s.
91 The reference is to Alfred Lord Tennyson's poem *The Lady of Shalott*.
92 Stavro, possibly Steve Caramondanis.

to be self-indulgent this winter. It's the only way I can get the work going well again.

I don't know what you're doing. Enjoying your good press and getting your strength back, I hope. You must be wiped out by that big novel. Hope you've seen the good *Ms.* review.[93]

Thank you for comforting Howard. I don't know what to do with him at the moment except not live with him, but he is learning a fair amount about himself and is capable of gratitude, now declares, however painful, the break was a good thing: wants back on different terms. I waver.

Won't tell you any more about all this until it's over or started again, resolved, smashed, frapped or something. Just want to say I am grateful to you.

love,
Marian

Had a good meeting with ACTRA.
Harold [Horwood]made them realize we are not amateurs.

To Brigid Brophy[94]
[England]

10 February 1975

Dear Brigid Brophy,
First, thanks for the personal letter. It was astonishing to get good reviews in England, but very pleasant. I expected most of them to

93 Joan Larkin, 'Laurence of Canada,' *Ms.*, November 1974, pp. 96, 100.
94 See note 5, p. 86. Brophy's *Guide to Public Lending Right* was published in 1983 (Aldershot, Hampshire: Gower).

be along the lines of the *TLS*.[95] But the Ronald Blythe one was a knockout.[96] Usually the English HATE books by Canadians.

I am enclosing a document I obtained from the Copyright Institute which deals with your case. It has apparently gone no further. It sounds like another loathsome American Imperialist deal. We are quite used to them: they must be fought tooth and claw.

Here, the Secretary of State is thinking of leaving PLR out of the Copyright Act but declaring it a provincial matter (i.e. hopeless) and we will have to fight that; the Union devilled away on the remaindering business (over-printings of our U.S. editions are brought in and sold in competition of Canadian editions at no revenue to us) and got nowhere; the courts decided remaindering of foreign editions of our books was legal because the Copyright Act is so vague and Schedule C of the customs act isn't very satisfactory either – so now we're reduced to demos and huge ads in newspapers. Of course the public thinks us rich authors are trying to keep them from getting cheap books, so it's all complicated.

Meanwhile, two of us (Jas Lorimer[97] and me) are on the Toronto Library Board trying to get librarians to Buy Canadian and save the book business. There's a huge wrangle between the old-style, largely U.S.-dominated publishers and the new young men who in spite of subsidies haven't been able to break into any distribution network. Merrily, merrily, and, it turns out, very expensively, we roll along.

95 The unfavourable review of *One Way Street* (*Monodromos* was reissued under a new title by PaperJacks in 1974) by Sylvia Miller appeared in the *Times Literary Supplement*, 24 January 1975, p. 73.

96 Ronald Blythe, 'A Novel Not to Be Missed,' *Sunday Times* [London], 5 January 1975, p. 31.

97 James Lorimer (1942–), Canadian writer and founder of the publishing house which bears his name.

Hope this is some use to you, and good luck. Friday we start negotiating with publishers.

Cheers,
Marian Engel

From Hugh MacLennan
Montreal, Quebec

1 May 1975

My Dear Marian,
A few days ago, by some weird accident, your letter of April 23 leaked through the postal strikes and arrived. Today we are threatened here with another police strike. Yesterday, income tax day, parliament voted itself a better than 33% raise. Men tend always to satisfy their needs and desires with the least possible exertion and on the inexorable workings of this law, our thirty year matrist social-democratic ramp is foundering. How appallingly apt that the day before May Day, Saigon should have been renamed Ho Chi Minh City! And why does the government do nothing to stop the strikes? Because in this climate of opinion nobody will consent to be governed and also, as a spendthrift government's fundamental need is to have more money to spend, why should it stop strikes? Every strike results in a huge pay hike and that means more money for the government, which has no money of its own. If the postal workers win their raise, that will mean an extra tax bonus to the government to the amount, roughly, of $600,000,000.

Hélas, dear Marian, what a letter of yours! You've always been ferociously honest and extremely determined and fundamentally you're a woman of action, and action is clearly claiming you. I'm sorry about the marriage. It's never been an easy institution, but in a time like the present it is worse than ever, for the simple reason that its basis is a shared territory, together with the hope of improving it, retaining it and being secure in it. In this present public marriage of multi-national capitalism and national socialisms, the individual is the inevitable victim. His house can be expropriated for a high rise. The services he strips his savings for are diminishing increasingly and he sees a general wipe-out of his life's work as certain. How, then, can his territory hold him, and how can it sustain a marriage? Your children may not do too badly after all. At least they may have a chance to see the rebirth of a culture which now is dying, which indeed is committing suicide. To have lived through the past fifteen years in Montreal was to live through an entire cycle of history. In 1960 the Church still ruled here. The word 'divorce' was censored out of the movie screens. The birth-rate was what it was. By 1967 there were 22 skin flicks in Montreal, more than half of them made in Quebec. The birth rate had sunk to the lowest in Canada and there was a riot a week. So the people turned like sheep to the new religion of Quebec nationalism, which opened the door to a horde of office-seekers and job holders of every kind, and to bullying union leaders who claimed (and it was granted) that an audit of union books was undemocratic.

However, out of this has emerged the best good students I ever knew, though what will become of them God only knows. But for the present, Yeats said it all in *The Second Coming*.[98] My poetry reading was always sporadic, and I never discovered that poem until two years after I wrote *Return of the Sphinx*. For some years I've been working on another novel – I put it aside for a year and a half for *Rivers of Canada* – and possibly I'll be able to finish it. Whether it's worth doing I don't know. Non-fiction is by far the strongest prose medium today, because for fiction to be success-ful, there must be a solid perspective in time or at least an ideol-

98 W.B. Yeats (1865–1939), Irish poet and playwright.

ogy in which one can believe. The only way I can write a novel of the present, or of the recent past, is by beginning it about fifty years ahead and flashing back.

Memoirs? Maybe. But the title I'd like for them is pre-empted by a book I have been re-reading every second year since its appearance in 1943 – Albert J. Nock's *Memoirs of a Superfluous Man*.[99]

But how can you handle a novel about a woman and a bear? It could be the success of a decade, for oddly enough, the time being what it is, it doesn't strike me as in the least bizarre. But good luck to you and God bless you. Quite possibly, He might.

Affectionately,
Hugh

P.S. The woman you met in Kamloops (originally from North Hatley) was christened Anne. When she was fifteen she told me she intended to get married when she was 19 and have four children in five years. She was a hard-working and good student, though with no sense of humour, and got into my old prose course and took a first-class. She graduated the year Dorothy died and immediately married a young Jugoslav emigré. They had two children, he took to drink and they were divorced. Her mother told me she got married again last summer to one of the professors at Kamloops. She sent me the script of a novel which had a good deal of promise but did not find a publisher. It was a mixture of her own personal life together with a certain amount of fantasy. Possibly she can come through as a novelist. Certainly women have been more successful in that medium lately than the men, for women seem able to concentrate on the details of actual life and disregard the larger canvas that men are lost without. No

99 Albert Jay Nock, *Memoirs of a Superfluous Man* (New York: Harper & Brothers, 1943).

man who ever lived could write the stuff Alice Munro is turning out.[100] Maybe the male of the species has been abolished by evolution?

H.

To Anna Porter
[McClelland and Stewart]
Toronto, Ontario

338 Brunswick Ave
Toronto

14 September 1975

Dear Ms Porter,
I'm sorry to be so long answering your kind letter of July 24 but I didn't receive it till I came back to Toronto early in September and since then I've been juggling my calendar.[101]

It sounds like a lovely thing to do but I don't think I can. I have 2 kids just too young to leave alone if I go away and all the leave-of-absence I can afford is booked for the Writers' Union conference in October. My husband is very good at helping out, but he's with CBC and doesn't get home early enough at night

---

100 Alice Munro (1931–), celebrated Canadian short story writer whose work has appeared regularly in the *New Yorker*. Author of *Lives of Girls and Women* (1971), she has won several awards for her work, including the Giller Prize for *The Love of a Good Woman* in 1997.

101 The letter is not included in the Marian Engel Archive, nor have we been able to locate a copy in the McClelland and Stewart Archive at McMaster University.

to take care of the children. So I'm afraid it's all impossible in December.

I therefore enclose a list of Writers' Union writers for you to peruse.

I'm really sorry. I thought I might be able to manage it, but it just doesn't seem possible. I hope you can find someone else. Harold Horwood or Cassie Brown, maybe?[102] Or do you want an outsider? Sylvia Fraser might be free, as she's got no dependents.[103] I don't know if Margaret Laurence likes doing these things. I think Margaret Atwood's probably tied up. Leo Simpson might be free – he's a good critic.[104] Let me know if I can help you in any other way.

Yours sincerely,
Marian Engel

---

102 Harold Horwood (1923–), Canadian writer, editor, and politician, author of *Joey* (1989), a commemoration of Newfoundland premier Joey Smallwood, with whom Horwood worked; Cassie Brown (1923–), Canadian author and playwright whose works focus on stories from her Newfoundland home.

103 Sylvia Fraser (1935–), Canadian novelist and journalist, author of *Pandora* (1972), *The Candy Factory* (1975), *A Casual Affair* (1978), *Berlin Solstice* (1984), and *My Father's House* (1987), a memoir of an abused childhood.

104 Leo Simpson (1934–), Canadian novelist and short story writer, noted for his comedic depictions of contemporary urban dilemmas.

From Dan Wickenden[105] via Timothy Seldes[106]

10 November 1975

Dear Marion:[107]
I thought you would like to see this letter, Cordially, T

Harcourt Brace Jovanovich, Inc.
New York

Mr. Timothy Seldes
Russell & Volkening
551 Fifth Avenue
New York, N.Y. 10017

7 November 1975

Dear Tim,
You call Marian Engel's *The Bear of Pennarth* unusual.[108] I call it extraordinary. Ever since we published *No Clouds of Glory*, which we should have published under its author's own title *Sarah Bastard's Notebook*, I've been convinced she's one of the most talented of the younger Canadian novelists, though the two novels that followed the first (I think there were two that came to

---

105 See note 9, p. 55.
106 Timothy Seldes (1926–) has spent most of his professional life in book publishing. He began his career with Doubleday and subsequently worked at Harcourt Brace and Macmillan. He has been the president of the New York literary agency Russell and Volkening since 1972.
107 Misspelled in the original.
108 'The Bear of Pennarth' and 'The Dog of God' both appear as titles on the final draft of Engel's manuscript of the book which was to become *Bear* (Marian Engel Archive, McMaster University, box 14, file 11).

H.B.J.) seemed to me not to come off altogether, and to be hopeless for the U.S.A. But I'm glad they both got published in Canada.

I wish I could see some hope for *The Bear of Pennarth* at H.B.J., but I can't. Its relative brevity coupled with its extreme strangeness presents, I'm afraid, an insuperable obstacle in present circumstances. I wonder how Marian herself would describe it. For the sake of ease and convenience, I call it a tale of sexual obsessions and for me it works almost totally. One is made to believe in Lou's obsession, understand it; accept it; to take it seriously, in short. A story that could have seemed incredible, or unintentionally comic, or merely grotesque, or of sheerly prurient interest, or wholly disgusting, or a combination of all of these things miraculously is not. (Oh, I admit to a few fleeting qualms.) For me it comes off. I respect and admire it and believe it ought to be published in the U.S.A., and hope it will be.

If we were going to publish it, I'd have a few small suggestions. The manuscript isn't at hand because I took it to the office yesterday, expecting to find time to write this letter there so I can't refer back to it. But, for instance, I was never clear how the chain was attached to the bear (to a collar? an ankle iron? what?), or about the points at which Lou kept the chain on or let the bear go free. I think maybe the author needs to be more specific about this. How, for instance, did it come to be roaming at large the first time it startled Lou by entering the house and climbing the stairs?... It's probably deliberate on the author's part to make Lou think of the bear as both 'it' and 'he' – as I recall, sometimes in the same sentence – but I suggest that he should become consistently 'he' fairly early in the proceedings ... To resort in novels to the device of dreams generally seems to me a mistake, and the dream or reverie around page 40 is an instance, I think, although I can see that the story needs to say, at that point, what it says by the dream device. Perhaps this could be handled somewhat differently ... I wonder if the reader should not learn at least a little more about Lou than the author now reveals – about her background, I mean. The startling effect of the first offhand reference to her sexual arrangement with the Director of the Institute is fine; but as the story progresses thereafter, maybe a few other details should be woven in, about other aspects of Lou's past ... For a U.S. reader, the geography is vague and rather confusing: I'd like more specifics here, too.

A gastronomic quibble: on page 97 there's what I consider a libel on *quenelles de brochet*, which on the basis of those I've had at five different Manhattan restaurants, I'd describe in quite other terms myself.

A usage quibble: in Canada too, it seems, hapless schoolchildren have had it pounded into their heads by schoolmarms who have never read Fowler that every 'if' or 'whether' or 'unless' must be followed by the subjunctive 'were.' '... they diffuse,' says Fowler of these subjunctives, 'an atmosphere of dullness and formalism over the writing in which they occur; the motive underlying them, & the effect they produce, are the same that attend the choosing of FORMAL WORDS, a reference to which article may save some repetition.' One of the great virtues of *The Bear of Pennarth* is its style, which in its unobtrusive transparent way is first rate, I think. What I call the False Subjunctive has no place in such a style, and I have made light annotations in the margin, *passim*, hoping to persuade Marian to avoid it henceforth.

No more. If I had a generous endowment and my own press, I'm pretty sure I'd publish *The Bear of Pennarth*. I hope some leading U.S. publisher will decide to do so ... The manuscript will go back to you separately, from the office, by messenger, probably on Monday.

Best wishes to you, and do pass along to Marian Engel my congratulations and my regrets.

Yours,
Dan Wickenden

4

Changing the Landscape, 1976–1980

Marian Engel shared two major items of news with her friend Pauline McGibbon in a New Year's letter of 10 January 1976. First, she had moved with the children into a house of her own on Marchmount Road in Toronto. The Engels had separated and would later divorce. Second, Engel had completed a 'very strange and rather obscene book' – the future Governor General's Award–winning *Bear*. This novel about a bookish woman who has a love affair with a bear marked a turning point in Engel's literary career. She had also moved in a professional sense, from a small press, Anansi, to the larger, more prestigious McClelland and Stewart. 'I've broken away from the one-horse, however lovely, publishers,' she told McGibbon. The move was a significant one for Engel and emblematic of the broader literary scene. As Douglas Fetherling saw it, 'the publishing landscape, thanks largely to Anansi's efforts but to a lot of other people's as well, had changed fundamentally – and for the better, so far as Canadian books were concerned. There were now Canadian publishers galore.'[1] If Fetherling was somewhat overstating the situation of Canadian publishing, there could be no denying that by the mid-1970s, McClelland and Stewart boasted a vigorous Canadian publishing program. Earlier concerns that the company was for sale and might be taken over by American interests had been laid to rest, and McClelland and Stewart's feisty president and publisher, Jack McClelland, was signing up the foremost Canadian writers of the day and bringing their works into print. His roster included Margaret Atwood, Earle Birney, Leonard Cohen, Irving Layton, Margaret Laurence, Al Purdy, W.O. Mitchell, Mordecai Richler, among others.[2] With *Bear*, Marian Engel joined their company.

Bear was a McClelland and Stewart success story. Canadian literary icon Robertson Davies enthusiastically endorsed the 'strange' and 'obscene' new novel Engel had produced.[3] 'The theme of *Bear* is one of the most significant and pressing in Canada in our time,' Davies declared, 'the necessity for us who are newcomers to the country, with hardly four hundred years of acquaintance with it, to ally ourselves with the spirit of one of the most ancient lands in the world. In our search for this spirit, we are indeed in search of ourselves' (12 January 1976). Timothy Findley conveyed flattering comments from Stanley Colbert,[4] who pronounced Engel's novel 'perfectly accomplished.' Not only was it one of 'the most brilliantly set down books' he had ever read, but it was also a perfect 'exercise book' or 'study book' to give to all writers to read (15 December 1976).

Timothy Findley, who makes his epistolary entrance in this chapter, was a close and understanding friend to Engel, who had encouraged and supported him in his early writing. Another of Engel's good friends and faithful correspondents, Jane Rule, also makes an epistolary debut in this chapter (24 May 1977). Rule's letters provide a glimpse of life on Galiano Island, home to many Canadian writers and the place where Engel was to seek some holiday respite in the summer of 1977. Engel's circle of writing friends was growing ever wider. Her correspondents now included new young writers like Sharon Riis (14 March 1977)[5] and Aritha van Herk (December 1979)[6] as well as old friends who continued to write, such as Gwendolyn MacEwan (March 1976),[7] Dennis Lee (7 June 1977),[8] Margaret Atwood (1 December 1978),[9] Rudy Wiebe (17 April 1979),[10] and, reappearing, Margaret Laurence

(2 April 1976, 30 August 1977, 30 September 1978) and Hugh MacLennan (8 August 1976, 9 January 1980, 20 January 1980). As Timothy Findley rightly observed (18 October 1977), Engel had 'a lot of friends.' Laurence and Lee sent letters of moral support following a stinging review of *Bear* by Scott Symons,[11] which Laurence discounted as a vitriolic and hysterical (30 August 1977), and Lee described as obtuse and ungenerous, wonky and shrill, and 'just plain out-of-touch' (7 June 1977). Symons's review, however, was the exception that proved the rule. *Globe and Mail* literary editor William French wrote a 'rave' review, observed John Rich, Engel's psychotherapist, to whom *Bear* was dedicated (14 April 1976). The novel received an admiring notice in the London *Times* (7 June 1977) as well.[12] Engel had written a winner, and she earned a Governor General's Award for it.

Before the introduction of the Giller Prize in 1994, the Griffin Prize in September 2000, and an increasing number of other literary prizes, the Governor General's Awards for Canadian fiction, non-fiction, poetry, drama, children's literature, and translation constituted the country's premier recognition of its writers. Accompanied by a cash award, they brought financial relief as well as national notice. Among Engel's peers, Margaret Laurence, Alice Munro, Mordecai Richler, Brian Moore, Robert Kroetsch, and Rudy Wiebe had all received Governor General's Awards for fiction. After more than twenty years of fiction writing, Engel's time had finally arrived.

Hard on the heels of *Bear* and despite the demands and distractions of single motherhood and writer-in-residence appointments, Engel produced her next novel, *The Glassy Sea,* in 1978. The story of a Protestant nun, Engel's new novel was admired by writer friends young and old. '[A] thing of beauty and perception unparalleled in Canadian literature,' Aritha van Herk wrote (December 1979); 'a most remarkable feat of empathy with some lapidary prose,' MacLennan commented (9 January 1980). Rudy Wiebe appreciated the 'inspired' dedication of the novel (17

April 1979), while Margaret Laurence praised its orchestration, spareness, and beauty of structure. '[A] fine, strong and moving book,' she declared, disagreeing with Dennis Duffy's critical assessment. '[I]magine saying "No male character gets presented as fully as a female,"' Laurence huffed; 'Oh, by the way, Mr. Hemingway, no female character gets presented as fully as a male ... who would ever ever ever think of saying *that*?' (30 September 1978). Laurence's letter underscores the extent to which women writers were still battling critical stereotypes at the end of the 1970s. The impact of boldly experimental work by writers like Nicole Brossard, Madeleine Gagnon, and Gail Scott in Quebec, and Daphne Marlatt, Erin Mouré, Lola Lemire Tostevin, Aritha van Herk, and Betsy Warland, to name only a few from elsewhere in Canada, would not be widely noted by the critical establishment until the 1980s.[13] In the interim, writers like Laurence and Engel introduced new, unconventional ideas, images, and visions for women within their novels and short stories. *The Glassy Sea* expressed Engel's deep concern with the social dichotomies and stereotypes that separate women into roles as saints or sinners, virgins or sex objects, Marthas or Marys.

Engel was disappointed that *The Glassy Sea* did not sell as well as anticipated and that, as a result, financial struggles continued. The author also faced a new battle as the 1970s drew to a close. In November 1979 she was diagnosed with cancer. This drastic development in her life seemed to break some old habits. 'I've changed in the oddest way,' she mused to Timothy Findley (28 December 1979); '... beginning to accept a lot, I think. Finally, my own imperfections. Finally, that I'm worth fighting for (and what a lot having good friends does towards one's feeling of self-love) ... But there's something else. I don't know quite what it is. Things are sliding into perspective. I've dropped conspiracy theories ... I'm just living. And that is good. Taking pleasure in weather and cats and just being. Not over-reaching, over-striving. It's as if I've finally had enough of that. I DON'T FEEL I HAVE TO JUSTIFY MY EXISTENCE ANYMORE. SOMEONE HAS GIVEN ME THE GRACE JUST TO BE. What a good feeling' (28 December 1979).

Closing this chapter of correspondence from friends and admirers is a letter from George Woodcock (3 July 1980).[14] He had reread all Engel's work in preparation for an essay he was preparing on her work. '[I]n *Bear* and *The Glassy Sea*,' he wrote, 'you're writing the best, most crystalline prose in Canadian fiction.' Engel was not finished writing. She would continue to practise her craft and hone her skills throughout the duration of her battle with cancer over the next five years.

Notes

1 Fetherling, *Travels by Night: A Memoir of the Sixties*, 163.
2 McClelland and Stewart counted many non-fiction writers on its lists as well, such as Pierre Berton, Peter Gzowski, Farley Mowat, and Peter Newman. In addition, titles continued to appear in the New Canadian Library series, established in 1958, and the Carleton Library series, established in 1963, through which the publishers reissued classic works of Canadian literature and history.
3 Robertson Davies (1913–95), Canadian novelist and playwright, creator of the fictional character Samuel Marchbanks and author of the best-selling Deptford Trilogy: *Fifth Business* (1970), *The Manticore* (1972), and *World of Wonders* (1975).
4 Stanley Colbert, Canadian-American writer, literary agent, and former president of HarperCollins Publishers.
5 Sharon Riis (1947–), Canadian writer, best known for her experimental first novel, *The True Story of Ida Johnson* (1976).
6 Aritha van Herk (1954–), Canadian novelist and professor of creative writing. Van Herk's first novel, *Judith* (1978), won the prestigious Seal First Novel Award. It was followed by four novels,

two collections of essays, and, in 2001, *Mavericks: An Incorrigible History of Alberta.*

7 Gwendolyn MacEwan (1941–87), Canadian poet, playwright, novelist, and short story writer. Her work and life are the subject of Rosemary Sullivan's biography *Shadow-Maker* (Toronto: HarperCollins, 1995).

8 See note 11, p. xxiv.

9 See note 18, p. xxv.

10 Rudy Wiebe (1934–), Canadian novelist and professor of creative writing. His first novel, *Peace Shall Destroy Many* (1962), cast a critical eye on the Mennonite community. Several novels followed, including two Governor General's Award winners, *The Temptations of Big Bear* (1973) and *A Discovery of Strangers* (1994).

11 Scott Symons, 'The Canadian Bestiary: Ongoing Literary Depravity,' *West Coast Review* [Simon Fraser University] 11.3 (January 1977): 3–16.

12 See note 31, p. 175.

13 Nicole Brossard (1943–), Quebec poet, novelist, essayist, and Governor General's Award winner, internationally recognized for her experimental explorations of feminist and lesbian worlds and imaginations; Madeleine Gagnon (1938–), another pioneer writer of feminist thought in Quebec; Gail Scott (1945–), journalist and writer, whose short stories and novels, written in English, were part of the feminist literary movement that animated Quebec literature during the 1970s and 1980s; Daphne Marlatt (1942–), poet, novelist, theorist, and founding member, together with Gail Scott, Barbara Godard, and Kathy Mezei, of *Tessera,* a journal that publishes Canadian women's writing in French and English; Erin Mouré (1955–), Montreal-based experimental poet, whose 1988 collection *Furious* won the Governor General's Award (English language); Lola Lemire Tostevin (1937–), bilingual poet and novelist, associate of Brossard, Scott, Marlatt, and other feminist writers of the 1970s and 1980s; Betsy Warland (1946–), feminist poet and activist, collaborator with Daphne Marlatt in the publication of *Double Negative* (1988) and *Two Women in a Birth* (1994).

14 George Woodcock (1912–95), Canadian editor, essayist, poet, and passionate advocate of Canadian culture.

To Pauline and Don McGibbon

70 Marchmount Road
Toronto

10 January 1976

Dear Pauline and Don,
My Christmas cards just turned up yesterday but they look good enough to send next year so I'll just drop you a line to say I've moved, with the kids, to this house, near Davenport and Christie (if I wanted to be tony I'd say 'Just west of Wychwood Park' but in actual fact it's just north of Frenkel steel yards), and I bought it, and if I'm a clever girl I might just manage to keep it!

It's a funny house – one of the old Toronto patterns, 3 up, 3 down, half-finished basement and lots of problems, but I think it's right for us as the spaces are relatively private. I didn't do very well over money in the preliminary court hearings because I SAVED last year and the judge held it against me. As my ma-in-law said years ago, I should have been extravagant.

On the other hand, it appears that a frugal childhood really is of use! If the wiring holds for a year we'll be okay.

It's been a rough 2 years. I still don't know whether I did the right thing, but it's done and that's that. I couldn't take marriage any longer; I don't like the alternative AT ALL but at least there's nobody telling me yesterday's sins every morning, when I goof it's my fault, when I succeed it's my own too. And Adele Wiseman's brother in Florida has come up with some information about new treatments for hyperactivity that sound more realistic than suppressing bubble gum and fluorescent light, so Will may come out of the woods at last.[1]

I don't know how you two have been such devoted public servants for so long. The Library Board has been an eye-opener. Meetings go on till one in the morning and much as I would like to skimp my duty, I'm the key member of the so-called reform group: if I leave, we lose. Reforms are, I think, much needed, so I stick with it. I've had the Forest Hill Yoga Lesson Crisis in my lap and am so afraid they'll call me anti-Semitic. But we really can't afford to give Yoga at the Learning Resources Centre any more and the citizens are furious. Finally, the community has organised to pressure. I was at a most interesting meeting last week where two men from the Y explained to the Forest Hill people the REAL cost of their luxury lessons. I had the pleasure of explaining that we had not been able to produce such excellent figures because we didn't have the money to hire a statistician. Nearly lost my temper at a woman who complained that poor immigrants got better services but at last got two groups to compromise, I think. We are also having very interesting negotiations with the Native Peoples' Centre who want a library in the Bible College on Spadina, which they have just bought.

All this has been a real insight into the kinds of things you've been doing. Volunteer work is EXPENSIVE though. I don't think I'd have taken it on if I hadn't thought I'd still have a salary behind me. However, (Cripes, this isn't a begging letter!) it's my one contact with the outside world and a very interesting one at that. Worth doing. Always wanted to know how Boards worked, why there were so many lawyers on them etc. Now I know.

---

1 Adele Wiseman (1928–92), Canadian novelist, author of *The Sacrifice* (1956), *Crackpot* (1974), and the non-fiction works *Old Woman at Play* (1978) and *Confessions of a Book-Molesting Childhood and Other Essays* (1987). Her *Selected Letters* to Margaret Laurence were edited by John Lennox and Ruth Panofsky in 1997.

I've just finished a very strange and rather obscene book which McClelland is publishing in May[2] – you may want soon to bid me fond adieu! It's a make-or-break job. I may be laughed out of town or make a fortune. *At least* people I meet at the libraries won't call me Dorothy Engel or Mrs. Eggles any more! And I've broken away from the one-horse, however lovely, publishers.[3]

Mother has had a slight stroke and is in Montreal with Helen.[4] We hope she'll be able to go back to Sarnia but are uncertain. She's in good shape considering – only a very slight speech impediment – but she's 79, so I don't know.

Well. Too long a letter as usual. But I wanted to get back in touch and say things are okay. The landlady is out of my life as a monster-figure, I'm working on a television play and more or less doing my duty by the libraries. The kids are well – and I hope you both have a good new year. And drop by if you're ever in the neighbourhood. The place is too small for parties but there's a tiny little parlour like a snug in a pub.

Love,
Marian Engel

---

2 *Bear* (Toronto: McClelland and Stewart, 1976).
3 The publication of *Bear* marked Engel's move from Anansi to McClelland and Stewart.
4 Engel's sister, Helen Crawford.

From Dan Wickenden
Harcourt Brace Jovanovich
New York, N.Y.

12 January 1976

Dear Marian:
Is it possible that when you and I last corresponded directly with each other, Women's Lib hadn't yet made the scene? I don't know how you feel about Ms., about which I feel ambivalent, but I do find it useful. But one is still occasionally confronted with the dilemma of addressing somebody whose name could be either m. or f., as for instance if I didn't know you and you spelled your name Marion.

After which wordy preamble I go on to say how pleased I am to have heard from you. I really was impressed by that manuscript, as I hope my letter to Tim Seldes conveyed, and it goes on haunting me. Perhaps it was dense of me to refer to it as a story of sexual obsession rather than as a love story. One thinks of it as being obsessive when the lover's passion for the beloved seems incomprehensible to all outsiders. Like, for instance, Philip's obsession with Mildred in *Of Human Bondage*.[5] (I have a notion he spelled his name Phillip, and was her name Mildred? In my mind's eye they are Leslie Howard and Bette Davis.)[6] Anyway, your Bear is more than just a bear to me, he's a symbol for all unsuitable or unlikely loved ones; and you make us believe absolutely in him, and in your heroine's passion for him. But it would be pornographic only if it made readers want to go forth and find bears of their own, which I can't imagine its doing. *It* refers to the novel.

5 A 1915 novel by W. Somerset Maugham (1874–1965).
6 Leslie Howard (1893–1943) and Bette Davis (1908–89), Hollywood film stars. The classic 1934 film, starring Howard and Davis as Philip Carey and Mildred Rogers, was directed by John Cromwell.

I'm delighted that McClelland and Stewart have taken said novel on, and, with you, hope this will lead to publication in both the U.S.A. and England. Ultimate mass-paperback publication strikes me as being at least possible, and I've begun to wonder if I didn't too lightly dismiss the manuscript as a prospect for H.B.J. [Harcourt Brace Jovanovich]. Still, there's a tendency to shy away from most fiction just now, and I don't know how what has become the General Books Department, of which our mass-paperback subsidiary Pyramid is now an integral part, staffed almost entirely by relative newcomers, would have made of your Bear. I hope he goes on to wide success.

It's also fine news that *No Clouds of Glory* is out in paperback as *Sarah Bastard's Notebook*, from which title it should of course never have departed and that it's going quite well. And that the serial novel written for radio is going well, too. It has pleased me to see you continuing to bob up as a reviewer for the *NYTBR*,[7] and I hope they'll give you further assignments, more frequently. Your reviews are always good reading, and although I don't suppose the *Times* pays large sums of money for them, what it does pay must help at least a little with the finances. I've forgotten how many children you have, to be on your own with, but may everything work out well.

Warm best wishes.
Yours as ever,
Dan Wickenden

Talking of pet pedantries, I have just observed, above, that the *NYTBR* is 'they' but the *Times* is 'it.' Now how do I justify that? My only excuse is that it's still pretty early in the morning, 9:05, and I didn't go jogging because of yesterday's daylong snowfall, and what it left behind.

7 *New York Times Book Review.*

From Jack McClelland[8]
McClelland and Stewart Limited
Toronto, Canada

12 January 1976

Dear Marian:
You will be glad to know that Rob Davies has joined the team of supporters for your novel. His comment is as follows:

> 'The theme of *Bear* is one of the most significant and pressing in Canada in our time – the necessity for us who are newcomers to the country, with hardly four hundred years of acquaintance with it, to ally ourselves with the spirit of one of the most ancient lands in the world. In our search for this spirit, we are indeed in search of ourselves.'

Incidentally he put this comment in a brilliant and wildly amusing letter about the book and how it will be received by various critics across the country. Regrettably I don't have permission to show it to anyone, but when you next encounter Rob, you might ask him if I may have his permission to show it to you. He ends up his letter 'I wish you luck, and my congratulations to Miss Engel, whom I do not know, but whose work I have long admired.'

With all good wishes.
Sincerely,
Jack

8 See note 42, p. 111.

From Robertson Davies[9]
Massey College
University of Toronto
Master

20 January 1976

Dear Ms. Engel:
Thanks for your kind letter of January 14th. What I wrote to Jack about your book was sincerely meant, but it was not all that I had to say, and perhaps Jack will show you the letter that I addressed to him. I am fearful that the book might not be taken as seriously as it is intended and that you might be exposed to comment and criticism of a kind which, in the long run, would not be helpful to you. Everything would depend on the tone of two or three influential reviews. I am afraid I have grown very cynical about our Canadian book reviewers, who suffer so much from the troubles of their kind – too much work that must be done too quickly, and, in many cases, submerged hostility towards authors.

I admire your courage in writing the book and I need hardly say that I wish you every success with it.

Yours sincerely,
Robertson Davies

9 See note 3, p. 155. This letter is published with permission of Pendragon Ink.

From Gwendolyn MacEwan[10]

GOD IS NOT YET BORN

My friend, if everything were finished, and we could say
We'd given birth to stars, if we could say *give over*,
It is done, things would be wild, and fair. But
Hairs in the nostrils keep on coming, and teeth
Confess their doom. It is not over. It has not yet begun.

It has not yet begun, because stallions dare to be horses
Even here, right in this room. The night pretends
To scare us. The night is wrong. Night is not yet born.
God is not yet born. I will repeat that: *God is not yet born.*

We want it all to end before the breathless prologue says
In the Beginning was the Word, and yet we want to come
Into being. We want horses to run and keep on running.
God is not yet born. The dual axis turns. Twins
Of night and morning summon
Stars.

God is not yet born. Day-mares race towards their destiny
And the end is dawn. Nothing is wrong.
The clouds have merely indicated sun. And O my friend,
Our God is not yet born. We bleed the chaos of His coming.

For Marian
March/76
Gwendolyn

10 See note 7, p. 156. This poem appears to be previously unpublished.

From Margaret Laurence

2 April 1976

Dear Marian –
Take heart. Finances *will* get better. Everything will get better. Just hang on. Survival is all.

Much love,
Margaret

From John Rich[11]
Faculty of Education
University of Toronto
Toronto, Ontario

14 April 1976

Dear Marian,
Bill French liked *Bear!* He continues to be the most sensible regular reviewer that I know of. Considering the prevailing coolness of his reviews, I'd call that one a rave. It's in the windows as you walk down Yonge Street, too (your book, that is). Next thing is which company to sell the movie rights to. If you have a voice in the casting, I'd appreciate a good word. With the right skin on I do a pretty good bear act. The part would have its compensations.

On Monday, the endodontist came at me with scissors, knife and drill. I faced him with clenched teeth and now here I am with a mouthful of suture string and a front tooth whose root is 25% ferrous oxide.

11 See note 90, p. 140.

Such, such were the joys.

Be happy that you've got two marvellous kids and a rare talent, *in trust*.

Your sententious pal,
John

From Hugh MacLennan
McGill University
Montreal, Quebec

8 August 1976

My Dear Marion:[12]

Luther said of St. Paul: 'His sentences have limbs; they bleed.' So do a great many of yours. Your letter of July 9 from P.E.I. was for me rewarding to a greater degree than you could guess. First, because I always, I think, have been able to sense ability and I sensed it in you and you have proved it. Secondly, because courage in isolation is to me the most admirable, which is why I have admired the Duke of Wellington and so honour Solzhenitsyn today.[13] And you have that.

Alas, dear Marion, people with those qualities are always hard on themselves.

Bob Weaver is a man I liked when we met, which was only once. Fulford and French I never met, but some of my friends like them

---

12 Engel's name is misspelled throughout.
13 Arthur Wellesley, Duke of Wellington (1769–1852), British prime minister and military leader; Aleksandr Solzhenitsyn (1918–), Russian novelist, winner of the 1970 Nobel Prize for literature, best known for his books *One Day in the Life of Ivan Denisovich* (1962), *Cancer Ward* (1968), and *The Gulag Archipelago*, first published in English in 1974.

and admire them. I can easily understand why *Sphinx* bothered them; it bothered me more, because I had to write it. But at least Weaver laid off *Rivers of Canada*. At the appalling price of $28.00 it was a success with the public, for it sold 19,000 copies. But my publisher told me that if I did not accept a short speaking tour, French and Fulford would have killed it dead. Fulford was syndicated in Toronto, Montreal and Ottawa, which for a book of that sort amounted to 80% of the market.

I was interested in your statement that they were Callaghan supporters.[14] And I'm thankful that as such they did not destroy my genuine admiration and friendship for Morley. God knows some people in Toronto tried to, but whenever Morley and I meet, we meet as a pair of old pros. His son Barry is apparently something different.[15] I've never met him.

Out of your letter I gathered a sense of an immense life-force accepting itself, accepting its position and its past experience, and knowing it can cope against whatever difficulties may arise, and you have many. But – don't laugh – you still have youth with you. At fifty, when Dorothy died, I still had youth with me. Now, perhaps, I have more wisdom and wisdom enough to ask what wisdom is worth. Still a good deal of vitality, and an open mind. I'm less pessimistic of the future than when I wrote you last because this June I revisited Germany, and Germany and East Europe at the Olympics showed this continent just how soft it is. Also, talking to Germans in Freiburg (an innocent city, very beautiful and unnecessarily destroyed by the Allies in 1944, but

14 Morley Edward Callaghan (1903–90), Canadian novelist and short story writer. He and Ernest Hemingway met when the two writers worked briefly at the *Toronto Star Weekly* in the early 1920s. Callaghan's 1951 novel *The Loved and the Lost* received the Governor General's Award.

15 Barry Callaghan (1937–), Canadian novelist, editor, and academic, son of Morley Callaghan, and author of several books of poetry and prose, including *Black Queen Stories* (1982), *A Kiss Is Still a Kiss* (1995), and *Barrelhouse Kings* (1998), a memoir. See also note 36, p. 108.

rebuilt to the inch) I realized that they had indeed recovered. They had learned that on account of Hitler they could expect no pity for the horrifying retribution they suffered – and Freiburg was never Nazi.

It seemed to me that the old German guilt-neurosis, based on sex, had finally been expiated. But that colossal German energy had not been destroyed.

Let's meet again, one of these days, dear Marion,

As ever,
Hugh

From Timothy Findley
[Cannington, Ontario]

15 December 1976

Dear Marian –
The typewriter is set up for television and the spacing for letters may not work out – but it shows you how lazy I am that I won't change the tabs ...

My knees are fine. Well, do shin bones count if they hurt?

Funny story: my friend Marigold Charlesworth[16] – who works in Ottawa – met an old friend on the street. The old friend was a sweet, Hungarian mime and M'gold said to him, 'Heaven's! What are you doing in town?' And he said, 'Oh – I have very exciting job in cabaret. We are doing a music-and-comedy called "Sax and Violins" – very nice, very nice.' So M' gold said, 'Good. Sounds

---

16 Marigold Charlesworth, Canadian actor, producer, and, with William White-head and Jean Roberts, artistic director of the Red Barn Theatre at Jackson's Point on Lake Simcoe, Ontario.

Viennese. I'll come round and see it. Where are you playing?' So
he told her 'Blue Gardinya' and later that week she turned up to
buy her ticket to – you guessed it – '*SEX AND VIOLENCE!!!*' It wasn't
Viennese.

Nice anecdote: there's a gent at the CBC who is an old friend of
mine from California – once an agent – also in the movie business. Now he's here as a script consultant – because he is a superb
editor – a real Pascal Covici.[17] Brilliant. His name is Stanley
Colbert.[18] Well – I was in his office the other week and spied a
copy of *Bear* on his desk. I said, 'What did you think?' and he said,
'I think it's the best thing I've read since I got here and one of
the most brilliantly set down books I've *ever* read. You know –' he
said, '– this is an exercise book. A study book. I give it to all my
writers to read – not just 'cause it's good – but because it's been
perfectly accomplished.' I thought you might like to hear that
one. (And, by the way, I agree with him.)

love in an old kimona –
Tiff

Sorry about the paste-job – the blind cat spilled tea on the table
while I was typing the envelope for this – and I'm afraid I didn't
have time to retype –
Congratulations re: divorce. Having gone through it myself – I
know it's hell. Try not to think badly of us all – none of us men are
perfect ladies – .

P.S. My 'soldiers' are fine.[19] The first draft is okay and now I know
it will be good. Willy is fine, too.[20] So am I. Be well. T.

---

17 Pascal Covici (1868–1964), Romanian publisher and editor.
18 Stanley Colbert, writer and literary agent.
19 Reference to Findley's *The Wars* (Toronto: Clarke, Irwin, 1977).
20 Findley's partner, William Whitehead.

From Sharon Riis[21]
Lac La Biche
Alberta

14 March 1977

Dear Marian Engel,

First I'd like to thank you for your generous review of *Ida.*[22] On Friday, Jan. 28 I was delivered of my first kid – a beauty of a boy, by the way – and on Saturday morning the call came from the Press exclaiming over the review. It seemed almost too much good fortune to handle at once. I had just read *Bear* the previous week: I must say you write like a very funky articulate lady indeed. At the risk of sounding ingratiating I must tell you that there's not another writer in the country who I'd rather have had that review from.

Second, will you excuse my presumption in asking you to support my appeal for a Canada Council Grant by writing a note of appraisal for them? My problem *re* this application business is that I don't actually *know* any writers. If you feel you cannot in good conscience perform such a task, I will understand and ask only that you return the appraisal form as soon as possible. I've enclosed postage for that purpose.

I hope someday we might meet and overdose on coffee and cigarettes and good conversation together. Meanwhile, thanks again.

Sincerely,
Sharon Riis

21 See note 5, p. 155.
22 *The True Story of Ida Johnson* (Toronto: Women's Press, 1976). The typescript of Engel's review can be found in the Marian Engel Archive, McMaster University, box 25, file 6.

From Jane Rule[23]
Galiano
British Columbia

24 May 1977

Dear Marian:

We got back to the island just a week ago, having taken a fine detour to Montreal for a visit with Marie-Claire Blais,[24] and I began to ask around about houses for you and the children. There are, as I told you, very few houses for rent here, and some of the few that are, are tiny, and some are at the north end, 17 miles from the ferry, far too isolated for you without a car. Tonight I think I've seen a house you might well find right for your needs. It would cost $800 for the last two weeks in July and the month of August, utilities included. It has a bathroom with a shower, three small bedrooms, one with bunk beds, one with a single bed, one with an old-fashioned three quarters bed, a comfortable living room with fireplace, couches and comfortable chairs and a table with six chairs, a small kitchen with fridge, table top burners, a toaster oven and a grill, but no proper oven. It's all electric: hot water heater, room heaters. There's an adequate amount of china and cutlery but no bedding because the family that owns it uses sleeping bags, partly because there's nothing but the kitchen sink for dealing with laundry, and the only laundromat

---

23 Jane Rule (1931–), Canadian novelist and short story writer. Rule's first novel, *Desert of the Heart* (1964), and subsequent works, presented lesbian characters and introduced new voices in Canadian fiction. Her partner (the 'we' of the letter's opening sentence) was the teacher and writer Helen W. Sonthoff (1916–2000).

24 Marie-Claire Blais (1939–), Québécoise novelist and poet, whose 1965 *Une Saison dans la vie d'Emmanuel* was a scathing portrait of Catholic Quebec during the 1950s. Winner of three Governor General's Awards, Blais's work has enjoyed much international attention.

on the island is at the north end, out of your reach. There is also no phone. The house is set in arbutus and fir trees, has a deck and picnic table but no garden or yard to tend. You glimpse the sea through the trees, and it's about a three minute walk to the beach, which is a rock shelf so warmer than other beaches on the island and with no dangerous currents. There are fairly near neighbours, but there are no houses visible from anywhere we looked. It has a good sense of privacy without isolation. There are two good sized boys' bikes which will be left there, and the store is about 2 miles, over the car road a pretty steep hill, but on two different trails very easy biking. Community mail box is just a couple of minutes away with six day delivery.

I should probably also give you more sense of the island's location. You get to it either by sea plane, twenty minutes from downtown Vancouver, or by bus and car ferry, a trip of about 2 1/2 hours from downtown Vancouver. There are three ferries each way a day during the summer, also three a day each way to Vancouver Island. You'd be about 3 to 4 miles from the mainland ferry dock and post office, both very easy biking. There is one taxi on the island. If you want relative quiet, good open space for the kids to explore without your worrying about them, I think the inconveniences of the house (ovenless, laundryless, phoneless) wouldn't trouble much. There is no liquor store on the island. There are several food stores, the one nearest you (2 miles) the best, and, though they don't bring in a great deal of fresh meat, they will bring in anything you want to order specially. Fresh produce comes in on Friday mornings. There's also a pay phone at the store. There's a fair amount of expected rural entertainment, pot luck suppers, bingo games, country dances, at the community hall, also two miles from you, a golf club, a lodge with a restaurant and bar about 4 miles away, a marvellous restaurant at the north end, which we'd take you to if you came. Quite a number of children turn up in the summer, and I'm sure your kids could find friends if they wanted to. The climate is mild and there's a fair amount of rain: blue jeans, rubber boots, and rain jackets, along with swimming suits, are what you'd need. There are more interesting women than men on this island because there are a great many widows. About 500 in population in winter, a good many more in summer. You'd be just up the road from the present president of UBC, whose kids are older than yours; I don't know about your other neighbours. Our closest friends are an 83 year old painter you can read about in *The Canadian* on the 18th of June,[25] Margaret Hollingsworth,[26] a playwright and novelist in her thirties, Charlie and Kathleen Partington, potters and weavers, Charlie also the new fire chief, young Tom and Ann Hennessy who are making their own life on a few acres, Tom's framing business supporting them, Ken and Marie Hardy, earnest teachers with a bunch of kids. We have a lot – too many in the summer – of visitors from the mainland and elsewhere all year long and mostly like that. For the last two weeks in August we'll have my three nieces with us, 10, 12, and 15, and all summer we'll have our marvellous friend Monica around, who has a boat and a dodge van and is very good at taking kids off into the woods, on fishing trips.

I shyly do not want to rave about the island, knowing its real limitations, but it has been a wonderful place for us, for Audrey Thomas,[27] for Earle Birney,[28] the mix of everyone from loggers to musicians, from the very old to the very young with the lively lore they weave together a good human world. It's easy to take ferries to other islands, bikes on board, to explore for the day. Our friends

---

25 John Hofsess, 'Escaping Old Age at 80: How Elisabeth Hopkins Painted Her Way out of a Corner,' *Canadian*, 18 June 1977, pp. 12–14.
26 Margaret Hollingsworth (1939–), Canadian playwright whose work focuses on women's experiences and gender relations.
27 Audrey Thomas (1935–), Canadian novelist, short story writer, and radio playwright. Her work extends from a first collection of stories in 1967, *Ten Green Bottles*, to the recent novel, *Isobel Gunn* (1999).
28 Earle Birney (1904–95), Canadian poet, best known for the poem 'David' from his first collection, *David and Other Poems*, which won the Governor General's Award in 1942.

would all welcome you warmly but not intrude on your space, and we'd be delighted to share the island with you for those six weeks. We could see to it that you had a good supply of salmon, crab, cod, show you fine places for black berry and huckleberry picking. The real estate agent said, 'Tell her, I'm sorry there are no bears, but plenty of deer and racoon, eagles and whales.'

The family who own the house are going off to Europe, and they'd, of course, like to know as soon as possible whether or not you'd like the place. It might be best if you'd phone me about it.

Oh, there's a doctor and a dentist on the island. We'd certainly meet your boat, get you to the store for first major stock ups, and be emergency transportation when you needed it – we're about 4 miles from you. And we have various extras we could lend you if you found anything in the house importantly missing. But I think you'd be located comfortably enough so that you wouldn't feel uneasily dependent on us for your needs.

So let me know. I'd be delighted if it sounded to you a good place to land for the summer holiday.

Jane

From Dennis Lee[29]
Toronto, Ontario

7 June 1977

Dear Marian,
I have been so wildly anti-social finishing *Savage Fields* that most of the world has been passing me by for months.[30] But a belated delight and congratulations on the award which you certainly

---

29 See note 11, p. xxiv.
30 *Savage Fields: An Essay in Literature and Cosmology* (Toronto: Anansi, 1977).

deserved. I was really tickled for you! And I noticed a neat little admiring review in the London *Times* (was it?) a while ago, which a friend sent over.[31] Huzzah some more!

This small object is something I thought you might enjoy – orphans from the last 10 years.[32]

I read Scott's *Bear* canker when it appeared a few months ago, and found myself shaking my head in dismay and sorrow.[33] I'd known he was working on it, but had no idea it would be so silly. (Those first 3–4 pages – whew! Scott trying to handle a stiletto is some kind of bad mannerist comedy; he must have stopped 3/4 of his readers before they even waded through that much.) I think it would be vaguely insulting to you if I offered 'sympathy' or anything of the kind; that would imply that we both thought it was a responsible, on-target piece of writing. And I presume that after the first shock wore off – and who likes to be the object of a sudden unpremeditated (I think I mean un-anticipated) attack by a near-stranger on the street? – you saw what a compulsive and out-of-synch piece of writing it was. Symons has been doing excellent things with his novel – which meant that the *West Coast Review* thing floored me even more than it would have otherwise because the obtuse and ungenerous spirit of it is exactly the opposite of the fictional work he's doing. But when I thought about it a bit more, I could see what happened. All his positive energy has flowed into *Helmet of Flesh*,[34] when he broke from that to secrete this piece he let out the bottled-up spleen, bile, frustration and bitchiness that accumulate when you've been writing hard. It latched onto his familiar critique of Canadian culture – and the sad part, to my mind, is that it ended up travestying and even prostituting what is sometimes a very cogent insight into all of us.

31 Jane Miller, 'Bear Essentials,' *Times Literary Supplement* [London], 1 April 1977, p. 393.
32 The object is unidentified.
33 See note 11, p. 156.
34 *Helmet of Flesh* (Toronto: McClelland and Stewart, 1986).

It came out so wonky, shrilly and just plain out-of-touch with what (to take the immediate excuse) *Bear* is doing, that it went a long way to discrediting that Tory critique of New World cultures which I imagine both of us feel at least partial sympathy to. Here, though, it was at the service of vindictive personal compulsions, which are Scott's problem, not yours.

Yergh. I can't imagine you want to hear anyone theorizing about the silly thing. For what it's worth, though, I owe Scott a letter (not having written since he left for Mexico) and will be saying in it essentially what I said above.

Much good will & affection. I'm just starting to stretch and realise that I've finished this wretched thing; I believe I'll have to try being a human being now, which will take a bit of an effort.

Ciao,
Dennis

From Margaret Laurence
Lakefield, Ontario

30 August 1977

Dear Marian:
Your letter is, I see, dated July 17! Gosh, can it be so long since I received it? The summer has fled, it seems. My brother and his wife and their 2 daughters (13 and 16) were with me all July, which was super, and we all had a splendid time, but hardly any work got done, or correspondence. During Aug, I've had quite a few visitors, too, but have managed to get a lot of strange and varied reading done ... it will all relate somehow to something, I'm sure, although I'm not at all sure how or when. Have done

some thinking, mostly fairly leisurely. I feel that it will come when it is ready. Am reading Jung's *Memories, Dreams, Reflections* now ... finding it very exciting and yet calming. Strange.

I'm so glad you have a house in Edmonton.[35] What a relief. I'm sure something will turn up for second term. I'm sending this to Galiano, with forwarding address if necessary, as I'm not at all sure when you'll be going to Edmonton. As the Irish joke goes, 'Please let me know if you don't receive this letter.'

During the last week I've read 2 of your stories ... the one in *Chatelaine* and the one in *Saturday Night*.[36] Coverage! Great! The one in *Chatelaine* I found so moving ... yes, it *is* always easier for the man to 'start again,' if anyone can ever be said to start again, and it is tough for women with children to come to this realization. I've been there, as you know. I thought it was a story you absolutely had to write, and I thought ... isn't it grand that she's got paid for it *as well!!* A good story. The one in *Sat. Night* was simply delightful and ... corny word but true here... haunting. I could *see* that bird-like little thing, hopping. And the ending was just right ... the one daughter wasn't going to be ordinary, not by a long shot!

Canadian Forum for Sept. has an issue on Canadian Cultural Policy,[37] and has, to my absolute *outrage*, included a long excerpt of Scott Symons' scurrilous piece in *West Coast Review*. I would like to know who on the editorial board made that decision. I have written a letter to the Editor, which I damn well hope they will print saying, among other things that seldom have I read such a piece of vitriolic, malicious, hysterical outpourings, and that I

35 Engel was preparing for a year as writer-in-residence at the University of Alberta.
36 'Forbesy,' *Chatelaine*, September 1977, pp. 53, 76–8, 80–1; 'Madame Hortensia, Equilibriste,' *Saturday Night*, September 1977, pp. 46–50.
37 Scott Symons, 'Lower Middle-Class Canada on the Make,' *Canadian Forum*, September 1977, p. 30.

think his attack on Can. women writers is sinister, and that he (Symons) would be better off trying to bring more of his own fiction to completion rather than standing outside the struggle and shrieking imprecations. I also say that I'm aware that in the original piece, myself and Marie Claire Blais were specifically exempted from the attack on such writers as you, [Sylvia] Fraser,[38] Atwood,[39] Munro,[40] *et al.* 'With friends like these,' I say, 'What need of enemies? I would rather have been placed with my colleagues.' I end up by saying that when the original piece came out, *West Coast Review* sent me a copy and, as I do not have a subscription, requested me to return it when I'd read it! I end the letter by saying I laughed, albeit with small amusement, as I dropped it into the garbage. How dare the *Forum*!

But I recall a vicious piece on Peggy [Margaret Atwood] a few years ago, published anonymously in the *Forum*. Sad to see that we scare the mostly male enclaves so much.

The Island sounds just wonderful. I hope the entire summer has gone beautifully for you all. Please drop a line when you get settled in Edmonton and let me know how things are. We'll miss you a lot this next year! But it's going to be A Good Year for you ... I feel it in my bones!!

Much love,
Margaret

38 See note 103, p. 147.
39 See note 18, p. xxv.
40 See note 100, p. 146.

From Timothy Findley
[Cannington, Ontario]

18 October 1977

Dear Marian,

Well – the book is now published – and I want to thank you for your part in getting it onto its feet and running.[41] Your praise of it is very moving – and you can't imagine what it's meant to me.

I was sorry you could not be here for the party. It was marvellous. We sang songs – and Graeme [Gibson] wore a suit!!! There were about forty-five or fifty of us and we sat down to dinner, after drinks, at tables of seven or eight. Every table had poppies on it – and red napkins. The food was great – and two kinds of wine – and liqueurs with the coffee! *CLASS.* I looked around the room and everyone was laughing and talking and having a good time. We all wore smashing clothes – and everyone was beautiful. Margaret [Laurence] wore a velvet gown. It made me feel extraordinary. There was no one there I didn't know – and no one I wouldn't have wanted. Margaret got up and praised the book – which left me ringing like a bell. I wish – I really do wish you'd been there. I particularly felt your physical absence – lots of people asked how you were and were pleased to hear about the house you'd found and I told them what sort of routine you have, etc. and I said you looked terrific and seemed to be enjoying what you were doing. *You have a lot of friends.* Physical absence or not – you were there in lots of people's minds.

I'll phone you on the 13th. Thanks for waiting. *The Globe* was a bust, too. Donald Jack reviewed it and 'said I had distorted the war.'[42] Oh well. Peggy is reviewing it in the *Financial Post* (!)[43] I

---

41 *The Wars* (Toronto: Clarke, Irwin, 1977).

42 Donald Jack, 'Two Views of War,' *Globe and Mail,* 15 October 1977, p. 43.

43 We have been unable to trace this review in either the *Financial Post* or the *Financial Times.* It is not included in the Atwood bibliography by Judith McCombs and Carole L. Palmer (*Margaret Atwood: A Reference Guide* [Boston: G.K. Hall, 1991]), nor is there a copy in the Atwood Archive at York University.

don't know yet how she felt about it. She's being quiet. I only hope to god it doesn't slip away into silence like my other books. Still – the silence is broken already by you + Gwen [MacEwan] + Pierre [Berton].

That's good enough for any book.

Be well.
Love, Tiff

From Doris H. Anderson[44]
Toronto, Ontario

10 June 1978

Dear Marian,
I'm off to Washington today to hob nob with David Rockefeller, the Japanese industrialists and decadent, jet-setting international experts on the Tri Lateral Commission.[45] Have a weighty brief-case full of papers I have to wade through for the meetings. No point in reading them except at 5 o'clock in the a.m. on the day they are to be given. My particular brain doesn't really retain information on trade relations and the law of the sea much longer than four hours. Very short attention span on such weighty subjects, I find.

I seem to be in a whirl of conferences – one on women in Ottawa put on by the B.C. status of women. Title: 'After Status – what?' And the answer seemed to be no status at all. We were cooped up in double rooms in Ottawa U. with two toilets and two

---

44 See note 77, p. 130.
45 David Rockefeller (1915–), American financier and philanthropist. The Trilateral Commission, established by David Rockefeller in 1973, aims to foster closer cooperation among Japan, Europe, and North America.

showers *per floor*. Most of the women moved out but since I arrived late and my room-mate had departed, I endured the lumpy bed and grubby walls one night. But would men be hauled to Ottawa and have to put up with such surroundings – and pay their own food and taxi bills to boot! Fortunately I had dinner with John Roberts[46] and Beverley and got the idea across to them (since the Sec. of State's dept. was funding the conference) that this was not good enough.

I love your vision of me in furs and gold rings. But it seems more and more remote. I'm told I won't get any royalties until January![47] Nobody seems to have the slightest idea of what sales might have taken place. I am at the top of the *Maclean's* Best Seller list and fourth on the *Toronto Star* (down from third) but does that mean anything? They keep telling me the paperback contract will be signed any day and I'll get a chunk of money – but when???

Meanwhile people keep circling around me, trying to figure out what to do with me. I get vague offers of full time jobs, half-time jobs, suggestions I set up some sort of magazine-writing school etc. And I seem to be subsisting on speeches, bits of non-fiction writing, a few paying board meetings etc.

I, too, was both mystified and amused by our encounter in Ottawa. At the moment I really find my mind running to very rich elderly men who will indulge my mad whim to pursue writing fiction. David Rockefeller???? I too read the Virginia-Vita correspondence[48] but the best letter was used in the *N.Y. Times* ad – about the white ball and the fountain. Got rather bored reading about making tea and headaches and whether it was going to rain.

Your summer sounds exciting and a new book[49] in the fall will be another solid addition to your already well-established reputa-

---

46 John Roberts (1933–), Canadian secretary of state, 1976–9.
47 Anderson's book, *Two Women* (Toronto: Macmillan), was published in 1978.
48 Probably *The Letters of Virginia Woolf* (New York: Harcourt Brace Jovanovich, 1975).
49 *The Glassy Sea* (Toronto: McClelland and Stewart, 1978).

tion. (Last night at a dinner party a nice Englishwoman from the London School of Economics said she had been told to read my book as an introduction to Canadian literature and I blushingly told her to start with you and Atwood and Laurence.)

I wish you would read the book, though, and write me and tell me about results from the laggard haematologists.

luv,
Doris

From Margaret Laurence
Lakefield, Ontario

30 September 1978

Dear Marian:
Last night I finished reading *The Glassy Sea* ... read it all in one sitting, as one should. (As one generally should, when possible, with every serious novel, in my view.) Marian, I was in tears at the end. It is a beautiful piece of work – strong, poetic, compassionate, profound, and a damn good story! You are going from strength to strength, dear friend, as I have long known that you would. Ethel Wilson once said to me when I had published only my first novel and some African stories, 'There is a spring of clear water in you; it will well up.'[50] I treasure that remark, and I now give it to you. Except that in your case, the spring has been welling up for some books now. It is a novel which in its spareness and beauty of structure, in its orchestration, is like a poem. The character of Rita/Mary/Peg (and how appropriate that her husband should

---

50 Ethel Wilson (1888–1980), Canadian novelist and short story writer, best known for her 1954 novel *Swamp Angel.*

have called her by a diminutive) is such a sympathetic and convincing and real person. And all the other nuns ... in ironic contrast to Asher's impression of them ... are such true individual characters. One trembled slightly, picking up the novel, because you had done such a marvelous thing with *Bear*. But after half a dozen pages, I knew this was a fine, strong and moving book, far and away the best Can novel I've read this year thus far.

I also read Dennis Daffy (Marian, that was a Freudian slip of a genuine nature ... I mean Duffy's) review in today's *Globe*, which I enclose, as it may take M & S awhile to send it to you.[51] I need hardly say that it infuriated me. This is the kind of review that is known to me as praising with faint damns. Marian, I'm afraid the conclusion of the novel is only too correct ... there *is* a war, alas, alas, alas, and there will be more casualties. Many men cannot bear us to do too well in writing, I'm afraid. They must quibble, especially on the lines that women aren't intellectually tough. If Duffy thinks the new convent has 'no more mind behind it than the Kate Greenaway (!)[52] convent it succeeds ...' then he is thinking with a very different set of brains than I am. The new convent has both mind and heart behind it. What is more, the entire novel has the kind of 'Lord, I believe, help thou my disbelief' sense to it, and if the ending is not a statement of the possibility of grace, then I don't know what it is. Also, imagine saying 'No male character gets presented as fully as a female ...' Oh, by the way, Mr. Hemingway,[53] no female character gets presented as fully as a male ... who would ever ever ever think of saying *that?* (Except those of us who long ago did *not* see ourselves in Hemingway's women.) I have had literally hundreds of people ask me why my

51 Dennis Duffy, 'When Early Life's So Cold, Later Years Must Pass in a Hothouse of Dreams,' *Globe and Mail*, 30 September 1978, p. 26.
52 Kate Greenaway (1846–1901), British children's book illustrator.
53 Ernest Hemingway (1899–1961), American novelist, author of such literary classics as *The Old Man and the Sea* (1952), *A Farewell to Arms* (1929), and *The Sun Also Rises* (1926).

protagonists are all women! No one ever asked a male novelist why his protagonists were all men, you can bet your life. My reply is always ... there are lots of male novelists to tell how men feel; I can tell how women feel and that is what I am going to keep on doing.

Also, your sense of place ... of growing up in S. Ontario, is just so authentic and so well conveyed. Of course, as no doubt many readers will tell you, that background has lots in common with, say, my own small town and many, many others in this land. And another thing I love about *The Glassy Sea*, as I did about *Bear* and *Monodromos*, is the way in which there are so many fascinating details of literature and history, etc., interwoven with such skill that they are like flowers in a large tapestry ... one comes upon them with surprise and delight.

I hope to God (I use the phrase advisedly) that Amiel doesn't review it for *Maclean's*.[54] But mean-spirited people do not matter. The work lives.

Much love,
Margaret

P.S. got a lovely long letter from Jocelyn this week ... she and Saro are safely in Corfu, and loving it thus far.
P.S.2. In confidence, what did you think of Aritha's *Judith*?[55] I am terribly glad she got the fifty thousand ... more power to any writer who can get a sum like that. But, truthfully, I hope she will not believe all the hype. It is, like nearly all first novels (the exceptions are there, of course, notably in this country *The Sacri-*

54 Barbara Amiel (1940–), Canadian author and journalist. Amiel did review the novel, admiring Engel's undeniable writing skill but not the novelist's 'sour' perspective on life (Barbara Amiel, 'Bearing Up under the Strain, Part II,' *Maclean's*, 9 October 1978, p. 64).
55 Aritha van Herk, *Judith* (Toronto: McClelland and Stewart, 1978).

fice and *As For Me And My House*)[56] it is a promising first novel. One should not expect it to be more than that. I hope she is neither persuaded to believe it is super-terrific, nor afraid to do another one ... either course would be possible, and unfortunate.

From Margaret Atwood
Edinburgh, Scotland

Marian Engel
Department of English
The University of Alberta
Edmonton

1 December 1978

Dear Marian:

I'm supposed to be writing recommendations for other people's Guggenheims,[57] which gives me a chortle since I applied for one myself when I could have used it, i.e. when I was writing *Surfacing*, and didn't get it; but your letter came this morning so I will be delinquent and write to you instead.

I haven't yet seen *Sea of Glass*,[58] or any other Canadian books, though some are supposed to be on their way. I have caught a few of the reviews (Dept. of Can. Studs. gets a few magazines) and, well, they could have been worse. Val Clery, I note, used you to beat Marg. L. & myself with; why not kill a few dogs with the same

---

56 Adele Wiseman, *The Sacrifice* (Toronto: Macmillan, 1956); Sinclair Ross, *As for Me and My House* (New York: Reynal & Hitchcock, 1941).

57 Guggenheim Fellowships, established in 1925 by American philanthropist Simon Guggenheim, to foster scholarship and international understanding.

58 *The Glassy Sea.*

stone?[59] Have there been any scatological ones? (Apart from Symons of course.) If not, wait. That comes next. Canada is the old sow that gives its young an apple but then makes you bloody well pay for it. No free rides! If success doesn't spoil you *per se* they'll help it along. Give them the finger & write another one. Soon we'll all be so old that they'll have to be nice to us.

It sounds as if you're about ready to move back East? Or further West? Get this job if you can and if you feel like a year away. You don't get paid much in pounds straight up front; but they get you a flat and pay all the heat & electricity for it, which helps considerably; and they've really been most considerate and wonderful. The man in charge is leaving, but hopefully as good a one will take his place.

With all good luck & best wishes,

love from all,
Peggy

From Timothy Findley
Cannington, Ontario

Marian Engel
7803 116th Street
Edmonton, Alberta

17 April 1979

Dear lady,
I'm glad we talked on the phone and I'm very glad you will be coming back this summer. The only unhappy note was that you sounded so exhausted by your university experience that it gave

---

59 Reginald Valentine Clery (1924–), 'Look Outward, Engel, Now,' *Books in Canada*, Aug.–Sept. 1978, p. 14.

me pause thinking that I am about to enter that world and do all that. Nonetheless I'm lucky in that at least I don't have to teach in the formal sense. I must also say I'm looking forward to the experience because for me it will be a unique occasion.

Good news about Willy and Charlotte. Bravo! It will take courage to let them go but that is a quality you have in spades.[60]

Now, about *The Glassy Sea*. Such very good writing. Some of the best episodes in the Engel canon. You have always, it seems to me, such a clear sense of how one fictional character perceives another. And what is seen is fingered like a coin being turned in someone's hand so that the three dimensions constantly spin as the characters float up into Heber's musings. She herself is a fascinating lady but of course you have tried to say too much about her which gave you a good deal of trouble with the time element in the book. Thornton Wilder faced this same problem writing *The Eighth Day* in which the whole variety of everyone's multiple experiences of life as they became defined staggered the reader's ability to pass the accumulation of so much experience so quickly through the media of a dozen characters.[61] I indicated on the phone my concern that you have come to the end of a cycle and I maintain this sense. All I really mean is that Engel's women must now make way for Engel's men. I should love to see you write a book about a man and I think, of all the women currently writing in Canada, you would bring us something extraordinarily valuable to our 'literature' by taking a stab at such a project. I sense so strongly – putting all your work on one shelf and looking at it – that the women are *there* for now and the next woman must hide some time inside you as fictional creature before you let her out. Ziggy is a 'character' and when I speak of your writing of a man or men, I mean that you seek him as profoundly as you have sought and found your women.

I have absolutely no right to have said any of that except in one

---

60 The news was probably that the twins were going to summer camp.
61 Thornton Wilder, *The Eighth Day* (New York: Harper and Row, 1967).

instance, as a reader who values what you have done so greatly that I want this circle widened.

We will talk soon I hope.

Much love,
Tiff

Looking at the sentence about the Ziggy stories, it might appear I mean there is no profundity in them and – of course – I don't mean that.

Today – the sun shone and the temp. began to climb. Winter may be over.

From Rudy Wiebe[62]
The University of Calgary
Dept. of English

17 April 1979

Dear Marian:
March has been a hard month; along with a tough (good) trip to the Maritimes, Tena's father died and we were much involved there. Thank you for your latest notes re E. 376–8; I hope I get your good batch in 407.[63] [ ][64] certainly seems to have prospered with you – 'Inner Circle' is a hummer of a story; I'm looking forward to what she will do this summer and fall. Thank you again for taking on that job: I was (and am) so happy you did, and I hope you had odd moments of enjoyment with it too. Teaching

62 See note 10, p. 156.
63 English courses Engel taught while in Edmonton.
64 The name of the student has been deleted at the author's request.

has its own rewards, though they're not necessarily visible every year one teaches. You are no doubt right: you are ready and willing to handle Toronto again. Spread the resourceful solidity and wild imagination of the west there: all that your two years of trial and testing have churned up in you. I hope you haven't lost all your free-lance contacts because of this past year. I'll see you in Ottawa, eh?

I sometimes have a great longing to write only; but then immediately I am surrounded by the vagaries of freelancing (the Riel CBC production is heavy in my mind now) and when I think of having to be dependent on those changelings, I vow 'Never, Never.' And then there's the good stuff like having a student like Aritha[65] or (in the far distant past) Kathy Govier[66] and more lately Helen Rosta (though I never taught her much, not that I can see)[67] or [ ][68] coming along – why the heck are they all women? Do only women have the nerve for imagination? It seems dreadful, all the world reading only women while the men are all ransacking the physical world for more oil and uranium: I've never been asked yet to speak to a men's reading group, but have been invited to dozens of women's. Is the entire intellectual and thoughtful development of our psyche to be placed in the scribbling and reading minds of women? If so, why aren't they the politicians of this country? I'm just asking you these questions because, presumably, you are in the van of all this reading and writing; I do believe you are one of those very rare women writers who are also philosophical: so you should be able to answer that. Nicht wahr?[69]

65 Aritha van Herk (1954–); see note 6, p. 155.
66 Katherine Govier (1948–), Canadian novelist, author of *Angel Walk* (1996) and winner of the 1997 Marian Engel Award, which recognizes a woman writer at mid-career.
67 Helen J. Rosta, Canadian writer, author of the collection of short stories *In the Blood* (1982).
68 The name of the fourth student has been deleted at the author's request.
69 German for 'Isn't it (so)?'

I've been reading Rilke lately;[70] his German is so much better than the clumsy translations (as always in translations, I know) but he is also very difficult. I really loved your dedication to *The Glassy Sea*: it was clearly inspired. But you knew as well as I that *GS* was not a big seller; in lieu of that, it will sell forever, so don't be bothered by it. Immortality is worth any amount of bucks in the bank! and that's no guff. My father-in-law was an incredibly good man, in a kind of aboriginal sense of Christian goodness; neither I nor any other person who knew him can remember a nasty or a vicious deed: he had compassion, and kindness, and hope to offer: that's all. He left a house paid for and a few thousand bucks in the bank for mother, after a life-time of work, but he had as good a death in the circle of his loved ones and as calm a funeral surrounded by hundreds of friends as one could pray for. Goodness: moral, artistic, spiritual – that is to be striven for. As you know; it's far harder to achieve than massive sales.

Peace, lovely lady. See you in Ottawa.

Rudy Wiebe

To Timothy Findley

15 September 1979

Dear Tiff,
Let me tell you first off that in the end I decided NOT to do the movie novel, because it would bore me stiff and I am going to treat this as a VERY precious year, I feel I owe that to my own health, and the more Anna[71] talked about the job the more I

70 Rainer Maria Rilke (1875–1926), Czech/German lyric poet.
71 Probably Anna Porter of McClelland and Stewart. We have not been able to discover more about the project.

hated the idea of it in the end, since she did not give in about the name and since it became clear that she wanted me really to work my overheated already imagination on it, I said no. I may be wrong, but I did it.

Also, you know I have been having a ball lately, there is a thing I do, there are lots of things I do besides get stinko and phone. It's a question, though, of changing one's habits about time. I had got into the habit of getting up really early to get time; now I don't have to any more and that's good because if you get up at 7 there's too much day to put in, and if you want a drink, it tends to come too early. So I am beginning to adjust my hours.

And lately I have been having a really, really amusing time re-organizing my books. Now, I would do this better if the gent who built the bookcase had put the shelves a real 10" apart as requested instead of 10" COUNTING the lumber! Most books are about 9½. So the awesome fact is that I am stuck with an organization that puts BIG BIG books in my bedroom, paperbacks in the office on the new shelf (all 63' of shelving) and middlesized books wherever one can. Ridiculous, but stimulating and a cure for one's pedantry and absent-mindedness!

So after deciding first about size, one has to decide, what, being under 9½ inches, is to go on the 63 feet; most of the paperbound fiction, all the Pelicans, lots of potted psychology and philosophy, history ...

And who and what to put with whom? Well, Findley of course with Faulkner and Ray and Sylvia Fraser, and Fowke and the two disparate Forsters, Margaret whom I know and E.M whom I would rather.[72]

72 References are to William Faulkner (1897–1962), American novelist; Raymond Fraser (1941–), Canadian novelist and poet; Sylvia Fraser (1935–), Canadian novelist and journalist; Edith Fulton Fowke (1913–), Canadian author and folklorist; Margaret Forster (1938–), American novelist and biographer; E.M. (Edward Morgan) Forster (1879–1970), English novelist.

Atwood, Austen and John Aubrey. Leonard and Matt Cohen. Borges and Burgess and Burroughs and Buckler. Some of the conjunctions are happy; others are not. Findley and Faulkner are okay, but think of Proust and Harry Pollock (I removed him politely to the 10" shelf). The Steins, Gertrude and David Lewis, constantly amuse me. Mailer, Miller, Moore and Munro are okay on the same shelf. A.J.A. Symons and Scott are at least both bent. Thackeray and Tolstoy and Audrey Thomas are bound together by liking (the T's are on the whole likable). In short, desegregating the Canadians is a wonderful experience though I am afraid I have left the French in their ghetto.[73]

The Bibles (can one throw one out?) are down with the *Kama Sutra*, the Anglican Missal, and *The Perfumed Garden*.[74] I have not decided yet what to do with *The Blue Book of Toronto, 1939* with tinted photos of Their Majesties. It reeks of Zena Cherry.[75]

You know, I could get used to life without William, and I think I just bloody well will. To heck with anxiety. Again, it's a question of changing one's habits. Any tension-reliever is worth it when you

---

73 Previously unidentified references include: Jane Austen (1775–1817), English novelist; John Aubrey (1626–97), English historian, biographer, and playwright; Leonard Cohen (1934–), Canadian poet and novelist; Matt Cohen (1942–99), Canadian novelist; Jorge Luis Borges (1899–1986), Argentinean author and poet; Anthony Burgess (1917–93), English novelist; William S. Burroughs (1914–97), American novelist; Ernest Buckler (1908–84), Canadian novelist; Marcel Proust (1871–22), French novelist and writer; Harry Pollock (1920–), Canadian journalist, novelist, poet, and Joyce scholar; Gertrude Stein (1874–1946), American novelist; David Lewis Stein (1937–), Canadian novelist and journalist; Norman Mailer (1923–), American novelist and critic; Henry Miller (1891–1980), American novelist; Brian Moore (1921–99), Irish-Canadian novelist; A.J.A. (Alphonse James Albert) Symons (1900–41), English essayist and biographer; Scott Symons (1933–), Canadian novelist and essayist; William Mackepeace Thackeray (1811–63), English novelist; L.N. Tolstoy (1828–1910), Russian novelist.

74 *Kama Sutra*, an erotic Indian text by Vatsyayana; *The Perfumed Garden*, a sixteenth-century erotic text by Umar ibn Muhhamad al-Nafzawi.

75 *Foster's Blue Book or Ladies' Directory of Toronto* (Toronto: J.G. Fisher, 1900–), an annual publication. Zena Cherry was for many years the society columnist for the *Globe and Mail.*

are trying to live with a screwed-up child. But I don't need one, now. Do I need the tension? I don't think so. I thought it might be lonely in the pure serene but Charlotte is good if independent (having been pushed off so often) company. As for money, there are two possible thousands from short stories, there's the Arts Council, and I think I'll just try to make it. With all these books for company, who can fail?

Thanks for your good counsel. I'll see if I go on bad-boozing and if I do, do something about it.

Oh gosh, I can't write any more, I have to get all the natural history in one place or it will drive me nuts. Then move on to islands. Look, when you get to town we'll get together. Love to Willie, blessings on the book, and thanks,

Marian

From Jack McClelland
McClelland and Stewart Limited
Toronto, Ontario

6 November 1979

Dear Marian:
Thanks for your letter. I am really sorry to hear about the cancer. At the same time I am delighted to hear that it is curable. I know that you will have to go through a rough period in the interim but I know that you can cope with that – you are a survivor if I have ever known one – but I just wish you didn't have all these problems being visited on you at one time.

The main purpose of this letter is to assure you that my offer stands.[76] I have great respect for you and I hope you will not

---

76 We have not been able to identify an earlier written offer.

hesitate if at any point we can fill a gap financially. I mean that and believe it. There will be no questions, no hassle, no delay.

All the best.

Sincerely,
Jack

From Aritha van Herk
Calgary, Alberta

December [1979]

Dear Marian:
Here it is Christmas letter time and it reminded me that I wanted to talk to you. Since I always seem to miss you when I'm in Edmonton, thought I would write and let the post office take care of getting us together.

I wrote you a note way back in October before I went on tour, but Bob forgot to mail it; he's got his mind somewhere between the stars and his rocks.[77]

First of all, Marian, I read *The Glassy Sea* on the plane to Toronto (to give me courage), and I was not disappointed. Let me say, and this is truly without flattery on my part, that it is the finest Canadian novel I have ever read and you must be proud of it. I was so moved by the section 'Envoie' that I sat there weeping, and the gentleman in the seat beside me was so disturbed that he offered me a kleenex. Oh Marian, if only everyone would dare to speak for us women like that – life would be so much simpler and easier and more straightforward. Anyway, I think you have written a thing of beauty and perception unparalleled in Canadian literature.

77 Van Herk's husband, Robert Sharp, a geologist.

Branching Out will be doing a review in this upcoming issue – (Sylvia Vance) and I think it's a very good one, certainly more perceptive than most of the reviews I've seen.[78] Toronto is very jealous of you, isn't it? I talked about you quite a lot all across Canada, and Toronto was quite nasty. But then, I hated Toronto, to say the least. I have never felt more unhappy by the tone and atmosphere in a city in my life. In contrast, you are something of a heroine in Montreal, where every interviewer I talked to brought you up of their own accord and with a great deal of praise. A lot of people there are dying to talk to you. Oh well, Canada is a strange country for a writer who is selling a book. They very rarely recognize quality.

I've survived alright. I am so happy to be home that I don't ever feel like leaving again, but I'm still in one piece. I spent a week in bed after I got home, just babying myself, but now I'm writing and having a good time here. I see Rudy once in a while – I think he is homesick for Edmonton. Perhaps he is finally ready to admit that he needs to belong somewhere too. It is very comforting to have him here and to know that when I feel down, I can go over to the University and talk to him. Still, Calgary is better than I anticipated. Most of the arts community that I've met seems very open and accepting.

I'm trying to work on my stories and getting somewhere, but slowly. I think it will take my entire lifetime to live down *Judith*. Oh well, the book is alright, but I think I've left it behind forever. I'm interested in so many different things now that *Judith* seems only like a part of my adolescence.

How is the teaching going? Are the kids as egotistical as they were in my day? Rudy was always complaining that I never said anything in his classes, but he never understood that when everyone is having an ego trip, it seems futile to say anything. I guess it's a function of trying to write.

78 Sylvia Phillips Vance, 'A Novel Worth the Wait,' *Branching Out* [fifth anniversary issue] 6.1 (1979), p. 52.

How is Satya doing? I miss his humour – he had a funny story for every thing.

Hell, letter writing always seems to futile to me. I wish I could spend 5 hours getting absolutely drunk with you. Is there any chance that you're coming to Calgary? I'll be in Edmonton for Christmas, but these family things are horrors – I can't get away. Maybe in the new year I'll come up for a week just to clean up old business and we can get together. I miss you a lot – just the fact that you were there was a good thought in my mind. And I guess there's always the Writers' Union meeting – I am looking forward to that.

So, have yourself a lovely Christmas. Say hello to William and Charlotte. You've written a wonderful book and if I can ever write anything as good as that, I'll be the happiest woman in the world.

Love,
Aritha

P.S. Bob says hello, too.

To Timothy Findley

28 December 1979

Dear Tiff,
I wrote the enclosed this morning.[79] God knows if it helps. It's not practical. Thoughts carried over from the middle of the night. But it's what I feel.

I've changed in the oddest way. I accepted your cheque. I went and paid the phone bill with it. Just accepted. Said, oh, he's

---

79 We have been unable to locate the enclosure.

having a good year and I'm having a bad one and think of the money I've dropped, the money I've given away ... I'm not ordinarily like that. But I just accept with thanks. Thanks.

I'm in a funny space; beginning to accept a lot, I think. Finally, my own imperfections. Finally, that I'm worth fighting for (and what a lot having good friends does towards one's feeling of self-love), finally, that nobody's going to take care of me if I don't take care of myself.

But there's something else. I don't quite know what it is. Things are sliding into perspective. I've dropped conspiracy theories (when I was in the *Bear* stage I had a counter-paranoid delusion that God was putting money in my bank account, John Rich says) in both directions. I'm just living. And that is good. Taking pleasure in weather and cats and just being. Not over-reaching, over-striving. It's as if I've finally had enough of that. I DON'T FEEL I HAVE TO JUSTIFY MY EXISTENCE ANY MORE. SOMEONE HAS GIVEN ME THE GRACE JUST TO BE.

What a good feeling.

I don't know that the enclosed addresses itself very directly to your problems; but I think some of it is right and good. It isn't very consoling to those of us who accept virtue as its own reward and can't make ends meet. But life just is unfair and it's childish to expect it not to be.

The novel's not going to die, you know. It's just having twinges, thinking of getting a divorce, etc. Probably from lack of critical support in the right quarters. But it will recover.

Lots of love,
M.

From Hugh MacLennan
McGill University
Montreal, Quebec

9 January 1980

Dear Marian:
Yours of Jan. 3 reached me only this morning – 6 days in the coming, the inefficiency of the post office expanding exactly in time to the increase in the demands of their union.

Somebody told me that Bob Weaver hadn't been well, but from your letter it sounds very grim indeed. Somebody also told me you had not been well yourself, and I hope this isn't true.

I'd be glad to write Mr. Bartlett in support of Mordecai's nomination.[80] Bob has done a very great deal for a large number of writers and the fact that he had little or no use for my own work is, so far as my judgment is concerned, of no issue at all in this proposal. I will write as strongly as I can in support of him.

Your phrase about 'the one brass ring on the Canadian literary merry-go-round' is absolutely perfect. It's cursed the scene ever since I began writing. Actually the notion grew out of a satiric piece of Sinclair Lewis called 'The Great American Novel.'[81] In Canada, and in Toronto in particular, they took it seriously. Thank God there are now so many writers around that it may become outmoded.

---

80 Mordecai Richler (1931–99), Canadian novelist, among whose best-known works may be counted *The Apprenticeship of Duddy Kravitz* (1959), *Cocksure* (1968), *St Urbain's Horseman* (1971), *Joshua Then and Now* (1980), *Soloman Gursky Was Here* (1989), and *Barney's Version* (1997), which won the Giller Prize. The nomination referred to is for the Molson Prize (see note 83 below).

81 Sinclair Lewis (1885–1951), American novelist and essayist. MacLennan may have been referring to a 1968 film by Lewis, *The Great American Novel: Babbit.*

I was also glad to hear from you because I didn't know your new address. I have wanted for some time to congratulate you on *The Glassy Sea* – a most remarkable feat of empathy with some lapidary prose.

Just before Christmas I finished a novel I began ten years ago, laid aside for two years to write *Rivers of Canada*, and I still can't believe it's done with one script in N.Y. and the other in Toronto. Without the study of fluvial geology, I would never have been able to write anything. I had to reach the point where it seems quite natural to think, and believe, that 15,000 years ago is only yesterday in the human story. Elspeth Cameron recently gave an address on my work which she titled *The Reluctant Nationalist*.[82] I wish I'd thought of it myself, for reluctant I certainly was. When I began writing there were no literary maps here at all; there wasn't even a market for native work and the phrase 'Canadian novelist,' if translated into its true meaning, signified 'Bush league novelist.' I don't think that's quite the case now.

I'm back at McGill, though they made me an emeritus last spring – back part-time and with a much reduced salary, but I do enjoy working with students so long as I don't have to work with the bureaucracy.

Good luck & God bless you, dear Marian,

As ever,
Hugh

---

82 Elspeth Cameron (1943–), biographer and critic, author of *Hugh MacLennan: A Writer's Life* (1981). Subsequent Cameron biographies include *Irving Layton: A Life* (1985) and *Earle Birney: A Life* (1994).

From Hugh MacLennan
McGill University
Montreal, Quebec

20 January 1980

My Dear Marian:
Your letter arrived and I am moved to say how sorry I am that you have been beset by so many troubles. Thank God, anyway, that the cancer is curable. Somebody told me you had cancer, but there are so many rumours.

Canada Council has acknowledged with thanks my recommendation of Bob Weaver for the Molson Prize.[83] It was as strong a recommendation as I knew how to write.

From my long experience with the young, beginning at LCC[84] in 1935, I think that in many ways your generation had the most difficult time of all in this country. The post-war period was singularly dead as the world recharged its batteries after the depression and the War. Now there is a vast change, after the lunacies of the 1960s and the students I know are quiet and serious, though badly prepared by the school system, which has taken over the theories of the Progressive Schools just at the time when the Progressives were totally discredited. I'm not sure I understand exactly what kind of school your son Will is going to, apart from your description of it as military. However, if he is hyper-active and has resented learning, it's probably the best possible. Years ago in North Hatley I remember a young American boy of about 18 from a rich family who was insolent, lazy and quite horrible. Four years later I met him again after he had spent

83 The Canada Council for the Arts Molson Prize was established in 1964.
   Robert Weaver was one of the three winners selected in 1980.
84 Lower Canada College.

two compulsory years in the Army. He was a transformed character and a happy one. He told me the best thing that had ever
happened to him was to talk back to his sergeant his first day in
boot camp. He was given the treatment and he finally liked it.
There was a young boy somewhat like that in Irwin Shaw's Jordache
stories.[85]

Finally, don't be astonished if you discover, when my last book
appears, that you are responsible for its title. I sent it to the
publishers with a tentative title and suddenly, off your page, sprang
the phrase – 'An Ever Rolling Stream.' If the publishers like it,
this will mean that I'll have had two titles out of Isaac Watts'
paraphrase of the 90th psalm.[86]

As ever,
Hugh

From Jane Rule
Galiano, British Columbia

22 February 1980

Dear Marian:
I don't seem to know when you're going to Australia or for how
long. Hope this gets there before you leave, but never mind, if
not.

Life here has been a bit surreal the last couple of weeks, mostly
because of trying to help friends get themselves unsorted out

85 Rudy and Tom Jordache appear in Shaw's novel *Rich Man, Poor Man* (New
York: Delacorte Press, 1970).
86 Isaac Watts (1674–1748), English doctor of divinity and composer of almost
five hundred hymns. MacLennan's seventh and last novel was published as
Voices in Time (Toronto: Macmillan, 1980).

without the expense of law suits. Father says, 'A good way to lose two friends.' Probably. I learn what I've always known: I don't want to be a lawyer or a marriage counsellor. I confront something more personal, a terrible untoughness in me that gets hurt by other people's pain, even frightened. I know I live in a never-never land of gentleness, but it's the only way I could.

In the middle of all this, Kate Millett arrived full of sweetness I've never seen, liveliness I've had only glimpses of in the last years, enjoying the island, reading *Latakia* and wanting to help Audrey get a New York agent, courting Hoppy, sleeping well, eating well, taking the gift of the place with joy and ease, saying to me, 'You're the big sister I invented, and I did a good job.'[87] She brought us *Basement,* which I had vowed not to read.[88] I have just finished it, and I don't finally understand why it needed to be done, what ghosts had to be laid. Oh I can guess some, and, if it doesn't work on any other level but for exorcising that ghost for her, I can be glad of it. And it's as if it had somehow deeply set her free of the anger, anguish. She's now writing about Iran, tales of larking, erotic sculpture after years of nothing but victims in cages.[89] And she also brought us *Elegy for Sita,* privately printed, laying another ghost.[90] She talks of turning her farm into an artists' colony for women, of tree farming, of turning her Bowery building into a gallery and printing press, not all practical dreams but so much better than where she's been before, trying to figure out who she is by reading *Time.*

87 Kate Millett (1934–), American feminist author and artist, best known for her 1970 book *Sexual Politics*; Audrey Thomas, *Latakia* (Vancouver: Talonbooks, 1979); Hoppy, nickname for the painter Elisabeth Hopkins (1894–1991).

88 Kate Millett, *The Basement: Meditations on Human Sacrifice* (New York: Simon and Schuster, 1979).

89 The book appeared as *Going to Iran* (New York: Coward, McCann and Geoghegan, 1982).

90 *Elegy for Sita* (New York: Targ Editions, 1979).

I've been alone now for four days, reading the CBC manuscripts for the short fiction contest, reviewing the new biography of Natalie Barney, who like all those other rich, crazy ladies in Paris aren't politically acceptable just now, pondering how to deal with that for *The Body Politic*.[91] Dreaming a bit, oh so shyly, into a new book/several books, not at all ready for committing myself to anything.

Thank you for writing about the problems of the Writers' Union. You and I seem very much in the same place, a bit bewildered by the anger, mistrustful of its political translation. Adele [Wiseman], as you know, is someone I don't deal with, a chemical hostility neither of us can do much about, but I'd still try to listen to something if I could hear it. Well, we'll see how it goes in May. Hoppy's show opens the 8th of May. I'll get into Toronto the night of the 5th. Once the Union meetings are over, I'll meet Helen at the Toronto airport and fly on to Montreal to spend a week with Mary[92] and Marie Claire – I hope. Marie Claire has just heard her latest book comes out in France in May; so she may have to go there. But we'll visit Mary in any case. Then home for the summer to use this pool I moon over at any sunny moment.

I'll be doing city things for the next couple of weeks in a way I haven't since we left, going to the Literary Store Front reopening, Alice Munro's reception, etc. Then finally I get to come home.

We had a good, funny visit in the south, earth quakes and family reunions and shoe sales. We even went swimming and to the symphony in the opera house where I heard/saw Flagstad right after the war when the veterans were threatening to throw bombs because of her quisling husband.[93] My brother, whom we

---

91 George Wickes, *The Amazon of Letters: The Life and Loves of Natalie Barney* (New York: Putnam, 1977). The *Body Politic* was a Gay liberation journal, published in Toronto, 1971–87.

92 Mary Meigs (1917–2002), writer and painter, author of *Lily Bricoe: A Self-Portrait* (1981) and long-time companion of Marie-Claire Blais.

93 Kirsten Flagstad (1895–1962), internationally acclaimed Norwegian soprano.

sent off in splendour, is now in Saudi Arabia playing solitaire and earning lots of money. Because of an old great aunt (the very last one) who got drunk at the banquet for Art, I want to write a story about hearing aids. Hers sent out distress signals as if she were lost in a snow drift, which perhaps she was. But that stuff takes a long time to filter down to where I can cope.

Be well. Hugs to the kids.

Love,
Jane

To Margaret Atwood
Adelaide, Australia

16 March 1980

Dear Peggy –
It's 4 a.m. in Adelaide – the light fading up over the palm trees. I fell asleep about 7 p.m. instead of going to a cocktail party. Very good for the health!

I've had a marvellous time for writers' week. The weather is fall & the landscape like Cyprus, so I feel superbly at home. My darned sprained ankle has kept me from roving – things don't heal very fast anymore – & that is just as well.

The speech & readings have gone off very well. I really like the women here – not the bleached blondes from England, but the Committee women. The nicest thing for me at the Festival was lunch with Christina Stead.[94] No fool that woman & a privilege to meet. I read *Bear* & they loved it. I find it flossily romantic now but never mind.

94 Christina Stead (1902–83), Australian novelist, whose works include *The Man Who Loved Children* (1940), *For Love Alone* (1945), and *Cotter's England* (1967).

Well, I'm off to do a university tour. I'm afraid I don't like our woman in Sydney AT ALL.

You were splendid with Piercy[95] – you are gracious & firm at the same time, an accomplishment.

I suppose you are in England now – what a running-around year. I don't envy you. I'm a bit homesick, for about the first time in my life.

Well – I can sleep again – love to Graeme & Jess & to you.

Marian

From George Woodcock[96]
Vancouver, B.C.

3 July 1980

Dear Marian,
I felt I really had to write to you. I've just read all your six novels in about ten days, and it really was an extraordinary experience – a great consistency and also a great stylistic development, so that it seems to me in *Bear* and *The Glassy Sea* you're writing the best, most crystalline prose in Canadian fiction. You'll see later, in detail, what I think of the individual books, since I've done an essay on them for one of David Helwig's collections of criticism, but I felt I must send you a fairly immediate note of appreciation and greeting.[97]

---

95 Possibly Marge Piercy (1936–), American poet, novelist, and essayist, best known for her novel *Woman on the Edge of Time* (1976). We have been unable to trace this reference.

96 See note 14, p. 157.

97 David Helwig, ed., *The Human Elements: Second Series* (Ottawa: Oberon Press, 1981). Woodcock's essay was entitled 'Casting Down Their Golden Crowns: The Novels of Marian Engel,' 10–37.

How are you? And do you ever come this way?

And, incidentally, 'Casting down their golden crowns around the glassy sea' always thrilled me also as a child, and I'm still convinced it's one of the great lines of English poetry.[98]

Ever,
George Woodcock

To Robert Weaver
[CBC, Toronto]

70 Marchmount Rd
Toronto, Ontario

2 November [1980]

Dear Bob,

I've been trying to do you a fresh story, but what with finishing the novel, and being writer-in-res. and finishing Hurtig's Island book, there isn't much hope.[99] The one I'm working on is a mess.

Meanwhile, here's a story I wrote for a book Anna Porter was getting together, and discarded. It was to be a Canadian ghost story and I read a lot of M.R. James and wrote this.[100]

---

98 The hymn, from which Engel took the title of her novel, is 'Holy, Holy, Holy,' with words by Reginald Heber (1783–1826). The second verse reads:
   Holy, holy, holy! Angels adore Thee,
   Casting down their golden crowns around the glassy sea;
   Cherubim and seraphim falling down before Thee,
   Which wert and art and evermore shall be.
99 The novel referred to is *Lunatic Villas* (Toronto: McClelland and Stewart, 1981). Engel was writer-in-residence at the University of Toronto, 1980–1. The Hurtig book is *The Islands of Canada* (Edmonton: Hurtig, 1981).
100 M.R. James (1862–1936), English author of tales of the supernatural, including *A Warning to the Curious and Other Ghost Stories* (1925).

After she decided not to do the book, I sent it to two women's magazines, but it wasn't their meat. I got it out and re-read it and thought that though it's a tiny bit over your length, you might like it for radio. I don't think it's an absolutely wonderful ghost story, but it's a good story about the ghostly side of lonely people picking up strangers. I'm a bit pleased that it's rather like the real Newfoundland I found, and I set it in an imaginary Newfoundland.[101]

I'm a bit confused these days because I seem to have picked out two or three subjects lately that Atwood is also working on and as she's much cleverer than me – though I think I have my own solidity – I'm going to have to cast around for the sort of things she doesn't do. There ARE coincidences of environment, and we never choose the same methods, but it's a bit like having someone walking over your grave a bit too soon.

John Rich died last week; his pallbearers were his wolf-hounds. I wonder if anyone will write about that?

I seem to be getting on okay with the Great Disease and am much comforted by a medical friend in California who phones every once in a while to tell me I'm being well handled. Both the children are happy in their schools this year and though I feel harassed at the university, I'm rubbing up against some excellent minds, which is good for me. I hope you're having good internal weather also.

I won't mind if you don't want this, I suppose, but it might amuse you. It could probably be cut a little if it's too long.

Sincere good wishes,
Marian

101 This was probably the story (apparently unpublished) called 'The Red Haired Man.' See Marian Engel Archive, McMaster University, box 21, files 20 and 21.

5

A Woman among Friends, 1981–1985

Engel's travels abroad, her terms as writer-in-residence, her literary activism, and her writing generated many friendships; as she
remarked to Margaret Laurence, 30 March 1984, 'friends old &
new' wrote with care and concern about her health and well-
being. This final chapter includes a sampling of letters that arrived during the early 1980s as Engel battled with cancer. Judith
Rodriguez (26 March 1982) and Heidi von Born (6 October
1982), for example, were writers befriended on travels to Australia and Sweden respectively.[1] Closer to home, Jack McClelland,
Claire Mowat, Alice Munro, and Helen Weinzweig, among others,
sent letters,[2] while Margaret Atwood, Doris Anderson, and other
friends helped with errands. Setting aside an earlier falling out,
Margaret Laurence wrote devotedly to her friend throughout the
early 1980s, as did Timothy Findley.

Engel was grateful for the attentions of her friends and family,
'and loving, too, though in an undemonstrative way,' she wrote to
Findley (11 September 1984). Influenced by her father's advice to
avoid being 'beholden' to people, she did not find expressions of
gratitude easy, she explained to her friend. Amidst fevers, strange
appetites, and other symptoms of her disease, however, came a
sense of calm and quiet acceptance. The author put a brave and
often good-humoured face on her deteriorating physical condi-

tion. 'I'm in fantastic shape except of course for being seriously ill,' she quipped to Findley. 'I've been happy as a lark and busy and progressive' (11 September 1984), although, she noted to Atwood, 'things don't heal very fast anymore' (16 March 1980) and she tired easily.

The fatigue Engel experienced in the 1980s was not on account of her illness alone. She was also profoundly tired of always 'nickeling and diming' it, as she put it to Jack McClelland (8 March 1982). 'Artistic successes are all very well, but the hungry little Engels can't eat them,' the Governor General's Award–winning novelist told her publisher (8 March 1982). *Bear* may have been a success, but the fact remained that life as a writer and single mother still meant 'doing columns at $250 and book reviews at $75' (8 March 1982), not to mention being asked to write without pay, as in the case of a request for an article about her students days at McGill (16 June 1983).[3] For a year, between 1981 and 1982, Engel wrote a series of thoughtful and provocative columns for the *Toronto Star*, an experience she found draining and demanding. She was 'exhausted and disillusioned' (8 March 1982).

Fatigued or not, Engel continued her efforts on behalf of Canadian writers. On 1 April 1982 she took the time to urge then secretary of state Francis Fox to endorse Public Lending Right for authors. 'The original proposal was by way of being my "baby" and I am most anxious that writers achieve some remuneration for the use of their books in libraries ... Writers' incomes, never great, are sliding down ... I worry, now that we have so many good writers, about how they are going to survive in these difficult times' (1 April 1982). Engel was especially concerned about single women, she told Fox, 'particularly about those who are getting older. The Council can't support them all. It does a fine job, but the numbers are too great.'

The number of Canadian writers gaining readership both at home and abroad had indeed increased steadily throughout the 1970s, and while financial uncertainty remained a reality for many, the future of Canadian literature looked far more secure at the outset of the 1980s than it had twenty years earlier, when Engel entered the literary arena. The 1980s coincided with a period of internationalization of Canadian literature and culture in two senses: Canadian literature was becoming better known on the international scene; as well, Canadian culture was beginning to reflect more clearly the international provenance of many of the country's citizens. By the 1980s, names such as Margaret Atwood, Margaret Laurence, and Alice Munro were familiar to readers abroad. Indeed, Canadian literature was one of the main vehicles by which readers around the world were coming to conceive of Canada. Even as these writers entered the canon, new names were emerging on the literary landscape. Canada's multiculturalism policy was one of the major influences on cultural and creative developments during the last two decades of the century.[4] Changes, long in coming, would eventually see writers such as Dionne Brand, George Elliott Clarke, and Engel's friend and neighbour Austin Clarke win leading literary awards.[5] These developments were in tune with Engel's early recognition of Canada's colonial history, her sensitivity to the challenges of being an outsider, and her commitment to writing about women's experiences.

Engel took up the topic of older women's poverty in a letter to Pauline McGibbon (15 August 1984). Watching the 'Women's Debate,'[6] Engel felt happy that 'AT LAST the facts are being publicly acknowledged': 'public acknowledgement from the major parties of older women's poverty is really something. One has not lived in vain!' Margaret Laurence was of like mind. In an exchange of letters toward the mid-1980s, Laurence praised the courage of Canadian women writers: 'Those of us who have had to earn our living and bring up our kids, virtually by ourselves, with a lot of moral support from friends and colleagues ... Personally, I think that a lot of women writers in this country, whether with children or not, and whether with mates or not, have been HEROIC' (1 April 1984). British women writers, from Virginia

Woolf to Jane Austen through the Brontës, Laurence stated, would have been awed by the strength, courage, and practical sense of Canadian women writers like Engel and herself, 'we who have coped with having reared our children writing our books, earning our livings, and not hiding the manuscripts under the desk blotter when the vicar came to tea' (17 September 1984). Writing in response, Engel observed that Virginia Woolf's writing had been important to her because 'no one was doing anything interesting at the time with traditional narrative, and perhaps because my life had been chopped, broken, cut off from its roots I felt good with disconnected writing' (25 April 1984).

Upon learning of her health problems, Engel's Swedish friend Heidi von Born urged her: 'Don't hassle too much with the world! Write and think! You are so good at that' (6 October 1982). In the face of illness, Engel did indeed remain a writer and thinker. She continued to work on stories and a new novel, 'Elizabeth and the Golden City.' This would be a 'slow, wilful one,' she announced to Jack McClelland (15 December 1981). '... I'm from now on just going to plug along doing whatever I damn well please and hoping for the best. I thought if I stopped being arty I'd sell. That didn't work and it left me full of a huge envy for experimenters.' McClelland's reply was astute and encouraging: 'Well that's a good letter but what you forget is the fact that you are a legend in your own whatever ... Whether money is made or not, it is a great lift to all our people and to the whole system to be able to say, yes, there is a new Marian Engel on the list' (22 December 1981). McClelland had already assured Engel that he was ready 'at any point' to 'fill a gap financially' with 'no questions, no hassle, no delay' (6 November 1979).

Writing and thinking went hand in hand for Engel, and letters from the early 1980s reveal that she was thinking a great deal about writing – writing, in general, and her own writing, in particular. 'Why do we write novels and who writes what I want to write and how is it done and am I doing it right?' she mused in a letter to Timothy Findley (3 December 1983). In the same letter, Engel rejected a comment by reviewer Sam Solecki that she was a 'one-note writer.'[7] '... I am a chronicler of longing and discontent,' she reflected to Findley, 'which I suppose, in his [Solecki's] books, women should never be. Funny, male readers can't see beyond the gender into the material ... Men don't want to see the texture of women's lives, when there's so much else to see; but they'll have to, some day.'

She was 'rather glorying in all this time to think,' Engel observed to Laurence on 25 April 1984. A more withdrawn life had some advantages: 'dozing, reading, writing a little, thinking a lot, suits me to a T' (3 December 1983). Engel's thoughtful self emerged as strongly as ever whenever the subject of religion arose in the correspondence. 'Protestant theology interests me a lot,' she remarked in a letter to Sara Stambaugh,[8] 'because I was soaked in it in my youth; but it turns me off now because it's like games in the school yard: it's all about who's in and who's out and there is really no way of changing one's status in spite of what salvationism is preached on tv. Us illegitimates are out by birth and that's that, and it's no fun to be born damned' (26 October 1983).

Engel returned to the theme of insiders and outsiders in a letter to Margaret Laurence on 16 May 1984: 'I don't know what to think of theology so haven't read your religious magazine. Every religion seems to have a heaven that's a bit like Forest Hill, big signs, "No one else allowed." If they won't be democratic about it I think I'll just go down to Friedbergs and buy myself a coin for Charon so I can go to the picnic in the Elysian fields. It will save me punching John Knox in the nose and getting sent to hell.' Thanking Laurence for yet another delivery of flowers (5 May 1984), Engel was feisty on the subject of a book another friend had sent: 'E. Kubler-Ross's new book about death, which is about being kind to cancer patients and full of photos. I got so mad I decided that the only return present was a stone angel with FUCK OFF engraved on it. One doesn't NEED pictures of people getting thinner and thinner and being grateful to their spirit-guides: one needs flowers and books and music and friends: a scented and satisfactory house.'

Family, friends, books, music, and flowers – these are the things Engel found meaningful as her disease progressed during the early 1980s. Piano lessons and psychological counselling were also helpful. A trip to Paris with her children at Christmas 1984 was a long-time wish fulfilled, even though this time she visited the city in a wheelchair. Engel also derived great pleasure from her garden; she was transforming her backyard with the help of money left to her by her mother, Mary Passmore, who died 24 May 1982. Tulips, daffodils, iris, colchicums, poppies, lilacs, coneflower, clematis, and if possible 'an old-fashioned, dense pink climbing rose,' she instructed the gardeners, 'or maybe two' (29 March 1983).

Marian Engel died 16 February 1985. A year later, in her memory and honour, Timothy Findley and a large group of Engel's writer friends created the Marian Engel Memorial Garden, located on the grounds of the Toronto Reference Library, the central branch of the Toronto Public Library system, on whose board Engel had served and whose holdings include autographed copies of all her published works. Also in 1986, the Marian Engel Award was launched. Administered by the Writers' Development Trust, this is an annual award presented to a Canadian woman writer at mid-career for her achievements in fiction. The first recipient was Alice Munro. Her reminiscence of Marian Engel captures the novelist's unique contribution, particularly in her depiction of women's lives:

It was as if she had caught something – our tone, our female bravado, subversive wit, desperate flashes of honesty, and she had gone right through to the spirit beneath that ... You have to remember how shunned, despised, misused, this material was at the time ... most of us thought there was no way to deal with it except to turn it into the layer-cake fiction of the women's magazines, or hype it up to the manic level of the humour of the harried housewives who write newspaper columns ... Marian Engel's bravery in tackling this, her skill in pulling it off, seemed to me quite revolutionary. She gave me the feeling that I hadn't quite understood what was possible.[9]

Engel would have wanted no higher praise.

Notes

1 Judith Rodriguez (1936–), Australian poet and translator, whose *Witch Heart Poems* appeared in 1982; Heidi von Born (1936–), Swedish novelist and translator of *Bear* into Swedish.

2 Claire Mowat (1933–), Canadian artist and writer, author of *The Outport People* (1983), *Pomp and Circumstance* (1989), *The Girl from Away* (1992), and *The French Isles* (1994); Helen Weinzweig (1915–), Canadian novelist and short-story writer whose works include *Passing Ceremony* (1973), *Basic Black with Pearls* (1980), and *A View from the Roof* (1989).

3 See the draft of Engel's tart reply, 16 June 1983. The professional Engel prevailed, however, and she substituted a more restrained reply recommending that the organizers contact Vera Frenkel for the cause.

4 Along with feminism, postmodernism, and postcolonialism.

5 Dionne Brand (1953–), Governor General's Award for poetry in 1997 for *Land to Light On* (Toronto: McClelland and Stewart, 1997); George Elliott Clarke (1960–), Governor General's Award for poetry in 2001 for *Execution Poems* (Wolfville, Nova Scotia: Gaspereau Press, 2001); Austin Clarke (1934–), Giller Prize in 2002 for *The Polished Hoe* (Toronto: Thomas Allen, 2002).

6 Election year 1984 saw the first – and thus far only – televised debate among the three major federal parties specifically on women's issues. The bilingual debate, organized by the National Action Committee

on the Status of Women, was held on 15 August 1984 and televised nationally.

7 Sam Solecki (1946–), Canadian editor, writer, and critic.

8 Sara Stambaugh (1936–2002), Canadian author and academic. Stambaugh's study of Isak Dinesen, *The Witch and the Goddess in the Stories of Isak Dinesen*, was published in 1988.

9 Alice Munro, 'An Appreciation,' *Room of One's Own* 9.2 (June 1984): 33.

To Sara Stambaugh
[Edmonton, Alberta]

70 Marchmount Rd
Toronto

12 May 1981

Dear Sara,

Glorious to have your letter yesterday; and I'm glad there's time and energy to answer tonight.

I cleared out my office at the U today and have only, now, to go and see the President, one Dr Ham, and make a little speech of thanks-and-utility. Well, tomorrow I'm taking Doris the staff out for lunch if I remember to make the reservation. Even if I forget. She's one of the poor-in-spirit if I ever saw one, and a distant cousin as well, but we'll do ourselves well anyway.

Pleasant lunch today to celebrate end of term at the College. Very different setup from U of A but this college is a good one and several people will remain friends.

Speaking of your U, I saw Rudy [Wiebe] and Aritha [van Herk] at the Writer's Union meeting: both hale and well. There wasn't much time to talk as I missed one day because of Will's school meeting; then got in a fight with Reshard over room reservations, which consumed most of my energy – he's been such a friend but I don't want him bunking with me at a conference, esp since Hilda's his wife.[1] He took my room KNOWING I wouldn't go for the arrangement – so he got one to himself and I had to share; trying not to snore kept me awake all night.

Re: hidden meanings, there weren't any in *Bear*. It was meant to be all surface but capable of being spied-behind; and *Glassy Sea* is confused, though Pelagia the harlot-saint was behind it. *Lunatic Villas* just came out that way; it was written in bits and from different points of view because it had to be; all-Harriet was too boring and not true to that book. The structure was more *Vile Bodies* than anything else.[2]

I've just decided the new one will be called *Elizabeth and the Golden City* but I've only got 2 pages done & anything can happen – and it will be trad[itional] I suppose but with postmodernist touches if I can remember what they are; I've already got 4 characters worked out but goodness knows what will happen and I'd rather play the piano.

Margaret [Laurence] is writing again!

Well, shall I read *Fat is a Feminist Issue* in the bath?[3] I'm dying to shed weight but what with fevers and strange appetites will have to consult Dr Scott first. I'm very interested in men at the moment and there seem to be some around at last. I went and had my hair chopped and permed and look a bit ridiculous.

---

1 Reshard Gool (1931–89), Canadian academic and author of novels exploring South African and Canadian politics, including the trilogy *The Nemesis Casket* (1979), published under the pseudonym Ved Devajee; Hilda Woolnough (1934–), Canadian artist.

2 *Vile Bodies*, a novel by English author Evelyn Waugh (London: Chapman and Hall, 1930).

3 Susie Orbach, *Fat Is a Feminist Issue: The Anti-Diet Guide to Permanent Weight Loss* (New York: Paddington Press, 1978).

Will's well and beautiful; Char's well and thinking of doing some modelling, though the braces get in the way. Paully is in town to do a performance – her own text – for the Theatre Festival and it was super to have her over for tea this afternoon.[4] She's happy and really writing well.

My typing has changed because of the piano finger-exercises and I'm not quite used to myself yet – the weak 4th and 5th fingers are much stronger so I zip along faster than I think most of the time.

No great ideas at the moment. My eyes are very tired these days – mostly I'm tired in fact; but think of what I did this year!

Schumann is a neat guy to play.[5] I'm spending a fortune on music! But I'm much better than I was before, I understand a bit about it and though bifocals are a struggle, I'm enjoying myself enormously. Charlotte says it's awful!

Oh, Mother's had a crisis and is in hospital but is apparently okay. Helen and I fought over who was going up; then the trains crashed and the line was blocked, the planes were full and Ma turned out to be more or less okay. I guess she's still in hospital but one can't get through the switchboard there ... we've tried again and again, the operator and I ... so I'm waiting till she gets home. Touch of heart and pneumonia and the neighbours are there every day.

Wed a.m.: letter from my Swedish translator re: special terms in *Bear* ... fun to answer.

Will do it now. Much love from all including Paully,

Marian

4 Paully Jardine, Canadian writer, producer, and actor.
5 Robert Schumann (1810–56), Romantic composer.

From Alice Munro[6]
Clinton, Ontario

13 May 1981

Dear Marion,[7]
It's snowing in May – pretty mushy-looking stuff at first but now it looks like business and the ground is white. One can have a proper sense of outrage. I'm just sorry it's Sunday and I can't go to the Post Office where this would set up a whole cantata of weather-talk with a very satisfactory theme of well-you-never-know, you-sure-don't, you-sure-can't-trust-it, maybe-won't-get-summer-at-all. I like that kind of talk, it makes me feel secure, you know nobody's going to come at you with some disquieting piece of wit and insight. But if it was all I had I'd be climbing the walls, I must remind myself.

Margaret L., on the telephone, says you're feeling better. That was a couple of weeks ago. I thought I'd get down to Toronto & ring you up – I still haven't heard about that party – and I did get down but spent all non-business time going to Oakville to see my ex-mother-in-law in her nursing-home. My ex-mother-in-law in her 80's is tolerant, cheerful, even *funny*. So – I thought I'd write you & ask – do you feel like visitors?

I guess you know about the *Room Of One's Own* deal so I'm not spoiling any surprise by telling you what a lovely time I had re-reading you.[8] I so much wanted to write something about the stories but J. Rule had already done something. I think there's a slant to those stories that's unique – they make me feel *loose*, somehow. I can't write anything approaching decent Lit. Crit. so I

---

6 See note 100, p. 146.
7 Engel's name is misspelled here.
8 The special issue of the periodical (volume 9, number 2), dedicated to Engel, appeared in June 1984.

wrote something about the excitement I felt when I first read what was then *No Clouds of Glory*. That was in the bookstore in Victoria. I read it at the desk, occasionally pausing to snarl at a customer. And the quality was still there – what I wanted was still there – this spring. And I was just as grateful as a writer and woman.

Have you heard from Tom & Judith?[9] Sibila wrote at Christmas a marvelous funny letter. She is a witty wonderful girl though probably can be as exasperating a daughter as any of them. She taught me how to make a Pavlova which has become a big show-off thing ever since.

My own daughter has just decided not to marry a man she doesn't (quite) love. She's right. I wouldn't have been that smart, or honourable. Oh, well. We all did what we did and here we all are and some things we didn't do too badly – and LOVE,

Alice

From Claire Mowat
Port Hope, Ontario

6 December 1981

Dear Marian,
I've been meaning to write to you for a long time but a couple of things by, and about, you that I read this week got me in the same room as my typewriter. I've had a horrible cold all week which means I languish in my room and actually get a chance to read newspapers and magazines which accumulate in huge piles all

9 Tom Shapcott, Australian novelist, and Judith Rodriguez, Australian poet. Engel met them during her visit to the Adelaide Festival in 1980. Sibila is Judith's daughter. Pavlova, an Australian dessert named after Russian ballerina Anna Pavlova (1881–1931).

over this house. They finally get thrown out by Farley in one of his whirlwind tidy-up sprees and mostly before I've read them. So while I was dallying over the favourite Christmas gifts of Pauline McGibbon and Maureen McTeer and you, I discovered that you and I share the same nostalgic favourite gift – a miniature brass-bound steamer trunk with fake stickers from faraway hotels. And I still have mine. It's sitting right here under my desk and it's full of my old high-school magazines, old photographs, pennants, and my Royal Life Saving Society swimming medals. It originally came full of doll's clothes that my grandmother had sewn herself. I treasure the thing. It got lost for a few years but it turned up 4 years ago when my mother moved out of her Bloor Street apartment. I had abandoned it in the course of my many moves, but she had kept it.

Then to-day I read that loneliness always attacks at twilight, and that rang another bell.[10] It sure does. About 3 winters ago Farley went off to our place in Cape Breton – to write – and I was effectively alone here for close to 3 months. And the one thing I remember was that dismal end-of-the-day loneliness. I was fine all day long, busy as a bee with writing and housework and a pile of other things. And I was fine late at night with a good book or the odd TV show. But around five when it was time to start getting my supper together – was just awful. People around here knew Farley was away and a number of them said 'Well, we'll have to have you over sometime for a meal.' But none of them did. They waited till Farley got back and then asked us *both* over. That winter I really did understand what it was like to be widowed or separated. I did ultimately find a friend – a gal up the street whose husband (a U. of T. professor) lectured 3 nights a week and who was left alone with two kids under the age of two. She got them to bed and then I'd bring over some food and she'd find some food and the two of us would quell the dinner-hour blues. I

10 The title of a *Toronto Star* column by Engel, 5 December 1981.

liked her a lot, but alas she's moved away now. Back to Toronto. This place is just a little too far for commuting.

I read *Lunatic Villas* last summer and enjoyed it. It reminded me of Harold Horwood's oddly extended family.[11] I was intrigued by the baby you named Winifred. I have more than a passing interest in the name since it is the name of my mother. She is 80 and her full name is Winifred Jessica. I note that Jessica (or Jesse, Jess, Jessie) is enjoying a very popular revival these days among newborn daughters. Maybe you'll have started a revival of the name Winifred. Watch the birth notices in the *Globe and Mail* and find out. It comes from Gwynfrydd, or some such, who was a Welsh saint about 1300 years ago.

And speaking of Gwynfrydds, have you heard anything of Gwen MacEwan? Do you by chance have her address. She phoned here one day last spring but there were a lot of distractions here at the time and I wanted to get back to her in a calmer moment. I prefer to write to people actually. I have trouble phoning people since I'm always sure I'm interrupting something that's vitally important. I tend to sound terse and unsympathetic and in a hurry.

What did you do last summer? Did you make it to the Magdalens or Miquelon?[12] We spent a quiet, and rather dull, summer at our place in Cape Breton. I don't know what I'll do next summer. I'm contemplating a summer course at O.C.A. [Ontario College of Art]. Well, maybe. Like you, I don't like the heat. But I don't want to spend four straight months of talking to no one but my husband.

That kind of isolation doesn't seem to bother Farley. One of the things I'm observing these days is the way men and women age. They do it differently. Men get grumpy and withdrawn. They cut down on their number of friends and don't make any new ones. Women mellow. They get sweeter, more philosophical, less com-

11 Harold Horwood (1923–), Canadian writer, editor, and politician.
12 Islands in the Gulf of St Lawrence and off the southern coast of Newfound-land respectively.

petitive. They keep their old friends and make new ones besides. I'm generalizing, I know, but I'm sure I'm right in essence.

I haven't seen your Island book yet. Gotta get one. Part of the trouble is that I've only been to Toronto once this Fall and that was a frantic day without anytime to browse in the bookstores. We have been to Ottawa twice.

Farley got an O.C. [Order of Canada] (which you probably knew) and it was nice that he got it from a GG who is a longtime personal friend.[13]

F. is fine and still ploughing through a mountain of research about the sea mammals of eastern Canada of four hundred years ago. He's alternately depressed by what we've done to eliminate them; and then boiling mad at Ronald Reagan and the whole central-American situation.[14] Either way he's not the best of company. But then writers are that way. I should know. I hope you are keeping well Marian. Your photo at the top of the *Star* column looks absolutely healthy and downright glamorous.[15] One of these days I have high hopes I'll have a chance to have lunch with you or something. I hope life at the Mowats will be less complicated after Christmas passes. How I hate Christmas. So I won't wish you a merry one. Just a fond wish that you, too, can somehow get through it.

Love from Farley
as well as from me,
Claire

13 Edward Schreyer, governor general, 1979–84.
14 Ronald Reagan, president of the United States, 1981–9.
15 Engel's 'Being Here' column for the *Toronto Star* appeared from 1981 to 1982.

To Jack McClelland
McClelland and Stewart Limited
Toronto, Ontario

70 Marchmount Rd
Toronto

15 December [1981]

Dear Jack,
So you're mad. So I am, but not very. I just like to mix in, it cuts the isolation.

I guess I remind you of all those ministers' wives your father used to publish. Sales in midstream seem to me a bit off, but I don't dispute your right to do whatever you want with your own company. You asked for my opinion, though, and you got it.

[What] I think about my own career is that because I don't make much money for either you or me, I'm from now on just going to plug along doing whatever I damn well please and hoping for the best. I thought if I stopped being arty I'd sell. That didn't work and it left me full of a huge envy for experimenters. So the thing I'm doing is going to be a slow, wilful one, and the *Star* can pick up the tab for our lives.

Your very generous advance on *Lunatic Villas* was a lifesaver and I now understand why Canadians can't have them unless they're the Top Ten. No way of earning them back.

I've gone to Ginger Barber in the U.S.A. as an agent. She's a woman I can talk to and I think we'll talk about letting you have foreign rights on the next one if you want the next one. Lorene beats going the Zurich-London-New York route by a long shot. But that's a long way away.

Carry on hating, it's good for the circulation.[16]

16 Engel's copy of this letter is unsigned.

From Jack McClelland
McClelland and Stewart Limited
Toronto, Ontario

22 December 1981

Dear Marian:
Well that's a good letter but what you forget is the fact that you are
a legend in your own whatever and as such you must keep producing. If you don't, the system breaks down. *The Star* doesn't answer
the requirement. So it doesn't make money for you or for me,
screw it. We live in the system. Whether money is made or not, it is
a great lift to all our people and to the whole system to be able to
say, yes there is a new Marian Engel on the list. That is the monkey
you carry. I hope it keeps scratching and I love you dearly.

Cheers,
Jack

To Jack McClelland
[McClelland and Stewart Limited
Toronto, Ontario]

8 March 1982

Dear Jack,
Thanks for your letter about the Toronto Book Award.[17] I liked
getting it: money from all those old pol[itician]s I worked for!
And I think I talked Roy Henderson and Michael Gee into raising
the prize at the party. So everything felt very good.

---

17 The Toronto Book Award for *Lunatic Villas* was presented to Engel in
   February 1982.

About writing another book, well, I guess I will one day. But at the moment, doing columns at $250 and book reviews at $75, I'm exhausted and disillusioned.

I don't know where my career is going; I do know that I've more of a physical future than I thought I had before, and that I want it to be a better time than I've had before. I'm sick of nickeling and diming, in fact.

Thought of applying for a Canada Council Grant: Margaret was keen as mustard to get me one. The fact is, though, we are now cheerfully spending more than $20,000 and it didn't seem right to take it and then work on top of it. So I'm freelancing, using a better agent, and hoping to sell stories more expensively later.

The other thing is reputation: though I seem to be all over the place, I'm not in the right places. Not in the NCL, not in the new *Anthology* collection (my stories are better than most: nobody sees it, damn them) ... still in the nickel and dime league.[18]

So what I'm doing is writing a movie for a guy in Montreal, and then, with that money, sitting down to have a think. I've a good idea for a novel, but I'm not going to write it unless I think it can be a success. Artistic successes are all very well, but the hungry little Engels can't eat them.

What I've got done on the new novel is incredibly bad, but the core idea is good. When I get going on it, it will be good. But it's Be Your Own Canada Council Grant Year, and it's taking me away from committing myself to anything that's not going to be – and go – first class. There'll be a gap, and I hope the hell they miss me when I'm gone.

Meanwhile, I'm getting both my health and my head together. Hope things are going well for you because we need you.

Sincerely,[19]

18 References are to the New Canadian Library editions of Canadian literary classics, established by McClelland and Stewart in 1958, and *The Anthology Anthology: A Selection from Thirty Years of CBC Radio's 'Anthology,'* edited by Robert Weaver (Toronto: Macmillan of Canada, 1984).
19 Engel's copy of the letter is unsigned.

From Judith Rodriguez
Victoria, Australia

26 March 1982

Dear Marian,
Extra to the little card we sent off: now back in Melbourne, I have
written the dedicatory poem to – my next book? or the next but
one? I don't know, haven't gone out and prospected with my
sheaf of MS. But the poem, which is written to Tom, has you in it;
and I couldn't wait till it gets into print or even till I see you. It is
the first in a whole lot of poems about lakes; and of course
Toronto Island was one of the wonderful places. Come to think of
it, you must have written about it in your island-book.

Dedication to Tom[20]

Because of the impossibility
that I should know your years, and you mine,
because we could not know
these children together
nor the first garden,

on Toronto Island spring comes
and the squatters in beach cottages
dance in the lake-dawns
and civic favour,[21]
and Marian dances,

20 A slightly revised version of this poem appeared as 'Lake Season' in Rod-
   riguez's *The House by Water: New and Selected Poems* (St Lucia: University of
   Queensland Press, 1988), 2. She had travelled across Canada with Tom
   Shapcott, winner of the Canada-Australia Prize, in 1980.
21 Engel had told Rodriguez about the struggle of the residents of Toronto
   Island to resist eviction.

by Lake Balaton[22]
winter reed-cutting is over,
under the mountain trees glow,
the boar rushes out,
the new antlers jostle –

these to your valley
of hanging gardens
assailed by the wrecker with new plans
I bring, a vision of lakes,
a second fruiting.

I'm sorry I haven't got in our swim at Maslins';[23] but it is just a matter of trying to regard the Antarctic Ocean as a lake! I shall succeed, after all I have already included poems about swimming at Pacific beaches. Tom, by the way, swims at Maslins' every few days; he is Resident Writer at Adelaide University.

The nicest person we met at this year's festival was Elaine Feinstein, whose new book *Survivor* you may know or have heard of.[24] I knew her translations of Marina Tsvetayeva's poems years ago,[25] and her own poems are terrific too. Anyway, we've just been showing her round Melbourne, Tom was across to have his birthday with us rather than alone, and we spent the whole weekend dashing about in pursuit of kangaroos, wombats, etc., an authentic Japanese meal, and the scientific bigheads her husband moves amongst, being an immunologist, from Cambridge.

Well, dear Marian, no *news*. Just chatter. How's your springtime coming along – and your big daughter – and writing? How are

---

22 A lake in Hungary. Tom Shapcott's next novel, *White Stag of Exile* (London: A. Lane, 1984), was to be about a Hungarian art gallery director.
23 A beach just south of Adelaide.
24 Elaine Feinstein (1930–), English poet, novelist, critic, and translator. Her biography of the poet Ted Hughes was published in 2001. The reference here is to *The Survivors* (London: Hutchinson, 1982).
25 Marina Tsvetayeva (1892–1941), Russian-Jewish poet.

you feeling? I had an operation in October and Tom has been pampering me in all of four cities one after another – now, back at work and with a bit of writing done, I begin to feel human – back with it – amazing what a long process it is.

Love,
Judith

To Hon. Francis Fox, Secretary of State[26]
Ottawa, Ontario

70 Marchmount Rd
Toronto

1 April 1982

Dear Mr Fox,
   RE: Canada Council Proposal, Payment for Public Use
I understand that this proposal is now before you, and I trust it has fallen into good hands. As Secretary of State you have proven yourself more understanding of the arts than others.

The original proposal was by way of being my 'baby' and I am most anxious that writers achieve some remuneration for the use of their books in libraries, particularly now, when we seem to be sliding into the Post-Gutenberg era, or just victims of inflation.[27] Writers' incomes, never great, are sliding down.

Few of us went into writing to get rich, which is just as well. The game is a lottery and the rewards have nothing to do with merit.

---

26 Francis Fox (1939–), lawyer and politician; secretary of state, 1980–2.
27 Engel had worked tirelessly, through the Writers' Union of Canada, for the creation of what was eventually to become Public Lending Right.

I worry, now that we have so many good writers, about how they are going to survive in these difficult times. I worry particularly about the single women, particularly about those who are getting older. The Council can't support them all. It does a fine job, but the numbers are too great.

I'm therefore asking that you give this plan your most sympathetic consideration. I'm not sure how it will mesh with the Applebaum-Hébert proposals;[28] but if it goes through it will make a big difference to the quality of writers' lives.

And when you're reading it, please, please think not of Arthur Hailey,[29] but of those of us who hack on doing book reviews for $75 and reading Canada Council manuscripts for $45 of which $6.50 is deducted for tax. We pay our cultural dues!

Sincerely yours,
Marian Engel

From Helen Weinzweig[30]
Toronto, Ontario

2 June 1982

Dear Marian –
Following an act of courage like yours – a public statement of where you stood, stand, with regard to Jews – I have to congratulate you. What comes through loud and clear in your *Daily Star*

---

28 Louis Applebaum and Jacques Hébert co-chaired the Federal Cultural Policy Review Committee, established 28 August 1980, to review cultural policies for Canada. Its report was published in November 1982.
29 Arthur Hailey (1920–), millionaire English-born Canadian popular novelist and movie script writer.
30 See note 2, p. 214.

column following that stupid attempt at humour at the awards dinner – what comes through is honesty.[31] No disclaimers, no mea culpas.

As for mentioning John[32] and me, you made your point: what is merely poor taste to some can be a source of shock and despair to those who have been rendered more 'sensitive' by persecution and prejudice. I don't have to tell you it includes blacks, women, cripples, as well as Jews.

Warm greetings and good wishes,
Helen W.

From Heidi von Born
Stockholm, Sweden

6 October 1982

Dearest Marian,
Some lines. You haven't heard from me for ages, sorry, sorry. I think of you often and so does the Publishing House. We are waiting to hear about your new work ... (*Lunatic Villas* was, unfortunately, considered a little too 'Canadian,' I'm sorry). We are well off now with the stately loan we finally got. We are so well off that this year we earned some money + have been able to move to

31 'Don't Talk to Me about Sensitivity,' *Toronto Star*, 8 May 1982, p. H1. In this article, in her 'Being There' series for the *Star*, Engel discusses the continued existence of anti-Semitism and admits that, despite having married a Jew and raising half-Jewish children, 'I know that anti-semitism lurks in me, because it's part of the culture I grew up with.' She mentions laughing during a sketch about Hitler at a celebration attended by Weinzweig and her husband; the Weinzweigs did not laugh.
32 John Weinzweig (1913–), Canadian composer and Helen's husband.

a posher address – and I have given the house a novel, coming this spring – I'm really hopeful about our house.

Your book [*Bear*] has sold well. Very well indeed. We are 8 millions and your book sold 2,000 copies; everyone is very pleased. Margareta sends her love and wants to know about your projects. She went off to Frankfurt yesterday. I'm glad I'm not going there ... I would like to go every 4th year.

You may know already that I'm coming to lecture in U.S.A. in March in the huge project, Scandinavia Today. The Swedish Institute is interested in sending me to Canada – Aritha mentioned that there were possibilities. So I would like to come in *February* or in *March* around my stay in U.S.A. I'm going to Minnesota, Seattle, and some other places, will know more about it on the 15/10. I have some parts of my books translated into English for my trip – well, I could talk about anything, like Swed. Cultural Policy, Swed. writers' work agency, the Publishing House and so on.

I have written to Aritha who said she could arrange something for me. Perhaps you could contact her. The Swedish Institute wants to send me so there would be no difficulties from their side. I could stay with Aritha in Vancouver and the lectures could be given free ... The system we had in Australia. Could you work on this, Marian?

A wonderful person, Dorothy Jones, gave a very good paper on your *Bear* at the Commonwealth Conference in Gothenburg the other month.[33] We had some copies of *Bear* there; they were all sold. I met Aritha [van Herk] and Matt Cohen there, both really wonderful persons. I sent a little gift for you with Aritha. It's just something to show that I *do* care ...

I wasn't too happy about your health report. Are you better now?? Don't hassle too much with the world! Write and think! You are so good at that.

---

33 Dorothy Jones, Australian academic and critic.

More later, but please answer me about the possibilities for me to come to Canada. I would love any minute. And I have got a huge beautiful order on Canadian Literature – an article for the Swedish Academy paper – deadline in some weeks. I just wrote a *big* one on Aritha and Matt, mentioning and analysing you there too, for a paper called 'Everything about Books' (15,000 copies). So I work with Canada here!

If you pass Longhouse Bookstore say hallo – I ordered a big book parcel. Tell them gently that I'm sleeping beside my mail-box to get my parcel ... I wrote the wrong street number, 162 instead of something like 602, and sent them 5 dollars to buy coffee buns. I hope they got my letter. Could you perhaps check on that – *if you have time*. I'm always in a hurry – my addresses turn out wrong all the time.

But this letter you'll get! All the best, a lot of good thoughts from the Publishing House and hugs and kisses from,

Heidi

To Timothy Findley

70 Marchmount
Toronto

27 October 1982

Dear Tiff,
I was comforted by your phone call today. I didn't like Margaret's letter at all, but I did feel that I'd been spreading gossip by talking to you. Hell, we can talk to each other, can't we? I mean, if Graeme had a cyst on the skull we could talk about that! But I

felt small and mean after I got that letter, and I was meant to feel that way.[34]

I don't know aboutyou [*sic*] but I'minfinitely [*sic*] suggestible (sorry, kids have been using the machine and spacing is off) and my interior voice is very weak. When someone I love tells me that my version of the truth is wrong, I strongly attempt to correct it, usually. This is where the shrink is useful because, although the ability to take on others' personalities is useful in writing novels, it plays hell with real life. I know because I've been checking out my perceptions (and drinking a lot less) [of] what I've been doing this year, and what Margaret has been saying, and her version is the one that's out. But somehow I want still to take on the guilt.

You sounded fine today and I hope you are fine. I've been getting on much better and we've had some family sessions that indicate that although Will is sometimes pretty shifty, he isn't responsible for everything that goes wrong in the family, and that 'goat' role is being removed from him.

If I sounded funny about your proposals of marriage – which Adele [Wiseman], I think, suggested in the first place – it's because I've been working out certain relationships I have with homosexuals, because I got a terrible crush on one of my doctors, who is. And I've decided that it's okay to have lots of gay friends, but only to marry them if they are chinchillas – fat and furry and elderly, and you're not one. So there. There's a bend in my libido somewhere; but what I really need is a straight guy who has the right chinchilla characteristics! A Nigerian with his arm in a sling would do. I haven't REALLY got my cap set for you or expect you to

---

34 Engel, along with Gibson, Atwood, and some other friends, concerned about Margaret Laurence's health, had attempted to persuade her to address her drinking problem. Laurence had been deeply hurt and had responded angrily, resigning from the Writers' Union. The rift between Engel and Laurence was soon healed, as Engel's letter of 12 January 1983 makes clear.

have yours set for me, but I'm rather amused by it: it acts out some stuff for me.

I don't think this is a storm in a teacup; I think there's a big blow coming out of this in the literary world, or maybe a little-big blow, but we've all got to stand firm and say Margaret, don't be an ass, we didn't intend to hurt you.

I've finally got new bookcases, the big one having collapsed when we tried to move it upstairs and I'm going, through the good offices of an athletic librarian-nephew, to get my books in order again. Right now I see Marx, Carol Shields, Joyce Carol Oates, Proust, and the Anglican Missal curling up beside *Writers at Work* and *Flaws in the Glass*,[35] but it doesn't help with 'Hey Ma, do we have anything on the Industrial Revolution.'

I got a cheque from Trans Canada Pipelines today, swelp-me [*sic*].[36] Never believed in unearned income before. I just stare at them and think, 'But I didn't have to write a book review!' Tomorrow I speak to the Simone de Beauvoir Institute in Montreal, however, and I think I'd better climb in the tub and have a think about that.

Hope you and Bill will come for tea some time while you're in town ... one or both or either or whatever: house is in decent shape now and Auntie Mary Ann's cups and saucers are a delight.

Be well, don't hurt yourself, and don't worry.

Marian E.

---

35 *Writers at Work*, a New York periodical containing interviews from the *Paris Review*; Patrick White, *Flaws in the Glass, a Self-Portrait* (London: J. Cape, 1981).
36 Engel was starting to draw income from her mother's estate.

From Dennis Lee
Toronto, Ontario

10 December 1982

Dear Marian,

Now that the *Descant* thing has come and gone, it's a relief to discover that my feet are just as clayish as before, while the marmorealization of my upper regions has not apparently proceeded to a lethal degree.[37]

I did want to let you know how much I enjoyed your piece. It called back that lovely bizarre discovery of working on *Honeyman* together, which I still recall as one of the treats of that period. I want to sit down and read it again soon; haven't done so for a number of years, and it's one of the books from then that I expect still to hold up well.

Hope things proceed as they should. As a mantle of currency settles around your shoulders, remember the poverties of thy youth & remain your good self. (Sounds like serious advice, which is hardly necessary!)

Love,
Dennis

---

37 *Descant*, a literary journal published by the University of Toronto. Issue no. 39 (Winter 1982) was a special issue on Dennis Lee.

To Margaret Laurence

70 Marchmount Rd
Toronto

12 January 1983

Dear Margaret,
The best thing about getting the Order of Canada was the letters
and phone calls it brought me – from you, Hugh MacLennan,
Doris Anderson and my dear Pauline [McGibbon] particularly.

I didn't expect the honour, nor do I feel I deserve it, but I love
it. Good things are good for people. It makes me want to drink my
orange juice!

I saw Edith Fowke the other day,[38] who says you are well. I'm
glad. Last summer I thought both of us were in bad shape but I
probably transferred a lot of my fears about myself to you. I,
however, am just fine; it was the shingles that knocked my blood
count down last year.

I'm blasting away on another book with the usual feeling that
it's dreck. I'm also feeling guiltily disloyal because I'm setting part
of it in Montreal and talking about the colonialism of the setting.
MacLennan would not approve but then he came from the east,
not the west.

Take care. It was lovely to hear from you.

Yours,
Marian

---

38 Edith Fowke (1913–), Canadian folklorist and musicologist.

To Mrs [Lois] Lister, Mrs Carley, Mr Muller[39]

70 Marchmount Rd
Toronto

29 March 1983

Dear Mrs Lister, Mrs Carley, Mr Muller,
I'm sorry I couldn't talk very well to you that last Monday. The
fates were hanging over me. However, they've decided to put me
in Hospital April 3 for 1 or 2 weeks depending on what they
decide to do. The house will be empty except for a visiting cat
sitter until April 8 when various friends will be moving in: so you'll
be able to knock and get what you need. Just say you're the
gardening people.

I'm enclosing a silly map of what's there based on what's coming up. You can't and shouldn't save everything. I'd like to hang
onto as many tulips and daffodils as I can and the iris are just new,
most of them; and the colchicums will probably move. I'd suggest
digging a trench in the front lawn in front of the hedge, where
the grass is bad anyway and has to be re-seeded, slinging them in
and hoping for the best. That way we get the fittest. I don't know
whether the lilac bush is worth saving. I KNOW the poppies won't
move. I'd like to keep the silly coneflower because it's a sensation-
ally silly one, covered with bees all summer. I'll put any plastic
vessels I can find in the basement outside the door for you, too.
The one fence-stake in the back yard should be put in the back
hall, and we ought to keep the eavestroughing out there until we
decide how to replace it. Could you come and talk to me about
planting when I'm back home and out of hospital? It would be a

---

39 Lois Lister, well-known Toronto landscape consultant and leader of Engel's
gardening team. The rest of the team is not further identified.

nice thing to think about while recovering, and your budget is a good one.

Don't put anything in the front flower bed: it's stuffed with tulips and the soil is very poor anyway. I'm trying to think of what the ideal things for the trellis would be, besides the worthy grapevine (but examine it for nasty orange rust, which is really obscene) and the half-dead clematis. I'd favour, I think, an old-fashioned, dense pink climbing rose, or maybe two, the thick fellas you see in old gardens.

While you're in the neighbourhood, go and look at the Italian seeds at Frederick market on Davenport Road just past Ossington, the old IGA store. There are about 10 varieties of chicory and many other goodies, none for me. But they are good seeds – I've got basil and other herbs from them – and you may find them a treat.

I'm off to the bank now to arrange to cover cheques, so I think everything is looked after.

Yours with thanks,
Marian Engel

To Margaret Gillett and Kay Sibbald[40]

70 Marchmount Rd
Toronto

16 June 1983

Dear Margaret Gillett and Kay Sibbald,
Your amazing letter turned up in my files again and this time I'm going to answer it. Before, I was too angry.

40 This draft of the letter was apparently unsent.

I guess some people write more easily and more gracefully than I do, but the thought of writing about 5,000 words of what amounts to autobiography, and doing it well, which means giving a couple of months to the project, and doing it for no fee, is outrageous.[41]

I should have answered you before, though, because I think Vera Frenkel, who was a REAL McGillian, would like to be included.[42] She is a much more distinguished graduate than I am, having been an undergraduate where I was just a grad student of uncertain status, and being higher in the ranks of the art world than I am in the literary. You should contact her at York University Fine Arts dept but she won't be back until the end of August. Anyway, your people won't make their deadlines. They'll sit down with your firm instructions and find it pretty hard to turn out 20 good pages. Though I dunno, maybe they all have secretaries.

McGill was my second university, not my first, and as such not really a formative influence except insofar as I existed there in a continual state of outrage. They kept asking me not to go out with Jews.

Dr Roscoe was wonderful and so was Joyce Hemlow, but other people have better stories to tell, and are more truly McGillites than I am, a mere McMaster guttersnipe hired to guard the gates at RVC.[43] I made some super friends but somehow I'm not terribly grateful to McGill. Not grateful enough to write without a fee. Life is tough enough.

Yours sincerely,

---

41 The book, edited by Gillett and Sibbald, appeared as *A Fair Shake: Autobiographical Essays by McGill Women* (Montreal: Eden Press, 1984).
42 Vera Frenkel (1938–), Canadian artist and video producer, professor emerita of York University.
43 Muriel V. Roscoe (1898–1990) taught botany at McGill for twenty-seven years. She was the second woman in McGill's history to be named a full professor (1945). Joyce Hemlow (1906–2001), biographer of the British eighteenth-century novelist Fanny Burney, taught at McGill from 1948 to 1984. RVC is Royal Victoria College.

To Margaret Gillett and Kay Sibbald

70 Marchmount Rd
Toronto

16 June 1983

Dear Margaret Gillett and Kay Sibbald,
Thank you for your letter of March 16.

I regret that I cannot at this time undertake such a lengthy project as 5,000 words for no fee. Perhaps other contributors write more easily than I do but this would be two months' work.

And McGill was not my Alma Mater. It was the university where in return for guarding the portals of RVC I was allowed to do an MA. I met some splendid people but my basic loyalty is to McMaster, where I was an undergraduate.

You should get in touch with the distinguished artist Vera Frenkel, who was an undergraduate at McGill. She is presently in Europe but will return soon to the Fine Arts dept of York University. McGill WAS a formative influence in her life.

Yours very sincerely,
Marian Engel

To Sara Stambaugh

ᵒᵒᵒᵒᵒᵒᵒᵒᵒᵒ ah good it's printing again; and I dropped it too.

26 October 1983

Dear Sara:
Still in hospital but going home tomorrow ... wheeeeee. I've had a good time playing around with this machine here; there are compensations. I am also thrilled to be walking on two canes. Much easier than crutches and faster and one can use the end of a cane to pull the bathroom door shut!

Char brought me the letter from you the other day and I read it and kind of saw red and made a cross reply which I didn't mail. Then this afternoon I re- read it, having finally decided that the code to your handwriting, which is really a kind of stitching, is that rs and es look the same, so in difficulty try the other. It worked and I gave it a more careful reading.

I guess we'll always disagree. Protestant theology interests me a lot because I was soaked in it in my youth; but it turns me off now because it's like games in the school yard: it's all about who's in and who's out and there is really no way of changing one's status in spite of what salvationism is preached on tv. Us illegitimates are out by birth and that's that, and it's no fun to be born damned. Besides who wants to go to heaven if Grandma P. runs it?[44]

I've been much happier since I decided it was better to put one's early beliefs on the back burner. I'm not Rita of *The Glassy Sea* any more than I'm Rebecca of Sunnybrook Farm.[45]

I'm not happy either, however, with the idea of guidance and

---

44 Grandma Passmore, Engel's paternal grandmother.
45 Kate Douglas Smith Wiggin, *Rebecca of Sunnybrook Farm* (New York: Houghton Mifflin, 1903). There are many subsequent editions.

direction from outside. I mean, who does it if it isn't God and what do you have to have lined up to get it and who shoves the tea leaves around? I'm much happier with the idea that our world is an interior world and that we are made happiest by our choices of affinities: you and Dinesen are beautifully matched,[46] you understand each other in terms of your similarities, which are many, and your differences too. I don't think it's a judgement on any of us that our guidance should come from inside. If you leave it in the outside you have to go from animism through the whole of world religion through the collective unconscious, which probably exists but is amoral (which is why people invent religions, for collective morality) but oh crud, spooks and witches and spells. But hell, I'm just a hopeless rationalist. I like it better that way. I don't have to look over my shoulder as much. Some people are wiser than others, some have more empathy etc, and, label them how you will, bits and pieces of people's personalities fly around and recombine and give richness or meanness to their experience. I don't think it's invalid for people to get a feeling that there's Something out there, Something more. I think it's human; but I'm damned sick of their fighting about their Somethings, their feelings of superiority.

I'm glad Rudy [Wiebe] likes the book. You should send a copy to Peggy [Margaret Atwood]. Publishing's in worse than ever shape, though. Laughable.

Well, sticks Engel has to get out there and practise.

I don't know why this subject makes me miserable. Just the feeling that the spirits have got it in for me because I don't believe in them. Wonder if I should play safe and turn Catholic. Nonsense. Stick it out. The inside world is more fun. Project whatever you want of it, wherever you want, but don't shake things at me

46 Isak Dinesen, pseudonym of Karen Blixen (1885–1962), Danish writer. Stambaugh worked on Dinesen for many years and later published *The Witch and the Goddess in the Stories of Isak Dinesen* (Ann Arbor: UMI Research Press, 1988).

for being a narrow prod.[47] I'm about the broadest prod. there is but you can't catch me with Ouija boards.

Marian

To Timothy Findley

70 Marchmount
Toronto

3 December 1983

Dear Tiff,
Hoped to see you on Tuesday, but my leg is kicking up and I talked to my shrink that aft and decided it was OK to be a convalescent and stay home. Gwen said anyhow the party was standing room only, which would not have been good. I've a little phlebitis and self-indulgence is indicated: LOTS of sleep. I think about novels – the conflict between technique and narrative drive when you want to cover a lot of time, etc., and what I'm doing with the shrink, getting back to that child.

Speaking of children, what on earth led you to call me Miggs? You wanna be my nephew? You may, if you wish ... but Miggs is a name I LONG to leave behind. Are you fond of Tiff? Would you rather be Timothy or something else? Those days as the baby-of-the-family are something I always hope to grow out of; besides, Miggs rhymes with Piggs and belongs to grubby infancy.

I like this withdrawn life; sometimes get restless to go shopping or to the ROM,[48] otherwise, dozing, reading, writing a little,

47 Protestant.
48 Royal Ontario Museum.

thinking a lot, suits me to a T. The groceries get delivered, when the house gets too thick, I'll hire a cleaning woman. Your tapes await a new set of AA batteries but Char will pick some up. Music makes up for a lot.

I dashed around the world so much ... I don't want to right now. Sleep seems the kingdom of the rich.

Why do we write novels and who writes what I want to write and how is it done and am I doing it right? Ideas about places, people, I am rife with them, but when I put them down sometimes the text is preachy and ponderous. Is Solecki right, I'm a one-note writer? No, he's never right. But I am a chronicler of longing and discontent, which I suppose, in his books, women should never be. Funny, male readers can't see beyond the gender into the material: the conflict between the glittering vision of life-as-it-should-be and life-as-it-is, romantic as a potato. An age-old theme and he sees me as one note. Well, having discovered that people farted, Rabelais trained himself to love the farts, that's one way.[49] I'm still trying to distil the essence; but since I failed alchemy in grade 2, it's a hard thing to do. Men don't want to see the texture of women's lives, when there's so much else to see; but they'll have to, some day.

Passing thought: could James Joyce have married anyone OTHER than a woman called Nora Barnacle?[50] It's as inevitable as Pound's marrying Mary [*sic*] Shakespear,[51] both being poets trapped by labels; but otherwise they were everywoman and anywoman because women weren't important, they were to bring you your tea.

---

49 François Rabelais (ca. 1483–1553), French writer, best known for his celebrated romance *La Vie de Gargantua et de Patagruel.*
50 Nora Barnacle (1884–1951), inspiration and mistress of James Joyce. They were finally married in 1931.
51 Ezra Pound (1885–1972), influential American poet, whose major work was the *Cantos*, published in ten sections between 1925 and 1969; Dorothy Shakespear (1886–1973), American artist, who married Pound in 1914.

Or perhaps they were too important and had to be reduced to bringing teas and bearing, like roses, labels on their stems.

Thanks for writing. Your cane is in use again, much more substantial and handsome than the hospital's pair and good for waving cats away in the middle of the night. Benny can interpret cane-signals far better than words and is getting quite good at going to the right door when I wave my Stone Orchard wand at it![52]

Take care now,
Marian

About naked males: how often does a heterosexual see a naked person of the same gender? Other women's real, not magazine, bodies always amaze me: for that you go to the Jewish Y, where they scrub and scrub in a way that us Xtian puritans were discouraged from, but that time we did the review for the Union I had a good prurient look at the bodies of the other Farley Mowat Dancers and was fascinated: women have changed since my day, they're much smaller than my generation of Percherons[53] was allowed to be and I don't understand their white fleshlessness. I NEVER see my kids whose dread of being Italian causes them to cover up their bodies even in summer. So I'm not surprised at what Suzuki says.[54]

The film looks like a success.[55] I'm so very pleased.

52 Benny, the family cat; Stone Orchard, Findley's home near Cannington Ontario.
53 A large and heavy breed of draught horse.
54 David Suzuki (1936–), Canadian scientist, writer, and broadcaster. The specific reference is unclear.
55 The film version of Findley's novel *The Wars*, directed by Robin Phillips, appeared in 1981.

To Judith Rodriguez

70 Marchmount Road
Toronto

5 December 1983

Dear Judith, dear Tom,
Judith, we were so glad to have your letter this morning; Char is
home from school for exams and we read it together. She thought
longingly of Richard's Queensland beaches![56] So what if he doesn't
like snow, she said. I guess Canadians like it because they associate
it with Xmas but it's pretty nasty stuff.

I'm glad to hear you're home and settling in, finding things to
do, making new plans – onward and upward, you didn't plan to
grow up and stay the same forever, did you? I'm getting stronger
day by day. I had a setback with a bit of a cold, some phlebitis. I
can't take much. I haven't been going out at all except to the
shrink because I've no resistance to viruses and don't want to be
in crowds. And there are so many good books to read!

I seem to be getting enough garbage out of my head to apply
myself to good literature again, instead of sitting round reading
detective novels. (Margaret Laurence sent me a bunch of bad
ones written by a Canadian woman in Boston; that sort of killed
the genre for me!) Struggling as ever with Thomas Mann who is
so bad and so good, but of course mostly good; it's Adrian
Leverkuhn I want to strangle and Sophocles, who seems to know a
little about pain.[57] Also my friend Leslie Armour gave me a copy
of his book, *The Conceptualization of the Inner Life*, and although the

---

56 Richard is Rodriguez's son.
57 Thomas Mann (1875–1955), German novelist, author of *Dr Faustus* (1947).
   The novel is framed as a posthumous biography of Adrian Leverkuhn,
   written by his best friend. Sophocles (ca. 496–06 BC), ancient Greek dramatist whose plays include *Oedipus Rex* and *Antigone*.

introductory chapters drive me mad, his examples further in the text are extremely interesting. If I get together the critical essays I'm thinking of, I want to do a piece on psychological criticism as both Ellman and Edel seem unfair and off-base to me.[58] And it would be interesting to talk about how landscape affects prose, the uses of minor characters as baroque decorations etc.

I'm not seeing many people but I celebrated the publication of *The Greatest Modern Woman in the World* with Sue Swan[59] and David Young[60] was over this morning, and Judith Merril[61] and I still talk a lot on the phone. She's getting on fairly well but will not be able to spend more than 30 days in Jamaica as her red corpuscle count must still be watched. She can't leave off her cortisone, and she's very upset. But she's much better and more active than she was. It's just that the life she planned, a really Bohemian one, isn't available now and it's very disappointing. I hope she's getting down to her book. But then I wish that happiness on all writers.

Well. it's 6 p.m. and pitch dark. Char is on her way home from her Math tutor and ought to be fed. I shall pick up my Findley cane ...

Ah, yes, the movie was excellent though I might have shortened it a bit. One critic hated it, the others didn't, and it's having a

58 Richard Ellman (1918–87), American literary critic and biographer, best known for his studies of Irish literary figures such as W.B. Yeats and James Joyce; Leon Edel (1907–98), American biographer and editor, whose work on Henry James won him a 1963 Pulitzer Prize. Engel eventually wrote her piece; see note 99, p. 267.

59 Susan Swan (1945–), Canadian novelist and professor of Canadian writing at York University, has published four novels since *The Biggest Modern Woman of the World* (1983), including *The Wives of Bath* (1993), which was adapted for the feature film *Lost and Delerious*, released in 2001.

60 David Young (1946–), Canadian playwright, novelist, and writer for television, film, and radio. His awards include the Chalmers and Dora Mavor Moore Awards and a Genie for most promising screenwriter.

61 Judith Merril (1923–97), Canadian novelist, editor, and science fiction writer. In August 1970, Merril donated her collection of some five thousand books to the Toronto Public Library, where it is preserved as the Merril Collection of Science Fiction, Speculation and Fantasy.

success in town. Tiff is very pleased, needless to say. I made it to the premier but was exhausted for days: it was a good debut, however.

Tues. a.m. What happens to the perceptions of letters which sleep all night in the typewriter? Do they sleep with one eye open? With their heads tucked under their wings? Do the words fly around and reassemble themselves like flocks of starlings, then get in order for the morning again?

Beginning to come alive, again, I am. But it worries me that if I want to write about writing I am going to have to plough through the last ten years' critical theory, which is going to be very boring indeed. However, I'm tending that way because the novel is sending me back to generational influences; I now giggle in reminiscence of us corn fed Canadian university students hanging around trying to be good little existentialists in black, trying also to be decadent. 'La chair est triste et j'ai lu tous les livres' she says, 140 pounds of good hand-made all wool Canadian knitting.[62] But what we were doing was quite honourable – leaping out of the more pious sector of the bush. It deserves to be recorded. It's a bit different from William and Charlotte's generation, cutting their teeth on cynicism via the telly.

I've just bankrupted myself ordering books by telephone but what I really want is a rainbow of new Shetland pullovers: it is cold and rainy today and it would be so pleasant to don rose and gold, turquoise, blue, a sort of pheasant green. I might go all the way and dream of tartan trousers! Must do something: captivity is finally causing me to lash out and love the world. Poach an egg? Do exercises? And you two doing USEFUL things. Love to all,

Marian

---

62 'The flesh is sad and I have read all the books'; quotation from Stéphane Mallarmé's poem 'Brise marine.'

To Margaret Laurence[63]

Toronto General [Hospital]

30 March [1984]

Dear Ms Laurence,
I have just finished *Emma* and feel I ought to address you in the formal way![64]

What a delight she is, and a consolation in tedious circumstances. I have only one more week here & am getting both impatient & fearful – can I cope at home? I've finally been ordered to wear a stiff girdle for my back in order to walk – discs are degenerating they say – and *hate* the idea. But the radiation is successful & I am more or less in one piece again.

The kids are both super – they *care* & friends old & new have rallied, which is a help. David Lewis Stein & David Young & Tiff Findley are all attentive, and of course my old gang from Huron St, Gwen, Adele, etc. And the neighbours *feed* Charlotte every night. Everyone is super & I shall walk again without support, I hope. Even if I need a cane – well, I'm alive.

I have *Persuasion* in the same pretty series as your two & will put the two together – doubly valuable because inscribed by you.[65]

Thanks, Margaret, and happy Spring.

Yours with love,
Marian

---

63 This letter is from the Margaret Laurence Archive at York University.

64 *Emma*, novel first published in 1815 by the celebrated English writer Jane Austen (1775–1817).

65 *Persuasion*, another Austen novel, first published in 1817.

From Margaret Laurence
Lakefield, Ont.

1 April 1984

Dear Marian:

It is April Fool's Day and I cannot think of anyone to play a silly joke upon ... when my kids were little, the standard April Fool's joke was to look out the window and yell 'Ye gods! It's snowing!' That was either in B.C. or England, where the very idea of snow in April was too absurd to be entertained for a second. However, I recall that here, about 4 years ago, we indeed did have a blizzard the first week in April.

Only found out your new room number yesterday, so I'm sending some stuff that I hope you may enjoy. The article on Bloomsbury folks is from the *N.Y. Review of Books*, and I really like the strong individual voice of the reviewer, whose views of Bloomsbury tend to agree with my own, and partly because I'm a Canadian who felt, years ago, somewhat like a naive colonial girl in literary London, and came to resent and then be amused by their attitudes ... much later than Bloomsbury but some of the same contempt for anything not Brit was there in my time, although the upper-class Brit by that time had all but vanished from the literary scene. It's interesting ... I've read Nigel Nicolson's book on his parents,[66] and a certain amount of the multitudinous material on the scene of those days, and of course Virginia [Woolf]'s books, although none of Vita [Sackville-West]'s, and I feel, as I always have felt, a profound sense of repulsion towards that group, not for their sexual inclinations, heaven knows ... I couldn't care less ... but for their amazing snobbism and hypoc-

---

66 Nigel Nicolson, *Portrait of a Marriage* (London: Weidenfeld and Nicolson, 1973).

risy, their malice and sheer *nastiness* towards everyone in the world
except their own little clique. Their lack of generosity, their terror
at standing up for any principle, is mind-boggling. Poor Leonard
Woolf must have been heroic, although I guess his
reasons were mixed also. I've always ... well, for years, anyhow ...
wondered what Virginia would have done if there had been no
one to look after her and keep helping her in her periodic bouts
of 'madness.' Maybe she would have written better ...? Those of us
who have had to earn our living and bring up our kids, virtually
by ourselves, with a lot of moral support from friends and colleagues, may well ponder this. Personally, I think that a lot of
women writers in this country, whether with children or not, and
whether with mates or not, have been HEROIC. But one thing we
have NOT been is bloodless, and you know, Virginia's writing,
much of which I read long ago, never did strike a chord in my
heart ... it always seemed so cerebral, so bloodless. Which is not to
say that she didn't have magnificent gifts in terms of writing ... she
did. But she never chose to write about things closest to her own
heart and spirit, and obviously I am not talking here about writing
in any direct autobiographical way. I think a lot of Canadian women
writers ... quite frankly ... have been braver. The incredible snob-
bishness ... the almost unbelievable ignorance in that way ... of the
Bloomsbury group ... seem now to have been a very limiting thing
in terms of their writing. I suppose it is an inability to know, really
know, the reality of others. I read with suitable reverence, as was
expected then, when I was young, Virginia Woolf's books, and
wondered why I didn't connect very much with them. Later, I saw
why. They were written out of an exclusive spirit, not an inclusive
one, and in some sense they were self-obsessed and unkind. We
are not always kind, kid, nor should we be, but damn, we aren't
exclusive!! And I believe that *caring* in the widest way does matter.
And *principles* matter. This may be my Scots Presbyterian background ... if so, okay. Poor Radclyffe (sp?) Hall,[67] thinking she

---

67 Marguerite Radclyffe Hall (1880–1943), pioneering lesbian poet and novelist.

might get some support, moral and vocal and financial, from those upper-class twits. Her novel was really a pretty awful one, in literary terms, but she fought her fight without the support she should surely have had.[68] Of course, what bothers me most and always has, is that those were the people who thought they had a natural right to all the goodies of this world, and who thought they had a right not only to rule England but to be the supportive colonial force that ruled the Empire. I suppose I detest them both in a human sense and in a political sense. They thought they were superior in every way, and they did not *care* at all or feel any sense of responsibility. Creeps.

I told you in my last letter that I had a new electric typewriter and that I was somewhat puzzled because I seemed to be hitting the letter 'l' without meaning to. I am surprised that it took me about 3 days to discover why, because the answer is so obvious. I have arthritis in my right hand, and my third finger is now bent-over. It is this finger that rests on the 'l' when the hands are positioned on the keyboard, so of course what has tended to happen is that when I move the hands up or down to type other letters, the arthritic finger tends to drag and to hit the 'l.'

I will write again soon. I haven't phoned because I don't want to intrude at an inconvenient time and also because I write a better letter than I talk a phone call.

God bless.

Love,
Margaret

68 *The Well of Loneliness* (Garden City, NY: Sun Dial Press, 1928).

To Judith Rodriguez[69]

70 Marchmount Road
Toronto

13 April [1984]

Dear Judith,
You're keeping the mails sizzling these days and it's lovely for me to have your news so regularly. I think there's a letter to you I wrote here somewhere and I'll add it to this, if I find it (can't find it) (ha! found it).

First, congrats on the house, it sounds super in its imperfect way and if you can see the harbour from the 3rd floor you can reach it on foot and take those glorious ferries. You must always take one on the day of a dinner party: let Tom polish the table and serve them Irish stew! I guess it is discouraging to put in a garden without reaching into your mind to know you'll see the harvest.

I'm sprung from hospital but I got into a contretemps whereby my GP popped me into another one for 2 days which angered my specialist and it's taken me all WEEK to sort it out; meanwhile I hope I open the door carefully enough to prevent the police taking me to hosp. It turned out that the difficulty was one I had had for years and the pain, a lymphoma pain, and now I have to go around soothing doctors and it's a great and insufferable bore. I am supposed to have known I had stuff in my liver; I'm sure I'd have remembered; but perhaps I protectively failed to hear. Anyway I'm sort of enraged because I lost control of the situation and alienated everybody and swore at my GP etc. and now I'm Mrs Mudd and if you come to my door, hide your doctor's bag.

69 This letter was provided by Judith Rodriguez.

I'm pretty tired but I walk better than I thought I would. Tell Richard the bulbs are coming up in the garden and he's not to worry what's in front of what because there's nothing else growing; we've just had some splendid days in the 60s and now it's raining so the flowers are starting up at last. But I usually don't plan on seeing bloom until the twins' birthday, 30 April. One of the good things I've done is order 4 new phones so I don't have to stagger the length of the house on canes when it rings; and we're having them coloured this time – beige here, blue there, ivory in the kitchen etc. and I'll take them off as a business expense. I'm tired of limping around all the time.

Margaret Laurence sent me her *Emma* when I was in hosp. and also told me she has a new typewriter she calls Pearl Cavewoman, which is what Margaret Wemyss, her maiden name, really means. Atwood and Gibson are in Berlin, having spent some happy time in England, where Jess rode, and was a Brownie, not a Famous Child.[70] The neighbours are dropping in again tonight to make sure I'm still alive. I'm half inclined to go to a party for Robin Skelton,[71] take them with me. Wonder if I could get away with it? Tiff's been charming lately too. The benefit of being ill is seeing everyone. He ripens, is better every time I see him.

Char's gone to see a play about Canadian history, of all things (Salutin's *1837*),[72] goodness knows where dear Will is, and I should settle down to the galloping Major if I don't get dressed and Skelton. Love from Friday the 13th and think of me attempting to preserve my freedom with my sword stick!

Cheers and thanks,
Marian

70 Jess, the daughter of Atwood and Gibson.
71 Robin Skelton (1925–97), prolific Canadian poet, editor, and academic, author of more than seventy books of poetry, drama, and prose; founder of the *Malahat Review*.
72 Rick Salutin (1942–), Canadian writer, lecturer, and social activist.

To Margaret Laurence

70 Marchmount Rd
Toronto

25 April [1984]

Dear Margaret,
A woman from the Ontario Status of Women commission presented me today with a) her cleaning woman and b) a huge stash
of office supplies – paper, envelopes, pens, markers, memo pads,
white-out etc., an adorable present. I am having such a lot of
trouble getting about and there isn't much hope the situation will
improve. However, if I can hobble out to the garden with a coffee
every morning, and people keep on bringing me things, I can't
really complain, can I? I won't be seeing you at Adele's party,
though, because I haven't started going out at night and don't
intend to for a good while.

But oh, goodness, after what I saw in hospital, to be able to sit
up, to hobble at all, is a blessing, and I'm writing because I've
been thinking of your good letter, which was a boon.

You know, I've always loved V. Woolf in spite of her snobbery
because I started her with *A Writer's Diary* and *A Room of One's Own*
as a young teenager and I suppose I just accepted snobbery
because there was so much around us (we were the people with
the trailer after all) – and then there were the Common Readers
which I loved and I became quite the snob myself, living in those
towns with so many people I couldn't stand because they couldn't
stand me. But I know mine is quite a different formation, because
it happened during the propagandising of the war and not earlier, so I'm much less left-wing than you and Adele [Wiseman]
and Judy [Merril]. I begin to think that politics are generational
and part of the zeitgeist.

And V. Woolf's writing was important to me because no one was doing anything interesting at the time with traditional narrative, and perhaps because my life had been chopped, broken, cut off from its roots I felt good with disconnected writing. I don't know. I still can't manage *The Waves* but *To The Lighthouse, Orlando, Jacob's Room* and *Between the Acts* are key books for me. But then I have always gone for the decadents, the sexually ambivalent, Proust, Gide, Pater, Woolf, Eliot, James, to a degree.[73] It seems odd to me now that my fresh-faced apple-cheeked generation tried so hard to be decadent: us in our black sweaters and trousers trying to be existentialists. It was a relief from the Billy Graham Crusades, which we felt university was somehow not about.[74]

I'm rather glorying in all this time to think, though some of the thoughts are not good. I've not been much to the psychiatrist lately though he was a help in laying out that strange childhood. I didn't realise it HURT so much to be a foster-child and orphan etc. until I read *In Search of April Raintree* and things started to break open.[75] I got that pain more or less out of my system and totter along fairly contentedly now. I'm getting the garden lady to plant my bower again and tomorrow David Young is taking me out to shop for the kids' 19th birthday presents. It's lovely to have grown children. And no adolescents!

I loved your detective novel, and thanks for writing,

Marian

---

73 André Gide (1869–1951), French writer and moralist; Walter Pater (1839–94), English writer and art critic; T.S. Eliot (1888–1965), American-English poet, whose 1922 work *The Waste Land* established him as the voice of a disillusioned generation; Henry James (1843–1916), American novelist and short-story writer.

74 Billy Graham (1918–), American evangelist.

75 Beatrice Culleton Mosionier, *In Search of April Raintree* (Winnipeg: Pemmican Publications, 1983).

To Margaret Laurence

70 Marchmount
Toronto

Saturday, 5 May [1984]

Dear Margaret, the flowers are lovely, an arrangement of pink roses and yellow tulips, but you spoil me! You must realise that this year I shall be in and out of the hospital till I GET that tumour, it's the only way and the race is to the swift.

A psychiatrist I know in Winnipeg sent E. Kubler-Ross's new book about death, which is about being kind to cancer patients and full of photos.[76] I got so mad I decided that the only return present was a stone angel with FUCK OFF engraved on it. One doesn't NEED pictures of people getting thinner and thinner and being grateful to their spirit-guides: one needs flowers and books and music and friends; a scented and satisfactory house.

I am doing a little work, which makes me feel good. I can't sit up for marathon writing-sessions but I've always worked little-by-little, so the book is coming along.

Lots of love,
Marian

---

76 Probably Elisabeth Kubler-Ross's *Living with Death and Dying* (New York: Macmillan, 1981).

To Margaret Laurence[77]

70 Marchmount Rd
Toronto

16 May [1984]

Dear Margaret,
Books, letters, pins, flowers, my goodness, I am much in your debt.

Still here, too; all the doctors do is flatter. I wonder, I wonder. But my dr. friend from California, Maggie Deanesly, says, 'Well, you have to pay for all that radiation somehow' and my shrink, whom I almost left and then didn't, says the sciatic nerve is probably a bit damaged, after all, it's had a tumour for a long time. Isn't it a good think [*sic*] I like reading.

I enjoyed Posy Simmonds[78] enormously ... that was the life we led in the Annex, too, when I turned out not to be able to make Quiche. And 1066 took me to my old edition of Hume and Smollett, which makes modern wars seem unremarkable.[79] Henry III was a monster of martial adventures.[80] Funny, that Louis became a saint.[81]

I don't know what to think of theology so haven't read your religious magazine. Every religion seems to have a heaven that's a

---

77 This letter is from the Margaret Laurence Archive at York University.
78 British cartoonist and illustrator of children's books.
79 Probably Walter C. Sellar and Robert J. Yeatman, *1066 and All That* (London: Methuen, 1984); Tobias George Smollett, *The History of England from the Revolution in 1688 to the Death of George the Second: Designed As a Continuation of Hume* (London: Jones, 1835); David Hume (1711–76), *History of England, from the Invasion of Julius Caesar to the Revolution of 1688* (London: A. Millar, 1762).
80 Henry III (1216–72), King of England.
81 Louis IX (1226–70), King of France.

bit like Forest Hill, big signs, 'No one else allowed.' If they won't be democratic about it I think I'll just go down to Friedbergs and buy myself a coin for Charon so I can go to the picnic in the Elysian fields.[82] It will save me punching John Knox in the nose and getting sent to hell.[83]

I've been having lots of visitors. David Young is a darling and yesterday came and stapled some plastic netting for the clematis on the fence. The garden people are putting it in this year as I can't kneel enough. I've sent Tiff an agapanthus, a big blue Egyptian lily, which I think is his style.

I love things that come in the mail, now. Ted Phillips just sent me the Grade 7 Study Girls' cookbook. I was fascinated to find that crab bisque is made of 2 kinds of Campbell's soup and a can of crab. It used to be made by the maid. The Study's that private school I taught at.[84] He taught at the boys' equivalent. MacLennan's sister was Classics Mistress at Compton.

Joe came this morning and told me how nice I looked in my red nightie, which was very funny considering Basia Hunter made it for me because she found it shocking I wore hosp. gowns in front of her friend Gerry Scott,[85] who is the sort to run when confronted by red nighties ... we took on the mystery of any having been assigned to the scanner on a Sunday. I phoned and found out the intern had copied the date down wrong. So I shall be able to go at the RIGHT time and be photographed in the round.

Spent last weekend typing Char's huge geography report. She's getting on towards her exams and cutting down on movies, thank goodness.

---

82 In Greek mythology, Charon is the ferryman of the dead; Elysium is the home of the blessed after death.

83 John Knox (ca. 1505–72), Scottish religious reformer and founder of Presbyterianism in Scotland.

84 Engel taught at the private school in Montreal from 1958 to 1960.

85 Dr Joe Greenberg, the family physician; Dr Gerry Scott, Engel's cancer physician.

The garden in spite of the cold is lovely as the forget-me-nots have spread all over and the tulips are out. There's an orange-yellow one called General deWet that is scented that I like. Char put them in last fall, and very nicely, too, one pink, one gold, one purple in each clump and they're effective. The crab is out and looks like popcorn. For some reason this bank of the hill is a suntrap, the right place to have a garden. Lois Lister is having her man plant for me this spring ...

Listen, if the Secretary of State's office dined people off bad china all foreign heads of state would be insulted. Why shouldn't you have pheasant off good plates if Mrs Thatcher does?[86]

Oh, dither, I really ought to phone my alderman. The boys next door are fixing cars out of the store again ... they have no permit to run a garage and mess the whole corner by doing so. But it's so undemocratic to report them. I shall go off in a corner and fuss about what to do.

Have you read about Indian children in Manitoba being sent to the States to be abused? You'd think enough people did it here. I don't mind about being adopted except that it was treated as a dirty secret which, perhaps, to them in the end it was. I don't think Mother was really sure enough of herself for it. I still dream about her.

Time for a little zizz.

Take care, love,
Marian

---

86 Margaret Thatcher (1925–), British prime minister, 1979–90.

To Pauline McGibbon

70 Marchmount Rd
Toronto

15 August 1984

Dear Pauline,

Just out of hospital after my second chemo and your letter came. Glad we are thinking of each other. I don't think my typing is good enough for you but I hope you can accept it!

I'm getting on pretty well because I've accepted my limitations now and have a nurse who calls and a visiting homemaker. Needless to say any time you and Don had a moment to pop in in the fall would be wonderful! You might keep in mind that my cleaning woman comes on Mondays! On the other hand, my physio is talking about getting me out on the street again so you mustn't think of me as bedridden.

I thought I'd had it for a while, and so did the doctors but the chemo has done the right things. It could reverse itself at any time of course, so we keep our fingers crossed. On good days I can sit up and write. For the rest I'm reading. I'm on a Trollope kick and love it.[87] The writers we skip when we're young are there for later. I'm afraid I've read most of Dick Francis.[88]

How lucky you are to know William Stephenson![89] I'm glad you had a good holiday and Don has checked out all right.

Charlotte spent the day with Howard's second wife picking out

---

87 Anthony Trollope (1815–82), English novelist, author of over fifty books, including the Barset and Pallister series.
88 Dick Francis (1920–), British jockey, journalist, and mystery writer.
89 William Stephenson (1896–1989), Canadian member of the British secret service, author of the autobiography (as William Stevenson) *A Man Called Intrepid* (New York: Harcourt Brace Jovanovich, 1976).

Vic courses. Then Howard phoned and we worked out the finances: we're splitting the fees and he's contributing to books while I lay on a good clothing allowance. She's a frugal girl and good about buying her stuff at the Hadassah sale but it's time she went to Holt's for a good winter coat, I think.[90]

I am thrilled with the resources I am finding. Home Care is very good and my friends are coming up trumps. The likes of Margaret Atwood and Doris Anderson shop for me, I've a good arrangement at the hospital now for emergencies and understand the signals better, so that everything that can be done is being done. And I have a super cleaning woman. I live a kind of life of Riley, and have decided it's ok to spend some of Mother's money doing it.

Later: I've just been watching the Women's Debate with a tremendous feeling that AT LAST the facts are being publicly acknowledged; when Mulroney promises credit for women, when even Honest John Turner admits that not everyone can afford to live in Buckingham Palace, perhaps we're going to get to some kind of fairness.[91] And I was tremendously proud of knowing Doris A[nderson] and Kay Macpherson and Eleanor Wachtel.[92] And of course, you Pauline and your Ma. And no skin off Don's nose. He get's the prize for being able to stand female achievers. I don't expect a lot to happen, but public acknowledgement from the major parties of older women's poverty is really something. One has not lived in vain!

Oh, dear, this is too long. I shall go back to bed and read more

90 Holt Renfrew, an exclusive store on Bloor Street West in Toronto.
91 Brian Mulroney (1939–), Canadian prime minister, 1984–93; John Turner (1929–), Canadian prime minister, June–September, 1984.
92 Kay Macpherson (1913–99), Canadian politician, feminist, and peace activist; Eleanor Wachtel (1947–), Canadian broadcaster and writer.

Trollope thanking you for your concern. I'm being well looked after.

Love and admiring thanks,
Marian

Sunday, May I put this in with *Room of One's Own?* My own special issue which I thought you might like to share. ME

To Judith Rodriguez[93]

70 Marchmount Road
Toronto

3 September [1984]

Dear Judith, dear Tom,
It's one of the hard days to get through: been raining so much the bugs are crawling in the back door for shelter, the rock concerts (Sinatra at the Exhibition, where Char is a ticket-taker, marvellous reggae somewhere else, to Judy's disappointment) were rained out last night. Maria, my new cleaning woman, is here civilizing us but of course it leaves me with nowhere but the typewriter to go! I am FABULOUSLY much better though I've been warned it won't last. I walk still with a crutch but to be able to sit up and type, get around the house and along the block is terrific.

My office is all mussed up with bits of novel again. Taking potassium by the spoonful rather than trying to produce it is

---

93 This letter was provided by Judith Rodriguez.

terrific for the IQ. I read *The Year of Living Dangerously* last week and then went on to *A Bend in the River* and back to my own ms, where I managed to haul part of it out of a quagmire of sentimentality.[94] Koch is really good; that was a hard book to write and he did it superbly. The Naipaul I had originally rejected because he's so mean to blacks but I went through it this time with Koch behind me and thought, well, he knows, and as a tract on not belonging, and being too intellectual to understand, it stands up as a fine book.

The season here looks exciting and I feel left out: Tiff Findley, Sylvia Fraser, David Lewis Stein and Matt Cohen all have big good books coming out, apparently. Tiff dedicated his Penguin short stories to me and I felt good about that. Any little thing helps. Also the Marian Engel *Room of One's Own* issue is out and I'll send you a copy as soon as I can. They chose praising articles and super photos, as they should have, and it looks like a put-up job and still sounds good. Alice [Munro] wrote a nice little piece, Jane Rule discussed the short stories etc. Gwen wrote a poem.

Will is turning out to be a good citizen second time round so he's still living here. He has to be limited but is otherwise reasonable and a lot of help. Char starts Orientation Week (mostly barcrawling, how times have changed!) at Vic next week and is very excited.[95] She's registered in English, sociology, two anthropologies and geography. I gave her a big clothes allowance and her choices have so far been VERY smart. She's very nervous of change, however. Her father's helping with the fees.

As for me, I'm living it up while I can, except for the booze. I don't miss it because I'm on a huge diet and I eat my way through the alphabet every day. I have put on weight, but then I lost about 30 lbs. I haven't lost my hair, though I've ordered a wig. Maybe it's

94 C.J. Koch, *The Year of Living Dangerously* (New York: St Martin's Press, 1979); V.S. Naipaul, *A Bend in the River* (New York: Knopf, 1979).
95 Victoria College, University of Toronto.

like taking an umbrella. The tips of my fingers and toes are numb, though, that's a side effect.

I presume from your silence that you've moved, but I know you've left forwarding instructions. I thought I ought to say I'm better for now. Love and hope that all your projects are turning out all right! Gotta go. Lots of other letters to write. Love, miss you,

Marian

To Timothy Findley

70 Marchmount Rd
Toronto

11 September 1984

Dear Tiff,
Although I know that you're this minute holed up in the Park Plaza canoodling with the Pope, thus have no need for a letter, when it's over, dear, you'll need your old friends again, and who better than old friends in silk shirts and beautiful blue pullovers? Though I must say I haven't ironed the shirt yet: both it and the new iron look too expensive for me to touch!

Today I started walking with a cane again, since the crutch hurt, and it was right, and of course the cane came from you too. If I appear not to notice your beneficence, I am remembering my father's lectures about being 'beholden' to people. He was wrong, of course, but it has taken me a long time to escape that formation. I *am* grateful.

And loving, too, though in an undemonstrative way. It didn't do Vanessa Bell much good to live with Duncan Grant, as I am reading in her biography.[96] Incomplete relationships are more hurtful than people think, though since most relationships MUST be incomplete, we have to put up with them. And maybe our writing compensates for the incompleteness so we maintain it. Still when ALL the men I have to do with are gay I begin to feel a sexual pariah, but it doesn't stop me feeling the greatest affection for you, even if I never say so and don't want you to call me Miggs.

I went in for chemo this afternoon. You wait in the Della Robbia lounge,[97] then get called into a room to see your doctor (who is back from Argentina but not talking about Gay Cabelleros), then have your blood tested and go into a room with big leatherette armchairs, where you sit back while a nurse (another fan!) injects your chemicals through a minute tube in your hand. It takes two hours from door to door. I went there and back alone in a taxi and felt very grown up. Graeme [Gibson] said he would drive me but he's having some teeth out today and why should I bother him. And going somewhere alone, hobble, hobble, was marvellous.

I'm in fantastic shape except of course for being seriously ill, and in the night got up and rewrote an article on psychological criticism I've been thinking of all year. I have a horrid feeling you might take offense as I said that 'even the marvellous Tiff Findley' confuses us when he mixes real people in fiction: it's a plea to abjure slandering the dead, especially psychiatrically. It contains, in reference to me and *Bear*, the line 'Excited was I when I saw Esau' and in reference to Jesus, a mention of clay feet that will get me in trouble. I also say I own a book called 'Boswell's Clap.'[98] I'm

---

96 Vanessa Bell (1879–1961), English painter and member of the Bloomsbury Group; Frances Spalding, *Vanessa Bell* (London: Weidenfeld and Nicolson, 1983).

97 Andrea della Robbia (ca. 1434–1525), Italian Renaissance sculptor.

98 William B. Ober, *Boswell's Clap and Other Essays* (Carbondale: Southern Illinois University Press, 1979).

really coming out of the closet, aren't I? Having fun, too, so I don't think you'll be totally offended.[99]

William, God bless us, is still going to Geo Brown[100] and has passed into the pre-business programme, more or less skipping most of high school. He's high on it, but still jealous of Char at Vic. He's working a LOT for me, and so is she and the three of us have a whole family going again. It cuts into the reading but I don't mind, except in the morning.

What other news? I've been happy as a lark and busy and progressive; get tired easily & lose my temper like a real human being. Happy reading the Vanessa Bell, and Ted Phillips has just sent me Diana Johnson's essays.[101] Updike is funny about the post modernists in *The New Yorker*, which is coming again.[102] The summer slump is in fact over. David Young's smoked lake trout was sensational, and I've connected him up with the T[oronto] P[ublic] Library reading programme as his Fraggle Rock book deserves to be read aloud to kids and he'll learn a lot from them because they only follow when it's good.[103]

Oh, I know what else I have for you: I was noodling around in my head. Here's Tom Graff's address: Vera says he'd be delighted to meet you in Big Van. Keep in touch, eh?

Love, M.

---

99 The article appeared as 'A Plea to Stop Turning the Knobs on Writers' Closets,' *Globe and Mail* [literary supplement], 17 November 1984, p. 1.

100 George Brown College, Toronto.

101 Possibly Diana L. Johnson, *Fantastic Illustration and Design in Britain, 1850–1930* (Providence: Rhode Island School of Design, 1979).

102 John Updike (1932–), American novelist, poet, and short-story writer. Updike's piece, one of his regular book review columns, appeared as 'Modernist, Postmodernist, What Will They Think of Next?' *New Yorker*, 3 September 1984, pp. 136–42.

103 David Young, *Marooned in Fraggle Rock* (New York: Holt, Rinehart and Winston, 1984).

From Margaret Laurence
Lakefield
Ontario

17 September 1984

Dear Marian –
It was so good to talk with you on the phone yesterday. Your voice
sounded so strong. How alike women writers are, or so it seems to
me. Your practical arrangements with your study, and plumbing
therein, seemed so sensible. But then, we *are* sensible, amidst
everything else, aren't we? I think Jane Austen would have loved
us, but I suspect she might have been a bit in awe of us, as well she
might, we who have coped with having and rearing our children,
writing our books, earning our livings, and not hiding the manuscripts under the desk blotter when the vicar came to tea. Wild
Emily, of the Brontës, wouldn't have understood our practicality,
as she had so little of it.[104] Charlotte Brontë would have understood, and yet I relate in some area of my heart more to Emily
than I do to Charlotte, although Charlotte was not only more like
I am, but also the better writer.[105]

I didn't talk to you about two wonderful things that will happen
this year ... the publication of Sylvia Fraser's novel, *Berlin Solstice*,
and Tiff Findley's novel, *Not Wanted on the Voyage*.[106] Both, in my
view, quite brilliant. I rejoice.

God bless, dear friend and colleague,

Love,
Margaret Laurence

104 Emily Brontë (1818–48), English poet and novelist, best known for her
    gothic masterpiece *Wuthering Heights* (1847).
105 Charlotte Brontë (1816–55), English novelist, author of *Jane Eyre* (1847),
    Shirley (1849), and *Villette* (1853).
106 Timothy Findley, *Not Wanted on the Voyage* (Toronto: Viking, 1984); Sylvia
    Fraser, *Berlin Solstice* (Toronto: McClelland and Stewart, 1984).

To Judith Rodriguez[107]

70 Marchmount Rd
Toronto

5 November [1984]

Dear Judith
and Tom etc.,
Can one say that one feels revelrous? I think, rather, grown up.
Joyce Wieland, the painter, just phoned to say that she's coming
over with some lampshades for my office so I asked her to bring a
bottle of wine.[108] I oughtn't to have it, it goes so badly with the
Tylenol, but I'm feeling perverse. The children have been buzz-
ing all weekend, keeping company with a [British new wave rock]
group called Frankie Goes to Hollywood. William has been putting on quite good Liverpool and Los Angeles accents and lying
his way into press conferences, and taking Char along. I think she,
being frugal and industrious, helps him out with drinks and bus
fare. Tonight, they're in a movie. For this I spent the morning
typing out 1,000 words on George Herbert's 'The Flower.'[109]

I'm up and down. Not walking, I think, as much as I should, or
perhaps the leg doesn't work, I don't know. But there was a flu
virus I had to beat off so I spent a long time in bed and now I'm
even less mobile. I'm probably writing letters and thinking of
drinking because I just can't bear to read one more Victorian
novel, having done 6 of Trollope this fall. Marriage settlements
turn me right off now. But as it's *Phineas Finn* I'm considering
starting, I think I'll come around.

My friends are producing novels again ... the men particularly.

107 This letter was provided by Judith Rodriguez.
108 Joyce Wieland (1931–98), Canadian artist.
109 George Herbert (1593–1633), English poet, whose poems were published
posthumously in 1633 under the title *The Temple.*

Matt Cohen's *The Spanish Doctor* is, I think, splendid; it got slain in the press for being violent and sensational.[110] I think they just didn't want to know what the Inquisition did to the Jews, how the Sephardim got to Kiev. Tiff's just put out a book called *Not Wanted on the Voyage* based on the Noah story. I'm afraid I react to it as I do to pink ice cream, but others find it profound and meaningful. David Lewis Stein's *The Golden Age Hotel* begins well.[111] It is set in the US and should sell there, but didn't. It has had rather luke-warm reviews. I haven't got hold of Sylvia Fraser's new novel yet. It's a Berlin in the thirties thing. I always think Isherwood was enough.[112] But then I can't make a fair judgement of Sylvia for some reason; find her rather unreadable and wonder if jealousy is behind it. Meanwhile Gwendolyn is happy as writer-in-residence at Western,[113] with a salary blessedly coming in, and Judith [Merril] is packing for Jamaica. I've been writing on the novel and prob-ably repeating myself, trying to cover 20 years in 45 pages for one chapter; but it's coming slowly. My God though, the desk is cov-ered with it. And the Penguin woman says she's coming to see me about getting the book of short stories together.

The doctor's putting me in the hospital again next week to see about this leg, which hurts as the chemo wears off. It's impossible to be civil to people who try to talk to me when the pain is ringing like a bell. I've read a couple of books on pain and come to the conclusion that you use whatever technique you believe in. The only thing I seem to believe in is the good old wet washrag, wot my mum used to put around my throat when I was a little kiddle (there used to be dolls called that, can you believe it?) and I put one on my thigh when it aches and it helps as well as anything else. Faith counts. Deep breathing does in grave emergencies but

110 Matt Cohen, *The Spanish Doctor* (Toronto: McClelland and Stewart, 1983).

111 David Lewis Stein, *The Golden Age Hotel* (Toronto: Macmillan of Canada, 1984).

112 Christopher Isherwood (1904–86), Anglo-American novelist and playwright, best known for his stories about Berlin in the 1930s.

113 University of Western Ontario.

of course it takes a long time to get going. Mostly I just grit my teeth and snarl. But people get distracted and babble at one.

Mostly, though I'm sluggish, things are rather pleasant. I've had a firm called Alternative Plumbing re-do the bathroom. We now have a basin between tub and toilet, built into a stand. It will have latticework doors. And it will have a splendid looking glass from an old dresser, and I've bought wallpaper with big loose pink and green flowers on it (Charlotte disapproves) and when it is done it will be lovely, I think. Then I'll buy new towels.

We've had an amazing fall, the garden still in bloom, the nasturtiums just got it last night and the trailing verbena is still being silly all over the place. And the prairies have been having snow for a month. For once we're lucky in the weather. My garden woman has become a friend and I enjoy her company.

I went to the 30th anniversary party for Anthology, Bob Weaver's radio programme, last week: SAW EVERYBODY. It was good. I got into the building okay as the room was on the ground floor of St. Mike's college, and sat on a sofa. Damn crutches take up a lot of room, though. Talked to Hugh Hood[114] and Alice Munro, Sandra Birdsell[115] etc., Matt Cohen, Tiff, Willy, my ex (about William and his plans in an expensive video co-op), Norman Levine,[116] who is turning out to be a constant visitor.

I like Alan Lawson and was glad to fill him in on Robertson Davies' early career, about which he knew nothing.[117] Important that, to remember people didn't spring from the forehead of Jove! I know the 30s background because it was my thesis topic.

114 Hugh Hood (1928–2000), Canadian novelist, author of thirty-two books, including the twelve-volume series 'The New Age,' in which Hood aimed to render the Canadian spirit in the way Proust and Tolstoy had done for their cultures.
115 Sandra Birdsell (1942–), Canadian novelist and short-story writer of Mennonite background, whose work explores women's experiences and gender relations.
116 Norman Levine (1923–), Canadian novelist and short-story writer.
117 Alan Lawson, Australian writer and editor (with Fred Lock) of *Australian Literature: A Reference Guide* (Oxford: Oxford University Press, 1980).

Must go now. You're getting into summer ... and are you going to Perth? Tell Tom I think explorer-botanists are a good idea. Something to get the teeth into. I've reread bits of *Voss* and decided it stands up.[118] Oh, and I've finally got hold of Somerville and Ross's *The Real Charlotte* which is a knockout of a novel.[119] Should write something about it.

Lots of love,
Marian

To A.L. Traversy, Order of Canada
Investitures and Records
Rideau Hall
Ottawa, Ontario

70 Marchmount Rd
Toronto

13 December 1984

Dear Mrs Traversy,
Thank you for your very kind letter of November 28th.[120]

I'm afraid my disease is progressive and goodness knows what state I will be in on April 10th, but I will let you know closer to the date if travel is possible.

My children are taking me away in a wheelchair for Christmas, which is how I would have to go to Ottawa. I would be able to attend a ceremony but not an evening party, alas.

The situation is not as tragic as it sounds: I LIKE reading in bed

---

118 A novel by Australian writer Patrick White (1919–90), published in 1957.
119 E. Somerville and Martin Ross, *The Real Charlotte* (London: Ward and Downey, 1894).
120 Engel had been appointed an Officer of the Order of Canada in December 1982. She had previously been invited to attend investiture ceremonies in Ottawa in April and August 1983 but had been too ill to attend.

and can continue to write when my back is good enough to sit up and type. But it does make social and professional activities awkward.

Yours very sincerely,
Marian Engel

From Margaret Laurence
Lakefield
Ontario

7 January 1985

Dear Marian –
Well, I didn't know you were going to Paris for Christmas, so you probably got back to find some *frozen* flowers on your doorstep, from me. As the saying goes, it's the thought that counts, but – oh shoot! – I'm sorry. I'm glad you went to Paris, though. I tried to phone several times today, but no answer. God bless, dear sister. As you've probably heard, the vigilantes are after me again in my own country. This time I'm *fighting back* – on behalf of us all. Tune in to CBC radio & TV & you'll probably hear & see me, because what the rednecks are trying to do to us all is *awful.*[121]

With love, prayers & blessings –
Margaret

You don't have to reply. Just know I'm thinking of you – & of all of us.

---

121 Laurence's novel *The Diviners* (New York: Knopf, 1974) was banned in 1979 by the Huron County School Board, the area in which she had made her home. She continued to be hounded by religious fundamentalist groups all her life; another initiative in 1985 also attempted to ban *A Jest of God* (New York: Knopf, 1966) and *The Stone Angel* (Toronto: McClelland and Stewart, 1964) on grounds of blasphemy and obscenity.

From Margaret Laurence
Lakefield
Ontario

12 January 1985

Dear Marian –
It was so good to hear your strong voice on the phone the other
day. Yes, we are fighting, and shortly after that, Janet Lunn[122]
phoned me to say what could the Writers' Union do, and I said,
write to the Peterborough Board of Education. I am so heartened
by the support of writers and of village people here. I am sending
you a novel by Barbara Pym ... only just recently has this writer
been, as it were, resurrected.[123] I have only read this one novel,
but I think she is splendid. I would not go so far as to compare her
with Jane Austen, frankly, but I do think she is good. Jane Austen,
the more I read her and think about her, was such a subtle and
strong feminist! *In them days!* But those days, apparently so far
back, are not so very different from our own. Is this not always the
way? I think so. Strong women did always have the difficulties that
Austen presents, and people like you and I have lived through
that, too. With, I may say, *success.* We pass on a whole lot of things
to the children, both female and male, or so I hope and pray and
know. Our generation, however, and I say this knowing I am older
than you are, did have our kids and reared them without any

122 Janet Lunn (1928–), award-winning Canadian author of books for children.
123 Barbara Pym (1913–80), English novelist, author of satirical tragi-comedies
of middle-class life, including *Excellent Women* (1952), *Less Than Angels*
(1955), *A Glass of Blessings* (1958), and *Quartet in Autumn* (1977).

colonial servant-type help, although I lived in Africa. Shoot, honey, we're heroic!

I am so glad that the flowers were not frozen!

Much much love,
M.

P.S. Canadian-type crisis ... my furnace was off for 6 hours one day this week it turned out that it had run out of fuel. I and a friend paced the floor, freezing. These mini-crises probably make us Canadians feel we are PIONEERS.

To Irene [ ][124]

70 Marchmount
Toronto

25 January 1985

Dear Irene –
I just woke in a kind of whinge of pain & I'll write to you while my pills are taking effect. I'm on 'Leritine' now, a bone-pain-killer, and it works on a deeper level than the others, but when it wears off the sensation is remarkable.

I was thrilled by your phone call. Three spathes & fourteen blooms! Ours has only 9-red-pink with a white centre, very frilly. I can see it through the hatch I've just had cut between my wall & the kitchen which increases my perspective when I am shut in.

124 No further identification provided.

Also the kids can leave food out for me easily. I am *terrified* of being left untended when I can't walk. Still, only 2 days before chemo.

There, things are calming down. It's frustrating. I feel I ought to write more but I also want to sleep. Wm & Charlotte are at each others' throats. There's no choosing between them. Char is in the 'Bob' show at Vic & very tired & cranky. Will *may* have a job at Hart House as a waiter. He's at a Trinity Square video party tonight. Hope that gets him into a good crowd. He wants to go back to Europe as soon as possible. Char wants to drop psychology.

I've just read Philip Kreiner's *Heartlands* about Jamaica.[125] I wonder how Judy Merril is. Gwen seems to have a new man. Vera went to Saskatoon to give a seminar today. She's in another martyred phase and I'd like to shake her. I keep wondering what her anger & distress are about. I guess she *needs* to be unhappy.

Joyce Wieland phoned from San Francisco last week, as she had met my friend Dr. Margaret Deanesly. She was just about to start teaching and we were both pleased that two of her friends had recommended Marg. Then Marg phoned & I told her about my 9-day trip & she was pleased. I must be doing well if I surprise the docs.

I'm ashamed of my handwriting! But have started to do the novel by hand.

All publishing news is dismal. I'm scratching around for $$ at the moment as we overspent at Xmas.

Well, I'm in shape to go to sleep again & my pen is running out so I'll say goodnight & thanks for phoning.

Love,
Marian

---

125 Philip Kreiner, *Heartlands* (Ottawa: Oberon Press, 1984).

Envoi

From Timothy Findley
Arkwright
Cannington
Ontario

To Donald F. Meadows
Regional Director
Metropolitan Toronto Library Board
Toronto, Ontario

28 April 1986

Dear Mr Meadows,
It has been suggested to me by Heather McCallum that you are
the proper person to receive this request.

It is now just over a year since Marian Engel died and, in the
time since her death, I have been making enquiries regarding the
possibility of having a hybrid iris created in her name. Gardens
were one of Marian's greatest loves and iris were her favourite
flowers. However – the results of my researches have been, for the
most part, negative. The project would take a very long time – the

process more than likely too costly. (Such hybrids must be created in Holland.)

Consequently, it occurred to me that Marian would as well – if not better – be honoured and her love of gardens remembered best if a Marian Engel Memorial Garden were to be established. And to this end, I turn to you. What better location for such a garden than The Metro Library? I can think of nowhere more appropriate.

It occurs to me that space for such a garden – however small – could be found in the open 'ampitheatre' on the north-east corner. This is a location that Marian herself was fond of – and, so far as I am aware, there are already places where flowers would be practical. I hasten to add that I myself – and perhaps a few others of Marian's friends – would be honoured to provide sufficient bulbs, perennials and, of course, iris to fill whatever space might be allotted. The dedication of such a Memorial Garden would, naturally, fall in the purview of the Metropolitan Toronto Library Board of which you are the Regional Director. I am certain such a project, in honour of Marian Engel, will receive enthusiastic support. Therefore, may I ask you to place this proposal before the Board? I should be more than happy to co-operate in whatever way I can to bring such a project to fruition.

Yours sincerely,
Timothy Findley

Bibliography

Atwood, Margaret. *Negotiating with the Dead: A Writer on Writing.* Cambridge: Cambridge University Press, 2002.

Cohen, Matt. *Typing: A Life in Twenty-Six Keys.* Toronto: Vintage Canada, 2000.

Djwa, Sandra. *Professing English: A Life of Roy Daniells.* Toronto: University of Toronto Press, 2002.

Fetherling, Douglas. *Travels by Night: A Memoir of the Sixties.* Toronto: McArthur & Co. 1994.

Matyas, Cathy, and Jennifer Joiner. 'Interpretation, Inspiration and the Irrelevant Questions: Interview with Marian Engel.' *University of Toronto Review* 5 (Spring 1981): 4–8.

Symons, T.H.B. *To Know Ourselves: The Report of the Commission on Canadian Studies.* 2 vols. Ottawa: Association of Universities and Colleges of Canada, 1975.

Verduyn, Christl. *Lifelines: Marian Engel's Writings.* Montreal and Kingston: McGill-Queen's University Press, 1995.

– ed. *Dear Marian, Dear Hugh: The MacLennan-Engel Correspondence.* Ottawa: University of Ottawa Press, 1995.

– ed. *Marian Engel's Notebooks: 'Ah, mon cahier, écoute ...'* Waterloo, ON: Wilfrid Laurier University Press, 1999.

Wadland, John. 'Voices in Search of a Conversation: An Unfinished Project.' *Journal of Canadian Studies* 35.1 (Spring 2000): 52–75.

Weintraub, William. *Getting Started: A Memoir of the 1950s.* Toronto: McClelland and Stewart, 2001.

Illustration Credits

Charlotte Engel: wedding; Cyprus, 1963; expecting; Cyprus, 1971; with her children; on Galiano Island; in 1981.

William Ready Division of Archives and Research Collections, McMaster University: embraced by a 'bear' at a Writers' Union meeting [1976?].

Permission to reproduce all the photographs was provided by Charlotte Engel and William Engel.

Index